# MESSIAH ENIGMA

by

## ÍRANṢẸ ÈLÉDÙMARÈ

A COORDINATED ENERGI Publication
Paperback ISBN : 978-0-9935934-0-6
EBOOK ISBN: 978-0-9935934-1-3

# DEDICATION

This writing is dedicated to all those who are autistic, those with sickle-cell anaemia genes, those extremely good with numbers, those bearing obsessive compulsive genes and those with a retentive memory; for in you all are vestiges of some traits that a fully evolved human should bear, though these appear as burdens or fragilities presently, and the world prefers to see you as bearers of imperfections and disorders, contrary to that you all are precious to Humanity, make that light shine.

**ACKNOWLEDGEMENTS**
Multitudes go to those heroes of the past who by living their lives have limned and etched into the consciousness of Humanity various possibilities and realities about coming into a duet with Divinity.

# INTRODUCTION

Humanity is caught up in a foggy war, one purposed at concealing their awareness about the inherent potentials and treasures of human existence, which is what the human body transforms into, when powered by the entity known as "the Spirit of the LORD" or "the Light force".

As always there are at least two sides in every battle; on one side are those intent on concealing this potential from Humanity's comprehension, because its revelation spurs what is best described as "Human Enlightenment" or "a New Beginning", also religiously described as "the Kingdom of God coming upon the Earth". They obfuscate this disclosure solely to prevent such happening because it contemporaneously puts an end to "The Existing Order" on the Earth and the hegemony of all its beneficiaries. On the other side of this battle, are those fighting for this "Truth" to be revealed to humans. They tirelessly labour like a political opposition from a disadvantaged position for realisation of the precious potentials bequeathed to Humanity in order to spur "A New Age" on the Earth.

A quite intriguing aspect of the ensuing battle is that, humans are both the pawns used for waging the war and also they are the prize to be won at its end. Despite such great intrigue most of Humanity remains unaware about an ongoing war to determine their inheritance and future for aeons. This is no happenstance.

Historical accounts about humans, who someway or somehow were able to activate traces of "their Hidden Inheritance", best perceived as "an Image of God", exist showing such people have lived and walked the earth simultaneously as mortals and divine one. But worryingly such records are surreptitiously converted into objects and subjects of worship, reverence and outright misinformation for other humans by various faiths or cultures spanning the Earth. Such is done at the whim of those in control of affairs on this planet, in order to ensure other humans don't wake up. With such trends persisting, there is also on-going a cloaked attempt aimed at unlocking this inheritance bequeathed to Humanity, without their knowledge or consent. One akin to a computer hacker trying out every possible combination of a password sequence in order to secure unauthorised access. Such subterfuge tactics are beamed at Humanity by some entities of the Universe, in their desperate quest to access the rarest treasure to ever exist. One which Humanity retains its sole custodian and its clueless benefactor status.

All of such strategies by coveters of Humanity's inheritance fits perfectly under the context of human genetic manipulations, alien abductions and cross-breeding of the human race with other entities of the Universe. Even though there has been persistent wolf cries about such via the noisome outburst of conspiracy theorists, this has never been considered seriously by the human race, for they presume those bearing such concerns as loonies.

The aim to unlock "Humanity's hidden inheritance", also described as "The God Abilities in Humans"; is a high stake one, and it is so for the "power and authority" it bequeaths unto whoever unlocks it first. This quest is simply one to unlock the encrypted "seed of God" embedded into Humanities genes. Just like cryptologists were working tirelessly to decode the German Enigma machine during the Second World War, various entities or aliens are similarly busy doing the same in their bid to win this prize.

Most of human genetic manipulation aims are purposed to dumb down the Human race, to ensure they will always do what they are told to or instructed by any entity triggering such manipulations, even if the instruction given is one to obliterate the entire human race. Manipulation attempts are also a second strategy by which such other entities or forces intend to control, via the back door this treasure encrypted within Humanity's genes, just in case it falls into Human hands as ordained. The shortcomings and failures of all humans who have tasted this treasure "or drank from its cup" in the past is best explained if perceived from this context.

Most religions embraced by various civilisations on the Earth make promises of blessings, good fortunes and gifts of better futures to those humans who affirm belief and obey their dictates. Thereby transforming them into creatures mindlessly dancing to a predetermined piper's tune, the pipers remain the other entities in the Universe behind such faiths.

Despite the high stakes race towards unlocking "Humanity's hidden Inheritance", and all disinformation about it, some humans have against all odds been able to overcome every prevailing strategies aimed at suppressing human ability to activate "the Seed of God potential" they all posses. Some of such humans have been called Sages; Gurus; Prophets or Servants of God. And Jesus Christ, the most famous in this category of humans, has somehow acquired other titles such as "the only Begotten Son of God"; "the Messiah of Humanity"; or "the Last Prophet"; from God. All these are labels and titles which the eponymous religion Christianity adorns him with. Those who accept such views about him, remain perennially saddled with a responsibility to convince all those who don't share their views, that it is not one laced with half-truths, lies, suppositions or misinterpretations.

Science and Religion obstinately maintain dogged opposing views about the source and peculiarity of the Human species in the Universe. Both are like two sides of the same coin, mining from the same resource but airing different perspectives about it, just to prove each other's view as inaccurate at times.

With both factions deep in their trenches, Humanity's ignorance could last perpetually. Thankfully, Biotechnology, Genetics, Archaeology, Artificial Intelligence and Automation are all now helping to efface some of their wilful blindness by coalescing views and opinions that were difficult to reconcile in the past.

This literature will attempt at understanding and deciphering sacred texts and knowledges considered sacred, by subjecting such to critical analysis, sound and unassuming reasoning, in order to discern and to clearly establish a relationship between "Humanity" and "the Divine" or that which is religiously called "the LORD God".

The author's mindset as a computer code writer has proved invaluable at spotting sine qua non attributes about "the expected Messiah or Christ", which are embedded into sacred texts and teachings all over the world. His appropriate repositioning of such upon the jigsaw-cum-rubric puzzle of "the Truths about God and Humans" will audaciously reveal facts to readers that rehash all perspectives and insights.

The base reference for this writing is the King James Version of the Holy Bible, and this is because as faulty as it is, it remains or appears the least adulterated by canonical and overzealous doctrinal innuendoes of our days, when compared to various other versions of the Bible. From it can be spotted strains of codes, assignment statements and declarations, which when put together create blueprints guiding humans towards the activation of a supernatural ability.

These extractions are better perceived as "God's Artificially Intelligent resource", for their purpose is one which automates Humanity to accomplish a specific purpose clearly illustrated in this writing. In addition to that, random references to undisputable facts and teaching of other world faiths, religions or cultures are cited when appropriate, to buttress, collaborate, validate or situate specific viewpoints and context that also thought provokingly highlights the suggested.

# DEFUSING ORIGINAL SIN CONNUMDRUM

Almost everyone has heard about the story of Adam & Eve consuming an apple. (In scriptural context it was actually eating of a tree) which they were forbidden to eat of by "the LORD God". But the same was later offered to them by the serpent, (or the devil) with fascinating embellishments about its potency and transformative attributes. All in his vile bid to get this couple into trouble with the LORD God as narratives depict. An act which eventually led to their expulsion from "the Garden of Eden or the place called Paradise". Multitudes of views, opinions and interpretations abound about that anecdote. However, the reasons for those views are simply because humans tend not to understand what was planned, that which transpired and that being communicated by such a simple message to Humanity.

To explain further, I must define explicitly that if the LORD God referenced in that account does really exist, then surely He must be smarter than all other entities or created things existing. And that is simply because to have created and put together everything in our Universe, He must bear consciousness or intelligence in the highest level of such attributes that may exist or aggregate.

With that prestated, I could then proceed to put any human with a child (or one playing the role of a guardian) into the same seat of the Adam & Eve story, which we have placed the LORD for ages, because He being our Creator is qualified to play such a parental role for Humans also. This positioning of any parent or guardian is simply for a predictive reaction analysis, one for the simple question that follows.

Which of us as parents fully aware that the chances of their child getting shot, stabbed, robbed or getting involved with drugs in the neighborhood park were high, due to presence of other bad kids known to visit and spend most of their days at the same park, would grant their child permission to play in the park whenever they desired?

The simple reason why that question is put forward is that for ages, we all presume that God knew of the risk associated with Adam & Eve consuming of "the Forbidden tree", but yet He did nothing to stop that from happening.

Some have attempted to explain that apparent lapse in God's judgment by introducing "the burden of freewill" and placing blame on Adam & Eve, a right borne by all humans to do whatever they desire, whether it be good or evil. Surely, such excuses can't rest with the presumption that God was smart enough to realize that freewill would ultimately become an attribute that frustrates all the good He purposed for Adam & Eve or planned for His creation Humanity in general, which is apparently what seems to have happened eventually. Clearly, the same logic applies, in the case of most parents; they would certainly not allow their child to manifest a right of freewill desire to play with a cigarette lighter anywhere inside their home, for the predictive cause of starting a fire that could burn down the house.

In view of that, is it right to conclude that if God indeed knew or could predict that the exercisable right to freewill borne by Adam & Eve, could one day lure them into the desire to consume of "the Forbidden tree", and He did not do anything about it, but left such a possibility to chance, surely such an act by human reasoning suggests that God may not have been as smart as we would think or expect He was initially. Because any smart human who could have identified such a risk, will not leave it open to chance considering the disastrous consequences. Or we could say any sane parent will have kept the cigarette lighter out of their child's reach in addition to instructing the child not to ever touch or play with it, just as the LORD God told the first humans.

Now to suggest that God is not as smart as the regular human (or sane parent or guardian) is in my view blasphemous, considering the wondrous works of Creation attributed to Him. As such, rapidly shifting past such a presumption, will only prompt those who can make that quantum leap in reasoning to wonder, why God knew or could predict that Adam & Eve will one day consume of "the Forbidden tree's fruit", and yet waited for it to happen?

That is a question that can only be appropriately answered by considering the consequences of allowing the expected to manifest someday. In the case of the parent or guardian, putting them back in the seat of our analysis, it surely would be downright stupid of them to anticipate or predict, that their child could burn down the house by playing with a cigarette lighter, and do nothing but yet wait for it to happen, just for the pure purpose of teaching the child a lesson about playing with fire, or for the opportunity to now say later on, I forgive you for burning down my house child, simply because I love you and I am full of love.

Well, the same should apply to God, if that was what He did in Humanity's case, then surely we can opine that allowing such to happen – meaning Adam and Eve to eat of "the Forbidden tree" — without acting to prevent it was quite stupid of Him.

Thankfully, the LORD didn't just allow Humanity to fall into "the Forbidden tree sin", for the sole purpose of having a chance to forgive them of such a sin later down the line, as peddled by heavily sponsored religious doctrine.

Rather, other intentions were at work. God created Humans in His Own Image. To be created in another's image, does not necessarily imply that the created bears all the attributes of the Creator. And such facts can be proven to check out in the Adam and Eve episode. Because the Creator was smart enough to know, avoid and advise His creation to stay away from what was considered "the Forbidden tree". However, the created entity was not that smart, just as little children remain less aware of danger not experienced even if they are warned about such.

The same logic can be perceived playing out in the field of Artificial Intelligence, where Humans know how to do and avoid certain operational pitfalls that Robots or other forms of Artificial Intelligence still can't figure out how to deal with when encountered, such as pronouncing certain letters, words, understanding voice speech commands or driving a car.

The sole purpose behind the Adam & Eve episode was simply, a strategy of the LORD to train, test and use Humans as proxies of His in order to explore, study, spy, and eventually conquer other entities and territories on the Earth in this case. Humans are not originally from the Earth, we were planted here for a purpose by that entity which we call God.

*Job 20:4*
*Knowest thou not this of old, since man was placed upon earth,*

*Genesis 1:27-28*
*So God created man in his own image, in the image of God created he him; male and female created he them.  28.  And God blessed them, and God said unto them, Be fruitful, and multiply, and replenish the earth, and subdue it: and have dominion over the fish of the sea, and over the fowl of the air, and over every living thing that moveth upon the earth.*

Such intents of the LORD expressed above cannot be easily accomplished by a sudden dumping or placing of humans in any territory or on the Earth, because as a new person (or a newbie) in any region, dimension or terrain, humans were bound to find themselves scant in local-knowledge. And if they were subjected to examination — (a phrase which also may be perceived as being tempted from other scriptural perspectives) — they will be subdued for lack of such knowledge. Or if they were attacked by aboriginal entities of such domain provided there are any there, how they perform under such circumstances determines how they will be perceived by such entities, and by what classification or designation they will be naturalized into the territory. No one gets threatened when another person not as smart as them shows up in their neighbourhood, but the reverse occurs when a smart ass arrives.

That in a way summarizes what happened when humans were introduced into the Earth, and the ultimate fall out of it was that humans were tested or tricked by the serpent (or devil) who by dwelling here had more local knowledge or experience here than them. To the extent that by such temptation he tricked Adam & Eve to do that which compromised their integrity as "Images of God", and such ultimately disconnected them and Humanity in general from the LORD God.

This disconnection if perceived as what happens when NASA loses contact with a space probe, which still functions in whatever part of space it was launched into, may help us to understand what "the Fall of man" connotes symbolically. Well, if that was what really played out in our case, then such a play out should cause anyone to wonder how the LORD's purposed objective of Humanity's dominion over the Earth will ever get accomplished, if His proxies Humans — or in this case Adam & Eve — had become separated or compromised, and thereby triggering an aborting of their mission.

Well, the answer to that is simply, because as compromised entities or one disconnected from the LORD, Humans now became perceived as a slave race on the Earth. And as a slave race, humans became accepted as harmless co-dwellers on the Earth. Simply because they were now a conquered or second class entity, by virtue of being disconnected from their source, hence their threat to other earth dwellers was now severely diminished. Most especially, since the LORD gave the serpent this opportunity of victory, by allowing him to easily outsmart His creations and get them to eat of "the Forbidden tree". Such a characteristic masterstroke to deceive a classically stupid devil, could only come from God or (an entity) thinking several steps ahead in the game.

By luring the devil into a false presumption of being victorious and still maintaining control over the Earth, even with a foreign army having their boots on the Earth's soil, though now presumed as captives of the serpent's craftiness. And by deceiving the devil into thinking he had conquered the LORD's army, in this case Adam & Eve — or Humanity — in general, this army got accepted and taken as hostage or spoils of war mindlessly. Unknown to their captors that they were a Trojan horse, which if given the opportunity to regroup and re-assemble could launch a blitz against those holding them hostage on Earth. Also to be noted is that from the position of being a conquered army, second class aborigines or slaves and maybe the spoils of war, now dwelling within the enemy's territory, humans get the opportunity to execute deft reconnaissance missions, studying and relaying of intelligence reports back to central control concerning everything the enemy is capable of and that which it intends to do or is planning to execute, making them moles for God on Earth.

All these possibilities arose, only because the LORD allowed a defeat He could anticipate and prevent from occurring, which was allowing the consumption of "the Forbidden tree" by Adam & Eve. A strategy which most humans still can't discern its intent, which is that by simply making His army, in this case Humans to play the vulnerable one of the temptation script; such availed the LORD to move His plans of taking over this world into level-two of execution.

This was just the same thing as having one's mobile phone hanging carelessly in a jacket pocket, such that it attracts any pickpocket's attention who may consider it an easy trophy catch only, for such a criminal to find out later that it was purposely left there for entrapment reasons as a bait of an anti-pickpocket sting operation. Such intents will only get revealed after tracking the phone's location by using its global-positioning-chip to locate the whereabouts of the thief who nicked it.

In the case of perceiving humans on the Earth as playing the role depicted by such a perspective, the follow on question is, if really that was the plan all along, by now we could say mission accomplished. Humans are now here accepted as a conquered army and a slave race living in misery on the Earth troubled everyday by evil. We have had enough time to regroup the human army. We have built its population to over 7 billion. We have acclimatized. We must have conducted enough reconnaissance and gathered enough intelligence about the enemy holding us hostage. When, just when is the LORD God going to lunch that blitz against the one that torments Humanity or has captured it as a slave race for generations as He may have planned?

The answer to that is simply, such will happen when Humanity successfully decodes all which is needed by them to launch the attack or blitz which triggers a take over of the Earth as purposed and planned by the LORD. This is so because everything needed, all asset; weapons; blueprints; strategies; and tactics for such an action has been handed over to humans or Humanity in the form of what may be considered "a Messianic Enigma". Which when it is decoded triggers or begins "the Apocalypse". The information to activate this had to be sent or given in such an encrypted format, simply because such details can not be handed out in manners that could alert the enemy of the intended strategy. Just as a plan to escape out of a prison cannot be discussed or revealed in a way that those guarding it will realize what is being planned.

Because the needed resource is already with Humanity, in order to lunch the blitz against the evil one, all that is holding back this mission is "one human" who can decode the encrypted information within "the Messianic Enigma" and execute it. Such a decoding is also considered as "Breaking the seal" or "Opening of the books" in scriptural perspectives. Such are actions known to kick start everything bringing about the plans of the LORD God for the Earth. The conundrum encapsulated by what is called "The Original Sin" of Humans becomes resolved, when "the Messiah" who bruises the serpent's head is birthed, and since the serpent is the one who plotted Humanity's fall in the first instance, its own fall is the last command and also constitutes part of the plans behind that conundrum as depicted in verses below.

*Genesis 3:15*
*And I will put enmity between thee and the woman, and between thy seed and her seed; it shall bruise thy head, and thou shalt bruise his heel.*

Was this a change to God's address?

It appears that one of the vital messages that the Jewish man by name "Yeshua", now called "Jesus Christ" by almost everyone, brought to those walking the Earth in his days was one to inform them about a change in God's address details. This crucial information appears to have been overlooked all through generations even though he stated clearly to the Samarian woman at Jacob's well. "Lady, God no longer needs to be worshipped in a mountain or any specific city as you presume is the ideal manner to worship, rather God must now be worshipped in spirit and in truth, because it is what He desires from humans."

> *John 4:21-24*
> *Jesus saith unto her, Woman, believe me, the hour cometh, when ye shall neither in this mountain, nor yet at Jerusalem, worship the Father. 22. Ye worship ye know not what: we know what we worship: for salvation is of the Jews. 23. But the hour cometh, and now is, when the true worshippers shall worship the Father in spirit and in truth: for the Father seeketh such to worship him. 24. God is a Spirit: and they that worship him must worship him in spirit and in truth.*

This message though it appears slightly cryptic and unclear, was one to awaken everyone from a slumber of misassumption that the LORD dwelt at sacred temples or locations as defined by sundry cultures.

Considering that if really the LORD dwelt in temples made by human hands, it could then be said by pure logical reasoning and conclusion that the LORD must have created humans to build Him temples made from wood, stones or mortar to live in. Such a conclusion makes no sense considering that it surely would have been easier for the LORD to build himself a house to live in, than it was to create humans, who appear to be a more complex creation of His, than any building built by humans in all our existence. This supposition is one confirmed by the LORD's comments as voiced by prophet Isaiah, about building a house for Him, when He stated clearly, "I can do that Myself guys, I don't need Humans to do it for me, if that is really what I wanted."

> *Isaiah 66:1-2*
> *Thus saith the LORD, The heaven is my throne, and the earth is my footstool: where is the house that ye build unto me? and where is the place of my rest? 2.For all those things hath mine hand made, and all those things have been, saith the LORD: but to this man will I look, even to him that is poor and of a contrite spirit, and trembleth at my word.*

King Solomon also revalidated that view put forward by the LORD in a rhetorical manner during the commissioning of the temple which he built for the LORD. This was despite him having gone to great extents to make it a wonder of the world in those days and perhaps in our days equally.

> *1 Kings 8:26-27*
> *And now, O God of Israel, let thy word, I pray thee, be verified, which thou speakest unto thy servant David my father. 27. But will God indeed dwell on the earth? behold, the heaven and heaven of heavens cannot contain thee; how much less this house that I have built?*

The last sentence of Isaiah 66: 2, hints the LORD's interest in a man whose ways are pleasing to Him, those were not mere words to gloss over. We need to consider why those characteristics and criteria were laid side-by-side within the discourse about "a place to dwell for the LORD". Because they were made to specify a preference of the LORD's which only those paying attention in such context will catch.

By taking a look at what the LORD told King David, a man who in his lifetime also desired to build God a house — usually called a temple now — to live in, and comparing similarities in the LORD's response to this gesture of King David with some other prophecies concerning the birth of Jesus Christ, we will arrive at a clear conclusion concerning where God lives or dwells.

King David was a man who had great love for the LORD; that appears obvious because it could only take intense care and fondness for God to provoke within him, thoughts about building the LORD a house to dwell in. Judging by accounts of his life, it was deeply thoughtful and thankful of him, to bring forth the gestures purposed on relocating "the Ark of God" from where it was, parked in a tent outside his palace, into a more elegant and secure location.

This insight of care about "the Ark of God" was one of extreme importance. A conclusion arrived at by standing back and considering the LORD's reaction from the ensuing dialogue. It appears that this was a gesture the LORD had been long awaiting from Humanity, one which was a vital signal of a desire for Humanity to be reunited with the LORD once again.

This gesture by King David was also in some ways a marriage proposal from a human to the LORD. Hence the effusive response evoked by it once manifested. One thing we need to pay close attention to, is that this gesture happened in King David's heart and wasn't a publicly declared gesture. Yet the LORD God clocked in on it once it was conceptualized.

Rationalizing such a gesture on a human level, we can all understand that any parent will be greatly touched by their child coming up to them and saying, "one day I will build you a big house and we will both live there happily forever".

Or if one day a parent gets to hear from the grapevine that their child has been begging around for odd jobs and seeking to run domestic errands, because he or she wanted to earn enough money sufficient to buy the parent a worthy gift on their impending birthday or anniversary.

Surely no sane parent will easily forget such a gesture of love from their offspring, and certainly some will have their eyes glazed with tears the moment they hear of such thoughtfulness, coming forth from their child towards them. Such it was when the LORD discovered King David's intentions to build Him a house to dwell.

*2 Samuel 7:5-14*
*Go and tell my servant David, Thus saith the LORD, Shalt thou build me a house for me to dwell in? 6. Whereas I have not dwelt in any house since*

*the time that I brought up the children of Israel out of Egypt, even to this day, but have walked in a tent and in a tabernacle. 7. In all the places wherein I have walked with all the children of Israel spake I a word with any of the tribes of Israel, whom I commanded to feed my people Israel, saying, Why build ye not me a house of cedar? 8.Now therefore so shalt thou say unto my servant David, Thus saith the LORD of hosts, I took thee from the sheepcote, from following the sheep, to be ruler over my people, over Israel: 9. And I was with thee whithersoever thou wentest, and have cut off all thine enemies out of thy sight, and have made thee a great name, like unto the name of the great men that are in the earth. 10. Moreover I will appoint a place for my people Israel, and will plant them, that they may dwell in a place of their own, and move no more; neither shall the children of wickedness afflict them any more, as beforetime, 11. And as since the time that I commanded judges to be over my people Israel, and have caused thee to rest from all thine enemies. Also the LORD telleth thee that he will make thee a house. 12. And when thy days be fulfilled, and thou shalt sleep with thy fathers, I will set up thy seed after thee, which shall proceed out of thy bowels, and I will establish his kingdom. 13. He shall build a house for my name, and I will establish the throne of his kingdom for ever. 14. I will be his father, and he shall be my son. If he commit iniquity, I will chasten him with the rod of men, and with the stripes of the children of men:*

Summarizing from above, it can be concluded that both King David and the LORD loved, appreciated and desired the best for each other. The LORD's response to King David's gesture was simply superfluous, I will give your child or seed a right to "the Throne of Israel", and I will cause your child or seed to build "a House for my Name" and establish his kingdom forever, just for your thoughtfulness.

The LORD's promises were for two main purposes, the first was securing "a place for the LORD's Name to dwell" with a seed of King David, while the second was a place which was to be "a Throne for the Kingdom which the LORD was to give to David's son", one to be occupied by this seed of his forever. The widespread doctrinal or religious interpretation of this passage was that the LORD did not let King David build him the house he desired to build, simply because he had so much blood on his hands from all the wars he had fought earlier.

So God alternatively chose his son and successor King Solomon as the one to build "a house for God" which was later called "Solomon's Temple". Without any crucial examination of the intentions of the LORD for King David, we can presume an outright fulfillment of the LORD God's promise to King David upon the ascendance of King Solomon to the Throne of his father in Israel. However, one of the intents of the LORD was to "establish the Throne of David's seed forever". History reveals that those words were not fulfilled by King Solomon or any of the other King David's sons down the generation, and for that reason, the promise remains outstanding. One we have a right to hold the LORD accountable for, since He made it, and also because God does not and cannot lie by His nature.

Strangely, the LORD himself confirms that this promise was still outstanding, and as a matter of fact, gave detailed requirements of the pre-requisites to become a beneficiary to it during His interactions with King Solomon. Which if he fulfilled would have made King Solomon the one to provide "The LORD's Name a dwelling place" with "a seed of David" and such would have automatically "established the Throne of a seed of David forever". Such was communicated when the LORD spoke directly to King Solomon on two different occasions, after he began to build and during his commissioning of the temple.

*1 Kings 6:11-13*
*And the word of the LORD came to Solomon, saying, 12. Concerning this house which thou art in building, if thou wilt walk in my statutes, and execute my judgments, and keep all my commandments to walk in them; then will I perform my word with thee, which I spake unto David thy father: 13. And I will dwell among the children of Israel, and will not forsake my people Israel.*

*1 Kings 9:3-8*
*And the LORD said unto him, I have heard thy prayer and thy supplication, that thou hast made before me: I have hallowed this house, which thou hast built, to put my name there forever; and mine eyes and mine heart shall be there perpetually. 4. And if thou wilt walk before me, as David thy father walked, in integrity of heart, and in uprightness, to do according to all that I have commanded thee, and wilt keep my statutes and my judgments: 5. Then I will establish the throne of thy kingdom upon Israel for ever, as I promised to David thy father, saying, There shall not fail thee a man upon the throne of Israel. 6. But if ye shall at all turn from following me, ye or your children, and will not keep my commandments and my statutes which I have set before you, but go and serve other gods, and worship them: 7. Then will I cut off Israel out of the land which I have given them; and this house, which I have hallowed for my name, will I cast out of my sight; and Israel shall be a proverb and a byword among all people: 8. And at this house, which is high, every one that passeth by it shall be astonished, and shall hiss; and they shall say, Why hath the LORD done thus unto this land, and to this house?*

"A place for the LORD God's name" is the place where the LORD's Spirit dwells. The place where He dwells is also the place where His Glory and Power are present, because it is the place where He can be petitioned, prayed to, or worshipped, but best of all it can be imagined as a place where contact with the LORD is experienced for any reason it is so desired.

Despite all these cautions and admonitions from the LORD, King Solomon's conduct remained yet unpleasing, his debauchery and undedicated lifestyle to his father's faith ultimately angered the LORD and provoked Him into decimating the control and influence of "the throne of David" also at that time "the throne of the King in Israel", upon which King Solomon sat, and such prompted a un-hallowing of the temple Solomon built for the LORD God. In light of what transpired, it becomes strikingly clear that the assumed fulfillment of the LORD's words, about giving King David's seed, both a throne and kingdom established forever was not accomplished via King Solomon. That which was accomplished was simply one for him to seat on "the throne of King in Israel" after King David died, and also the building of a temple which was hallowed by the LORD initially. We need to note clearly that "hallowing of a temple" is not the same as "dwelling in a temple", because such misinterpretations lead people to making wrong doctrinal conclusions about the whole promise.

Taking a holistic review of all the promises made to King David in detail, it was either a case of the LORD changing His mind down the road, thereby reversing some of His intents and words to King David after his death. Especially the one about giving his seed an everlasting throne and kingdom, because no human has ever had such a dynasty as history has shown clearly, neither King Solomon nor any of the other Kings of Israel after him fulfilled those words.

The alternative thought is presuming the LORD was still at work with plans to fulfill those promises made to King David because King Solomon and the rest were found unfit for the promise. In such a case the holistic fulfillment of those promises must be via "another son of David". But one thing we must not misunderstand is that all those promises were for just one son or seed of King David to manifest comprehensively.

Several centuries later after the death of King David, the birth of "a son of David" was prophesied by Isaiah and an angel too, as recorded in the New Testament. This son was to sit on King David's throne with a kingdom that will last for ever, and His name was "Emmanuel" meaning "God is with us". This son, if he actually lived up to those expectations will have fulfilled and accomplished both the LORD's and King David's intentions for each other that were outstanding as put forward earlier.

We do recall that King David's intent was also "to build the LORD a house to dwell in", just like he dwelt in a palace. This dwelling place is symbolic of a place where "God and a Human" will co-habit like best friends or one where a man and his wife will reside together as a married couple.

Isn't it strange that this son's name suggested that God was with him just as King David had pre-planned? We also need to recall and note the LORD's response to this gesture by King David was, "for this gesture I will give your seed a throne that lasts forever". This means or suggests that I will make your seed reign forever, because that is what a throne that lasts forever connotes in all sense of it. Strangely again, this appears as a fulfillment expected to be brought about or manifested by this son whose birth was proclaimed, because his throne too was expected to last forever.

*Isaiah 9:6-7*
*For unto us a child is born, unto us a son is given: and the government shall be upon his shoulder: and his name shall be called Wonderful, Counsellor,*

*The mighty God, The everlasting Father, The Prince of Peace. 7. Of the increase of his government and peace there shall be no end, upon the throne of David, and upon his kingdom, to order it, and to establish it with judgment and with justice from henceforth even for ever. The zeal of the LORD of hosts will perform this.*

*Matthew 1:23*
*Behold, a virgin shall be with child, and shall bring forth a son, and they shall call his name Emmanuel, which being interpreted is, God with us.*

*Luke 1:30-33*
*And the angel said unto her, Fear not, Mary: for thou hast found favour with God. 31. And, behold, thou shalt conceive in thy womb, and bring forth a son, and shalt call his name JESUS. 32..He shall be great, and shall be called the Son of the Highest: and the Lord God shall give unto him the throne of his father David: 33. And he shall reign over the house of Jacob for ever; and of his kingdom there shall be no end.*

Considering in clear perspective the interactions between the LORD and King David, what was being discussed by both parties was clearly "a bridge between Humanity and Divinity". One which when built creates a scenario where a human dwells and interacts with the LORD, and also one where a human in this case "a seed or son of King David", reigns on "a throne established by the LORD" forever as a result of this bridge.

The phrase — "God is with us" — suggests faintly and hints boldly that the LORD was present with those who named this son so. But to the bemused, it is not out of place to question how his parents came about such a name for their son. Because "the Ark of God" an insignia of the LORD had been missing and had not been spotted for centuries in Israel.

Also, considering the fact that Jerusalem was presently under foreign rule by the Romans, such a status for the nation of Israel did not support a view about the LORD's Presence being with His people the Israelites, or in any way reflects any influence of a king installed by the LORD God sitting upon King David's throne at Jerusalem as prophesied of his birth.

In those days it could be presumed that the LORD dwelt in or within the Ark, because it was a symbol of His Presence and Power, and wherever "the Ark of God" was, victory was certain for the Israelites. Because the LORD their God was present there too. At present when this boy was born, that was not the real play of events in Israel, because they were a territory occupied by their enemies. So suggesting that the LORD was present or in town without "the Ark of God" being spotted throws up some serious questions to those who knew much about its symbolism.

The first simply, is if that assertion of God being with us was true or was it just a canard provoked or somehow prodded by a delighted imagination of nursing parents who were excited about a newly born son. The second is what happened to all the apparatus of "the Ark of God", and protocols that accompanied it including all the sacrifices that followed the Ark, its house-keeping and the retinue of priests who usually catered for the Ark? The retinue of those charged with the Ark's upkeep was so large that if these people were present, their presence will be noticeable to those around the young lad, just like we will spot and notice more security operatives in a town, if it was visited by someone of a high political ranking or status or if they resided there with one of the locals.

Without any credible answer to those questions, anyone choosing not to suspend their disbelief concerning the boy's name could presume, the LORD wasn't dwelling in the Ark anymore, but now with this boy's family as claimed. Though questions about exactly where in their home God was dwelling still needed serious answers to make sense of that claimed by the name his parents gave him.

## The LORD dwells with Humans on the Earth

There is nothing new about the claim of God dwelling with us, as put forward by the boy's parents. Looking back it appears the LORD had actually been dwelling with Humans on the Earth, perhaps for longer than we can pre-date. Therefore making an attempt to put a date on it, our best guess should be since the day's of old when "Eternal Life" — a derivative of His Presence — was available to inhabitants of the Earth or just before its withdrawal from Humanity.

The withdrawal of "Eternal Life" and its associated privileges brought about the wrong notion of the LORD's absence from the Earth in the mind of some humans. And this is one caused by the fact that actually He became estranged from Humanity in some ways, but this is purely due to human actions or misdeeds under the freewill context.

We have to realize that the LORD remains present on the Earth with humans perpetually, such is because the LORD possesses omnipresent attributes which avails Him this privilege. In spite of that, humans are still unable to interact with Him, due to the reasons or conditions brought about by their estrangement from Him, — famously described as "Original sin of humans" or "the Fall of man" — and for such reasons they may conclude He is absent, which in actuality is a case of Him being withdrawn from their midst.

*Exodus 25:8*
*And let them make me a sanctuary; that I may dwell among them.*

*Exodus 29:45-46*
*And I will dwell among the children of Israel, and will be their God. 46.And they shall know that I am the LORD their God, that brought them forth out of the land of Egypt, that I may dwell among them: I am the LORD their God.*

The need to establish a means of interaction with the LORD who was also dwelling on the Earth, is brought forward by His command to Moses and the Israelites to make Him "a place to dwell amongst them". This request by the LORD for humans to make Him a place in order to dwell among them is given to ensure humans remain within reach or contact of the LORD's Glory and Power. And that is needed for Humanity's peace on the Earth. Whenever such is prepared for God, the LORD comes there becomes God on Earth and rules over Humanity's affairs. But in absence such "a place for Him to dwell", other entities are god and rule over or control Humanity on the Earth, thereby enslaving them, and perpetuating evil acts aimed purely to estrange Humanity further from the LORD, and such was what happened after the Israelites lost contact with their God after sojourning into Egypt, they became slave to people worshipping other gods, those of Egypt.

*Numbers 35:31-34*
*Moreover ye shall take no satisfaction for the life of a murderer, which is guilty of death: but he shall be surely put to death. 32. And ye shall take no satisfaction for him that is fled to the city of his refuge, that he should come again to dwell in the land, until the death of the priest. 33. So ye shall not pollute the land wherein ye are: for blood it defileth the land: and the land cannot be cleansed of the blood that is shed therein, but by the blood of him that shed it. 34. Defile not therefore the land which ye shall inhabit, wherein I dwell: for I the LORD dwell among the children of Israel.*

*Exodus 29:44-45*
*And I will sanctify the tabernacle of the congregation, and the altar: I will sanctify also both Aaron and his sons, to minister to me in the priest's office. 45. And I will dwell among the children of Israel, and will be their God.*

The verses above clearly suggest the following:
A request for a place to be made for God to dwell in amongst humans, this place is also a place where contact between the LORD and human beings is established whenever desired.

A demand to keep the land free from all things that defiles it, because the LORD was also dwelling in the land with humans. A recognition that the entity called the LORD having associated itself with this tribe Israel, was by such association responsible for bringing the Israelites out from Egypt, for that reason that entity became known as "the LORD their God" or "the God of Israel", all this happened because Moses encountered this entity called the LORD God during his wilderness experience.

We could summarize from all these that the Earth is shared with the LORD. Although, this sharing is in such a way as, living in the same house with someone who will not use or share the living room with you, if it is not kept in clean, tidy or perfect condition as desired by that person.

This housemate simply remains in their own room, isolated from other occupants of the house unless the common area is fit for their presence, or perhaps another way of understanding the LORD's Presence on the Earth is to imagine that from the multitudes of Wi-Fi networks available within a neighborhood, people can only access networks they have the password to with their own computer.



Prior to the rising up of Moses in Egypt, there could be this assumption that the LORD recently arrived back on the Earth. Like a space or time traveller who forsook His people. And it was after this arrival, that He began revealing His Presence magnificently to Humanity via the ensuing battles with the Pharaoh of Egypt. One which may have been to take over control of the Earth, if not that the army or his people were not ready for such accomplishments. That re-arrival presumption is quite inaccurate. The facts to consider are that the LORD had been protecting the interest of humans — in particular the tribe of Israelites — way long before then.

There are several accounts of the LORD's intervention in affairs of Abraham; his son Isaac; and even Jacob his grandson.  The LORD God made Abimelech return Abraham's wife to him, even though Abraham had lied to Abimelech that she was his sister. He did this to protect the human — in this case Abraham's interest — and to ensure His words about Sarah will not be prevented from coming to pass as a result of what we may call Abraham's stupidity or cluelessness about the greatness of the entity — "called Yahweh" which he had made contact with. I say that because, if Abraham was aware that no other king or entity could stand against Yahweh — the LORD God and the same entity — he has found favour with, then he will not have lied to another king in order to save his life.

> *Genesis 20:3-9*
> *But God came to Abimelech in a dream by night, and said to him, Behold, thou art but a dead man, for the woman which thou hast taken; for she is a man's wife.  4.  But Abimelech had not come near her: and he said, Lord, wilt thou slay also a righteous nation? 5.  Said he not unto me, She is my sister? and she, even she herself said, He is my brother: in the integrity of my heart and innocency of my hands have I done this.  6. And God said unto him in a dream, Yea, I know that thou didst this in the integrity of thy heart; for I also withheld thee from sinning against me: therefore suffered I thee not to touch her.  7.  Now therefore restore the man his wife; for he is a prophet, and he shall pray for thee, and thou shalt live: and if thou restore her not, know thou that thou shalt surely die, thou, and all that are thine.8. Therefore Abimelech rose early in the morning, and called all his servants, and told all these things in their ears: and the men were sore afraid.  9.  Then Abimelech called Abraham, and said unto him, What hast thou done unto us? and what have I offended thee, that thou hast brought on me and on my kingdom a great sin? thou hast done deeds unto me that ought not to be done.*

In prior times, the LORD also gave Isaac favour when he sojourned and He equally saved Jacob from the wrath of Laban's fury. All these show and hint about the perpetual presence of the LORD with Humanity, even though a hiatus of His interaction or interventions was noticeable before His Glory and Power was manifested in Egypt during the time of Moses.

> *Genesis 31:22-25*
> *And it was told Laban on the third day that Jacob was fled. 23. And he took his brethren with him, and pursued after him seven days' journey; and they overtook him in the mount Gilead. 24. And God came to Laban the Syrian in a dream by night, and said unto him, Take heed that thou speak not to Jacob either good or bad. 25. Then Laban overtook Jacob. Now Jacob had pitched his tent in the mount: and Laban with his brethren pitched in the mount of Gilead.*

Taking such acts into consideration, any opinion about the LORD deserting humans should be clearly understood to depict what occurs when humans efface their knowledge about God, or when they break communication, union or contact with Him. Because the LORD always dwells with humans on the Earth, although most times not in the same dimension or realm just like radio signals can be present with us in our room, yet we may only partially access them by using other devices. Manifestation of the LORD's Glory or Power gets staunched in any generation of Humanity, whenever their hearts become alienated from Him — or tuned out of His frequency. And this persists until one human among them re-establishes contact with Him; such is what transpired when Moses encountered the LORD God in the wilderness. That human who discovers God in every generation or age after contact with Him has been lost, is a Messiah for that period, just like Moses, Noah and Jesus Christ were in their various generations.

## The LORD's revealed Glory is always in proportion to Human's will for His Power and Glory

Although the LORD remains present with Humanity on the Earth, every limitation to the advancement of the knowledge about God and His purposes for us is purely characterized by human shortcomings and disinterest towards being in communion better perceived as "at One with Him", or also expressed as "uniting with the LORD", or experiencing "a close encounter with God". In order to expound this view let us consider these statements made by the LORD.

> *Genesis 15:13-16*
> *And he said unto Abram, Know of a surety that thy seed shall be a stranger in a land that is not theirs, and shall serve them; and they shall afflict them four hundred years; 14. And also that nation, whom they shall serve, will I judge: and afterward shall they come out with great substance. 15. And thou shalt go to thy fathers in peace; thou shalt be buried in a good old age.*

*16. But in the fourth generation they shall come hither again: for the iniquity of the Amorites is not yet full.*

We can discern from these statements that the LORD was already aware of the bad conduct of another league of people named as "the Amorites", occupying a land far away. These people were exhibiting bad conduct collectively termed as "iniquity", but known as "sin" in our days. Their conducts were inclined towards those things or practices, which estranged them from the LORD and such ultimately caused "the Amorites" to be driven off their land.

One known as "the Promised Land" by narrative, which was given to the Israelites for inheritance. Discerning from how He handled the Amorites, we can see the LORD was not one who acted spontaneously whenever a case of wrongdoing "or iniquity" was discovered or brought against a league of people on the Earth. Studying carefully the interplay of events from that narrative, it appears the LORD had an established protocol for dealing with human misconduct, hence His comments "for the iniquity of the Amorites is not yet full". My guess is part of such protocol would involve sending messengers or prophets to such people to forewarn them of impending destruction or harsh retribution if they fail to change their ways. I come to this view by also observing how the LORD handled the people of Nineveh and the role Prophet Jonah played in that account. The city of Nineveh was also pencilled for destruction by the LORD, for the misdeeds of its inhabitants, but the dialogue between God and Jonah showed they had not been given a notice or forewarning stating to them that if they do not cease and desist from their current behavioural ways, they would face the wrath of God, and a destruction of their land, Jonah was the Prophet sent to issue this warning.

*Jonah 4:10-11*
*Then said the LORD, Thou hast had pity on the gourd, for the which thou hast not laboured, neither madest it grow; which came up in a night, and perished in a night: 11. And should not I spare Nineveh, that great city, wherein are more than sixscore thousand persons that cannot discern between their right hand and their left hand; and also much cattle?*

In another instance, reports were brought to the LORD about the bad conduct of the people of the land of Sodom. In this instance it appears that, the LORD had not considered their case as ripe for judgment according to His protocols.

Most likely, it appears a league of desperate ones further petitioned the LORD again about the bad, and perhaps the worsening and abysmal conduct of these inhabitants of Sodom.

This may have earned them a label of being dangerous to Humanity as a whole, hence prompting for a fast action by the LORD, as opposed to following His identified protocol iterated above. This in my view spurred the LORD's need to inspect and confirm the case against the land personally via an expedition which ended by the absolute obliteration of the land of Sodom and its inhabitants.

*Genesis 18:20-25*
*And the LORD said, Because the cry of Sodom and Gomorrah is great, and because their sin is very grievous; 21. I will go down now, and see whether they have done altogether according to the cry of it, which is come unto me; and if not, I will know. 22. And the men turned their faces from thence, and went toward Sodom: but Abraham stood yet before the LORD. 23. And Abraham drew near, and said, Wilt thou also destroy the righteous with the wicked? 24. Peradventure there be fifty righteous within the city: wilt thou also destroy and not spare the place for the fifty righteous that are therein? 25. That be far from thee to do after this manner, to slay the righteous with the wicked: and that the righteous should be as the wicked, that be far from thee: Shall not the Judge of all the earth do right?*

# THE LORD'S PRESENCE AND ITS REASONS

Playing the role of "the Judge of the Earth" and other accounts concerning what happened at "the Beginning of time", suggests clearly that the LORD God had certain intents and interests for Humanity and most especially this planet. God's Spirit was described as moving over the Earth at the beginning of time here as we are informed by scriptures. It is my opinion that this movement was one for surveying the Earth, to determine if it was fit for His purposes. Such a condition had to be satisfied before the transformation of the Earth into a place of order pleasing to Him, would be executed. This order is what we may call Creation or the effects of "the Big Bang" phenomenon as Scientists will put it. We can surmise that all those were the first steps of a series of actions towards the LORD's desired purpose for Humanity who are created to be images, replicas or clones of God dwelling on Earth.

*Genesis 1:2*
*And the earth was without form, and void; and darkness was upon the face of the deep. And the Spirit of God moved upon the face of the waters.*

*Genesis 1:27-28*
*So God created man in his own image, in the image of God created he him; male and female created he them. 28. And God blessed them, and God said unto them, Be fruitful, and multiply, and replenish the earth, and subdue it: and have dominion over the fish of the sea, and over the fowl of the air, and over every living thing that moveth upon the earth.*

Transforming the Earth into the habitable climate it is, with its characteristic order after it had been found fit for the LORD's purpose, was not aimed at creating the Earth for Humans to dwell on or misuse. But rather it was to make it a place habitable for them, in order to fulfill a specific purpose for the LORD, which was to raise up "children or sons of God", who are those to ultimately bear His Image. This is so they could operate in His Power and Authority as vessels or proxies in order to execute His Desires and Purposes on the Earth and within the Universe in my opinion. This may prompt us to wonder once again how Humans could then have become second class entities on an Earth created for them, as put forward in the earlier context of Original sin conundrum. Well the answer will come as you read on. Going on that explains why the LORD created all other things according to their kind or attributes, and humans specifically with His Image and Attributes — and also an instruction to have dominion.

The sub phrase "according to their kind" in creation narratives, should hint the discerning about the existence of more than one source of creation, — be it a template or consciousness — during the creation process. Questions should be asked about the source of such templates, prototypes or blueprints used for other creatures or creations by anyone who really cares for answers to all unknowns. Did they eternally exist too, or did they show up as random results of the Creation process? Such are issues we need trouble our minds with. The same applies to darkness, which was overwhelmed by "the Light of God" at the Beginning. We should be curious about if God created darkness too, because some people like to presume God created everything, a view I do not agree with from these perspective.

Such perspective about other existing entities, sources or consciousness does not in any way diminish the Omnipotence of the LORD. That view of mine is best buttressed by and also explains why the LORD destroyed the Earth, at a point when Humanity had become consumed with evil imagination in the days of Noah, as opposed to being consumed with what may be called "A God-like imagination".

The prevailing imagination at that point in time was an opposite of that which He craved for, which is the reason He triggered the flood. If those other entities could stop Him from destroying the Earth back then, it is right to imagine they would have done so, to save both their selves and humans bearing their imaginations within them. Various narratives show us they couldn't and by such highlight His Omnipotence. Noah was noted as one who walked with the LORD and had or possessed a different imagination compared to others existing in his generation, perhaps if Noah's peculiar attributes are viewed as "a kind or source" in context of the narratives of the beginning of Creation perspective, it could helps us to get the point being stressed about the LORD's preferences and His Omnipotent attributes.

*Genesis 6:5-9*
*And GOD saw that the wickedness of man was great in the earth, and that every imagination of the thoughts of his heart was only evil continually. 6. And it repented the LORD that he had made man on the earth, and it grieved him at his heart. 7. And the LORD said, I will destroy man whom I have created from the face of the earth; both man, and beast, and the creeping thing, and the fowls of the air; for it repenteth me that I have made them. 8. But Noah found grace in the eyes of the LORD. 9. These are the*

It appears that in our days, such an act of obliterating the imperfect ones by the LORD is being steadily effaced out of regular religious doctrine. Such is done to suggest the God we worship is a more humane and politically correct one. It is patently obvious from scriptures that the LORD takes full responsibility for such actions and justifies it. Furthermore, He even goes on to say, "I will do such again" as voiced by His prophets.

All that should hint to those who care to listen that He — this entity we call the LORD God — has predetermined plans. This view also highlights why the Earth is expected to experience a cataclysmic purging at the end of our generation, because of the way things are going in our world. Humanity seems once again to have become consumed with evil imaginations as opposed to being imbued with an imagination fitted for the LORD's purposes. And such can only prompt a repeat of what happened in Noah's times. This view may also may explains why time-after-time, age-after-age, the LORD wipes off or destroys civilizations or generations that do not produce the desired fruits of His labours for the Earth.  Such desired fruits are simply humans who bear perfectly "the Image of God".  Such is also known as "the fruits of the Vineyard of the LORD" as can be gleaned from scriptural context.

Looking back to the history of the Earth, we can at best perceive such wiping away of civilization as depictions of what scientists describe as those unexplainable catastrophes befalling the Earth over millions of eras in the past. Or the reasons for those unexplainable gaps spotted in the human evolutionary profiles.  It may be that whenever such events are decreed, those who are left to die or be destroyed, would be those adjudged or marked by the LORD as the lot of Humanity or Creation that cannot be of any good towards His Purposes. Or those who cannot bring forth the yield He expects of them as "the Sower of this field", known as the Earth.

Perhaps that also explains why we find buried down deep in the Earth, remains of dead plants and animals dating million of years into the past which we collectively describe as fossil fuels resources. It could be that our generation is just one of many millions or even billions raised on this Earth. And periodically from such breeding, the yields are harvested while the tares are destroyed. Those tares would include the other entities that humans became a second class dweller to here on Earth, simply because humans are now subservient to them by human's own free will folly, which is part of a grand plan. The wheats will be the good ones and they are those who will make these unexplainable evolutionary leaps.

The parable told by Jesus Christ about sowing good seeds in a field hints clearly, that while the LORD is busy trying to raise up His children — meaning those perfectly bearing His Image on the Earth, other entities are also busy with the similar purposes on the Earth, and that is a perspective that should not be glossed over nor ignored. For its implications, hints something special about the Earth and the Humans dwelling on it and presence of other entities.

*Matthew 13:24-30*
*Another parable put he forth unto them, saying, The kingdom of heaven is likened unto a man which sowed good seed in his field: 25. But while men slept, his enemy came and sowed tares among the wheat, and went his way. 26. But when the blade was sprung up, and brought forth fruit, then appeared the tares also. 27. So the servants of the householder came and said unto him, Sir, didst not thou sow good seed in thy field? from whence then hath it tares? 28. He said unto them, An enemy hath done this. The servants said unto him, Wilt thou then that we go and gather them up? 29. But he said, Nay; lest while ye gather up the tares, ye root up also the wheat with them. 30. Let both grow together until the harvest: and in the time of harvest I will say to the reapers, Gather ye together first the tares, and bind them in bundles to burn them: but gather the wheat into my barn.*

This parable's interpretation follows hinting caution to those who are discerning enough to grasp what is being suggested by its narrative:

*Matthew 13:37-43*
*He answered and said unto them, He that soweth the good seed is the Son of man; 38. The field is the world; the good seed are the children of the kingdom; but the tares are the children of the wicked one; 39. The enemy that sowed them is the devil; the harvest is the end of the world; and the reapers are the angels. 40. As therefore the tares are gathered and burned in the fire; so shall it be in the end of this world. 41. The Son of man shall send forth his angels, and they shall gather out of his kingdom all things that offend, and them which do iniquity; 42. And shall cast them into a furnace of fire: there shall be wailing and gnashing of teeth. 43. Then shall the righteous shine forth as the sun in the kingdom of their Father. Who hath ears to hear, let him hear.*

That parable about the LORD using the Earth as a breeding place also indicates that those who are not found with "the good seeds in their heart", will eventually be condemned to hell or eternal condemnation. Such warnings are issued to emphasize that humans have a role to play in determination of their future, simply because, if a human doesn't bear "the good seed" in them, then a priori that human bears "the evil seed" within them. These seeds were also that descriptively represented as "imaginations of the hearts" in the context of Noah's story. And back then, all those with evil imaginations were destroyed by the flood triggered by the LORD God.

Noah in my perception was the only human bearing good imagination. The assumption that the other members of his family too must have been like him does not add up when we consider that the LORD allowed Lot and his family to escape from judgment coming upon the Land of Sodom. Not because they were any better than those killed, but rather because Abraham who was Lot's uncle found favour with and also had the LORD's audience, by such privileges he pleaded exemptions for all those who escaped. The ensuing narrative, between the LORD and Abraham showed, the criteria to save the city as a whole was never met, even though it was brought so low to just ten good people being found within the city.

Also, this view about Noah being the only righteous one is buttressed via a prophetic utterance, where the LORD states explicitly that, if He calls for judgment again Noah, Daniel, or Job, would not be allowed to plead for anyone. Such comments suggest clearly that they had been allowed to do so previously by the LORD God to me.

*Ezekiel 14:12-14*
*The word of the LORD came again to me, saying, 13. Son of man, when the land sinneth against me by trespassing grievously, then will I stretch out mine hand upon it, and will break the staff of the bread thereof, and will send famine upon it, and will cut off man and beast from it: 14. Though these three men, Noah, Daniel, and Job, were in it, they should deliver but their own souls by their righteousness, saith the Lord GOD.*

Undeniably, the judgments standards held by the LORD may appear strict and harsh, and such are bound to raise questions about why humans should be sent to eternal damnation or marked for destruction, by a supposedly loving God. But the answer to such resides deep within the context of the parable. Which is, the LORD has His plans and we can either choose to work with Him or face the consequences when the chickens come home to roost.

To highlight this, if we consider that in our days, spent nuclear fuel rods are kept safe and secured forever as opposed to disposing of them in such a way that anyone who would desire to make a dirty bomb could lay hold of one and misuse it.

Such a perspective could help us understand the reasons behind the harsh judgments against humans not meeting the mark, once the LORD chooses to reset the clock on Earth. It should also be noted that even though humans may be judged unfit for the LORD's purposes, which is so simply because their hearts now bear evil seeds or imaginations. Those attributes still makes them useful to other entities collectively describe as "the enemy" in the parable of the sower. Such entities were those responsible for planting the tares or such seeds in human hearts. The question to us is who amongst us helps their enemy achieve their purposes? If we as humans don't indulge in such, do we really expect the LORD who is way wiser than us to aid his enemies? Do we really expect Him to let the loose cannons filled with evil to wander freely in a domain he purposes to raise his own Image bearers?

A human only becomes imperfect in the LORD's Eyes, if his or her soul has evolved into one bearing "the image of another entity", and not that of the LORD God who created Humanity for His purposes. Such a person then fits the "son of evil"; "son of wickedness"; or "son of Belial" descriptions which shows up in the bible.

Since these entities we classify as evil do not hold or share the same standards of perfection and intentions as the LORD's does for Humanity, letting them have the humans bearing their images in order to use them for their own vile purposes, will surely be a big blunder by the LORD God. The equivalent of such a blunder will be making spent nuclear fuel rods available to terrorists because we are done with them. If the LORD continually permits evil seeds to grow and get harvested on the Earth, we must note that it sort of defeats His own aim of making the Earth a breeding places for His own sons, seeds or images bearers as purposed in the first place, and such exemptions will only encourage more sowing of evil seeds on the Earth in the future by other entities, and that is justification for what we may perceive as His harsh judgments.

It must be realized that these other entities and their influence on humans is reason for traditions where humans kill their children or other humans as an offering to appease a deity — or a spirit god — that has requested for such a sacrifice. Whenever such requests are granted by humans, the soul of the one who is killed or sacrificed gets handed over to these entities in order to be used in serving their vile purposes, which in most cases are surely an anti-God purpose.

We all must have heard about people who are presumed to have sold their soul to the devil. Such casual statements uttered flippantly should cause a discerning person to wonder why the devil would seek to posses or own a human soul. That is if it was really true that such a transaction took place.

Considering that the devil is ready to trade a human soul in exchange for money; fame; or power; throws up a serious question about what a human soul is really worth? And also why a market exists for human souls? When a human sells their soul to the devil, what happens is that the individual gets possessed by a clone of the devil or has "an image or replica of the devil" now planted in their heart. That happens in exchange for whatever the devil delivers to them as bargained. And from the moment such an exchange occurs, the person involved becomes an agent, pawn and proxy that dances whimsically to the demands of the devil on the Earth.

That is so because the person's heart has now becomes a safe dwelling place for "the image of the devil" or simply put "a demon". And just like a computer virus that will never stop replicating itself until full control over all programs or executable software processes of a computer system's functions are secured and controlled by it.

Likewise, the devil via its clone-in-the-person also strategizes to do all that is needed to own and control that person's soul completely.

Owing a soul completely means stripping it of its freewill abilities to reject instructions to execute evil acts or deeds by its conscientious override abilities, whenever such instructions are issued to the heart of the human hosting this resident demon by the devil via its installed demon.

That explains why other humans can perceive the strange transformation in characters of individuals who dine with the devil, into one being intensely vile, with a personality only fit for the devil. Such persons in whom these changes occur will suddenly find themselves doing things they don't want to do, or doing things they have difficulties explaining, resisting or stopping. Even though, they know such acts are not good for them or others and bear harmful consequences to everyone in the long run. Humans who fit this description are those we can aptly describe as demon possessed individuals.

It should be noted that any feeble attempt to rescue such a human soul from the iron grip which the devil has over it, is usually violently resisted. Simply because, that human soul is technically now a property of the devil, who over some time has laboured at fully possessing such soul, with the expectation that at the end of such labours, that soul becomes transformed into a fully conscious demon capable of acting independently for the devil.

One which hides its true persona behind the veil of masquerading like a normal harmless human, but that is only a cloak to conceal that known as "an evil imaginations" or "the seed of the wicked one" embedded in it, and it is for such reasons that such a soul is not fit for preserving at Judgment day by the LORD. Because it is has been violated and damaged beyond the point of repair, hence the reason why such are marked for obliteration or incineration in hell. Isn't it curious that no one has ever spotted the devil doing evil on the Earth, what we see regularly is humans acting like the devil or on his behalf everywhere on the Earth. Such humans are purposed to be wiped off the Earth by the LORD one day, if such tendencies or imaginations within them are not snuffed out. The responsibility to stop evil propagated among Humanity is ours; it is settled doctrine that it is better to make Heaven with one eye than to have confirmed reservation with the evil one in Hell or Eternal condemnation.

*Psalms 37:27-28*
*Depart from evil, and do good; and dwell for evermore.  28.  For the LORD loveth judgment, and forsaketh not his saints; they are preserved for ever: but the seed of the wicked shall be cut off.*

## Why does the LORD need a place to dwell with Humanity?

Understanding the view that Humans can become bearers or hosts to various types of images "also known as or perceived to be seeds or imaginations", can help us to see reason to why the LORD desires to have a permanent dwelling place among humans. This dwelling place is not one to lay His head and sleep at night as we may imagine, rather it is one from which the LORD can share His Glory, Power and Influence to raise, nourish, protect and guide humans as His own seeds bearers as other creatures do for their young ones.

This dwelling place is one from which knowledge from God can be handed over to humans in order for them to safely exist and dominate the Earth. We must note that while the LORD is not playing such roles or doing such on the Earth, other entities are always busy at work doing the same. So in order to put a final end to such interregnums, the LORD's desire is to be permanently domiciled here on Earth in order to play such roles perpetually, herein lies a strain of wisdom concerning Jerusalem or the New Jerusalem.

Over the ages we have noticed that humans who are in contact with the LORD appear to demonstrate exceptional abilities, these set of people are regarded as those on whom "the Spirit of the LORD" rest or comes upon spontaneously.

Such individuals are those who seem to have discovered or possess the ability to establish a link between God and humans. This link is usually one that exist through which the LORD steps into the human domain to provide solutions to Humanity's problems and to protect His interest here on Earth. It is purely a support link or a bridge of rescue for Humanity, whenever they are in dire straits in one way of perceiving it. In another way, it is also a means for the LORD to continue at perfecting "the Humanity Project", which is one aimed to merge "the Spirit of the LORD" with "the Soul of Humans" for the purpose of Eternal existence just as other entities desire likewise too.

In our days scientific research and advancements are already being made in the field of preserving or extending the human life span, such that humans may not die when they get old, but rather keep on living. Our scientists are even considering transferring of human soul or mind into that of a robot or synthetic life forms, because its body does not wither or die like ours does. Such aims are similar to that which is purposed by the LORD's desire to merge His Spirit or Presence with our mortal flesh bodies under the tag "Eternal Life" for humans.

We should all recall that when Jesus Christ was born, His birth was pre-announced as that of one bringing about "the Presence of God" into the domain of Humanity. He wasn't seen as one with the ability to link up to God momentarily if desired as compared to other prophets, but rather he was seen as one who bore "the Presence or Authority of God" as a human. Simply because the LORD's Presence was with or accessible within him, for this reason he was considered "a son of God", and by the virtue of this status, He was a plenipotentiary for the LORD in our world, an "Emmanuel" by name and its suggested interpretation was "one bearing God's Image" as a man.

## Verifying the name Emmanuel

The only way to verify if the LORD was really with the bearer of that name "Emmanuel", would have been to test for "the Presence of God". Going by several accounts of the life of Jesus Christ, it was noted that he did really demonstrate "the Presence of God" being with him. He demonstrated such the same way or even to a greater extent as Moses or any other prophets who had interacted with the entity called the LORD God — or entity called Yahweh — before him had done.

"The Presence of the Most High" another way of referencing having an open bridge or link to the LORD by a person, makes any human qualified for such status "a child of the Most High"; or "a Judge; or a Prophet; or an Anointed; or a Servant of the Most High"; to name a few of such appellations fitting that status. However, we need to note that if the desired requirements for such presence are not achieved during a human's life, then the Most High's Presence, Power or Glory will not be manifested in such humans. Those who fail at meeting this criterion remain mere humans, and they eventually die off like mortals, but those who meet the criteria become upgraded into immortals, the peak of human creation in my view. The sub context of "Eternal Life" promised by gospels is better understood if viewed from this perspective as an objective for all humans.

> *Psalms 82:6-7*
> *I have said, Ye are gods; and all of you are children of the most High.  7. But ye shall die like men, and fall like one of the princes.*



There is a need to understand how and why the LORD's could dwell with Humans without a need for the contraption called "the Ark of God". And for clarity on this, we need to go right back to the beginning of Creation to understand a few things. The bible explains that after the LORD made man; he gave Adam & Eve the instruction not to eat of "the Fruit of good and evil" (also called the Forbidden tree, fruit or apple).

> *Genesis 2:8-9*
> *And the LORD God planted a garden eastward in Eden; and there he put the man whom he had formed.  9.  And out of the ground made the LORD God to grow every tree that is pleasant to the sight, and good for food; the tree of life also in the midst of the garden, and the tree of knowledge of good and evil.*

This "Forbidden tree" can best be perceived as one with the ability to transform humans from being "good creations" into becoming "evil creations".  The preceding discourse about humans not becoming bearers of evil seeds or images can be fully understood from this context about good and evil creations. We should note clearly here that humans were made to be only good creations, (in fact very good ones) with no provision towards being evil ones in the plan.

> *Genesis 1:31*
> *And God saw every thing that he had made, and, behold, it was very good. And the evening and the morning were the sixth day.*

Being "good creations" or bearing such a status availed humans the right to dwell close or in proximity to something described as "the Tree of Life". However, from the moment Adam and Eve experienced or consumed of "the Forbidden tree" they became capable of being both good and evil creations.

We should observe here that the pure reason why "the Forbidden tree" was also named as "the tree of good and evil" is because of what it does. Which is it ultimately creates in humans the potential for duality and opens up the possibility in them to become "evil creations", even though humans were initially created as only "good creations". This change in the default intrinsic setting of humans can automatically transform them into vessels capable of holding or containing evil. Thus they potentially became both bearers and propagators of what is at best described as "evil imaginations or seeds", because the door was now opened within them for such possibilities.

From the moment this transformation occurred in Adam and Eve, it appears there was immediate need for an action to restore Humanity to their initial good status. This need is also one meant to counteract their newly acquired evil capabilities or status. Crucially, we have to bear in mind that humans dwelt in the same domain as "the Tree of Life", and hence they still retained the right to live forever, which is the benefit of being juxtaposed or being co-sanguine to that tree.

With the changes in their status, humans were now also bearers or containers for evil or better still propagators and perpetuators of evil imaginations by description.

In such a circumstance, humans retaining the right to live forever became a great risk and this was a problem, one that needed a swift solution in order to prevent more complexities arising. The most practical approach at a solution was to ensure that the humans did not live forever, and that is accomplished by revoking their right to live forever, because if that right to live forever was not revoked, humans as beings living forever were simply potential reproducers of evil seeds and propagators of evil imagination on an endless industrial scale.

This creates a threat of ultimately populating the Earth and possibly the Universe with pure evil that could never be destroyed or exterminated. Just imagining that should put chills in our spine, what a horrid place our world would become if a murderer or serial killer cannot be killed. Or if terrorists, rapists or child molesters cannot be stopped because they simply don't die, by virtue of living forever. And that in a way highlights why "Eternal life" is the prize which we all must strive for because it is what was purposed for our fore bearers, herein is wisdom for those with a heart full of love. From a scientific perspective, the experiencing of "the Forbidden tree" by humans had created a security breach in what can be described as "the Humanity Project". One planned and executed for the sole purpose of being exploited by the serpent "or devil" so he could raise seeds or image bearers too.

A perhaps equivalent faux pas in our days would be, if the military unwittingly revealed into the public domain details of passwords enabling access into computers controlling their nuclear arsenals or other defense missiles via an email not meant for the recipients. It would be right to presume that some terrorist cell somewhere in the world, will swiftly attempt to use such inadvertently disclosed information to their advantage, such individuals would try to login into the military's computers to maliciously take advantage of this military gaffe before the error or breach was discovered and remedied. In such a scenario there would be only one way to stop such people obtaining such access into the nuclear armaments computers, and that would be to permanently shut down computing access to all military installations until a fail safe mechanism or protocol is developed to ensure only truly authorized military personnel can remotely obtain access to the computers controlling those weapons at such installations.

Similarly in the case of Adam and Eve, the first disaster recovery strategy of stopping humans from living forever was taken after "the Forbidden fruit" breach occurred. This in my view appears to ensure that even if a human mind became completely taken over or possessed by the devil, via any of its demons as a result of that breach in the original Humanity configuration, also known as "the Fall of man". Such a human was destined to die one day and on the day of their death any evil acts they were capable of executing or propagating by virtue of becoming possessed by the devil or a demon ends.

However, if contrary to that such a day of this human's death never arose because they simply lived forever, this human now under the control and influence of evil entities could potentially be used to perpetuate evil endlessly without any cessation of such. Again that is scary just by imagining it.

> *Genesis 3:22-24*
> *And the LORD God said, Behold, the man is become as one of us, to know good and evil: and now, lest he put forth his hand, and take also of the tree of life, and eat, and live for ever: 23. Therefore the LORD God sent him forth from the garden of Eden, to till the ground from whence he was taken. 24. So he drove out the man; and he placed at the east of the garden of Eden Cherubims, and a flaming sword which turned every way, to keep the way of the tree of life.*

For such reasons enumerated above, this strategy was executed, and Humanity was zapped out of the dimension or realm where "the Tree of Life" was located. This action is subsequently described as "the Fall of Man", because from that moment onwards, humans became degraded in status to beings that had terminal lifetimes "or mortals", a consequence of being driven out of "the Garden of Eden" — which was the place where "the Tree of Life" was situated.

It was also a place where "Death" as we know it had no influence or power over humans; this is so because the effects of "the Tree of Life" also better perceived as "the Glory of the LORD" abounded in this place called "the Garden of Eden" and this kept death away.

This glory is also the source or essence of "Eternal Life", an attribute which humans have lost by their sin, that of consuming, encountering or experiencing "that Forbidden fruit" depicted by the Adam & Eve anecdote.

> *Rom 3:23*
> *For all have sinned, and come short of the glory of God;*

Since humans were no longer inhabitants of "the Garden of Eden", but now denizens of a new realm where a different influence called "Death" reigned, they were now beings in a place, dimension or realm where there was no "Glory of the LORD".

In such places there was another glory — "called that of Death" — and it causes all things living to eventually die off by snuffing out all life or living forces in them. Notably the resulting circumstances chimes with the warning from the LORD to Adam & Eve that, "if you eat of this fruit you will die". This dying or death process appears to be one where humans became lesser status creations that gradually disintegrate back to dust or died in one of many perspectives.

To me there is a correlation here with the fact that the LORD cursed (or pronounced to) the serpent, that it will eat dust all its life. Because that dust appears in my view as what Humanity is made up of and what they return to when they die as a result of their fall, if no repentance occurs, in a perspective.

*Romans 6:22-23*
*But now being made free from sin, and become servants to God, ye have your fruit unto holiness, and the end everlasting life. 23. For the wages of sin is death; but the gift of God is eternal life through Jesus Christ our Lord.*

A lot of other things happened at the withdrawal of the right of humans to eat from or be in the presence of "the Tree of Life" located within "the Garden of Eden". This withdrawal can be best half-explained as the act of unplugging a mobile phone from its power source and then waiting till its battery drains out all power stored in it, because it had to be in such a state before any attempts at fixing the problems in the mobile device's circuits can be made.

Baring that perspective, it is right to swiftly wonder why the LORD didn't fix Adam and Eve when they died — meaning after their life resource ran out — and simply turn them back on later, because considering that if this fix had been done then, surely it should have put an end to all the problems created by experiencing "the Forbidden tree" by Humanity shouldn't it?

Well, logically that sounds right, but it appears the human problem was not that simple to fix. Herein lies the second half of the explanation to help make sense of that view, in the case of a discharging battery what happens is that it drains out power or charge as electrons flow in one direction.

However, in the case of humans experiencing "the Forbidden tree", by that experience the tree corrupted the heart of humans by injecting into it something called evil, by this happening evil instructions, forces or entities were now being written or deposited into Humanity, hence Adam & Eve lost their intrinsic good characteristic as a result of this experience, even at death they were now some part good and some part evil.

Like a reprogrammable memory which overwrites on previously stored information, the heart or soul of Adam & Eve had now acquired or had written into it evil characteristics or attributes. Simply turning it off and simply restarting couldn't solve the problem or fix the inherent damage caused; just as it wouldn't if we had a virus installed in a computer system.

If we recall that the tree was called one of "good and evil" which meant it had an alternating effect on humans, by experiencing of the Forbidden tree. A reverse process began in humans that ultimately transformed the human heart into containers of both good and evil executable codes or instructions even though it was initially created to harbour only good ones.

Humans were not created to have hearts that harbour, contain, imagine or execute evil; this ability became acquired when "the Tree of knowledge of good and evil" was experienced. Having their hearts now capable of harbouring evil had now transformed human hearts into both a breeding place for evil entities and a launching pad for their operations. A breeding place because there hearts were being reprogrammed to host and reproduce evil entities also called demons. A launching pad because their hearts now became lunch pads or vessels that could be used to execute "evil instructions, imaginations or actions" fitting to the devil's agenda.

These changes essentially transformed humans into potential slaves for the evil entities, because "the door" had been open to these entities by "the Forbidden fruit gaffe of Adam and Eve" to manipulate humans. Such entities could now begin to dwell in the hearts of humans and utilize human will as they so wished. On the contrary if the human hearts was in the state it was initially made to operate in, which was only harbouring good, in such a state no evil entity could obtain access, dwell within, reproduce in or use human hearts to execute their vile purposes.

*Mark 7:20-23*
*And he said, That which cometh out of the man, that defileth the man. 21. For from within, out of the heart of men, proceed evil thoughts, adulteries, fornications, murders, 22. Thefts ,covetousness, wickedness, deceit, lasciviousness, an evil eye, blasphemy, pride, foolishness: 23. All these evil things come from within, and defile the man.*

Though evil dwelling within humans may appears a breach of the LORD's plan, it really isn't because it simply lures evil entities into a domain created by the LORD from which they can be analyzed, observed and tagged till he is ready to strike at them.

To help clarify the evil dwelling in human view point further, I will use the following perspective. We all know that you can't find fishes or other sea creatures in a hot dry desert because they simply can't survive there. However, if you flood or irrigate that same desert with sea water, within a short while you will begin to observe aquatic life forms thriving in the place that once was the preserve of desert life forms.

A place where only desert adapted life forms could thrive previously now becomes transformed into one where other life forms thrive. Such was the change the human hearts experienced after contact with "the Forbidden fruit" or "the Tree of good and evil".

This ability of the human heart to yield towards, or harbour evil is termed "the Original sin" of humans. It is that for which the prophets of God cry out to humans, that repentance is needed as desired by God. It is usually misconstrued with apologizing for wrong deeds humans have done, such as breaking one of the ten commandment rules or disobeying religious or moral laws and demands of a civil society, which are also labelled as "sins" too. The difference in both types of sin is that the second set of sins are all caused by evil entities influencing, controlling or subjecting the human heart to their whims as a result of now having access into it, thereby making such humans act vilely. If that vulnerability is stopped, and all evil entities are somehow kicked out of a human's heart or denied access to it, — that accomplished by the repentance clamour — then the human's heart becomes good once again, and that human will stop acting vilely or doing things labelled as "sins", which are such things that the religious and moral laws or commandments are made to preclude humans doing in the first place.

> *Luke 6:43-45*
> *For a good tree bringeth not forth corrupt fruit; neither doth a corrupt tree bring forth good fruit. 44. For every tree is known by his own fruit. For of thorns men do not gather figs, nor of a bramble bush gather they grapes. 45. A good man out of the good treasure of his heart bringeth forth that which is good; and an evil man out of the evil treasure of his heart bringeth forth that which is evil: for of the abundance of the heart his mouth speaketh.*

The word "repentance" is derived from another word "penance". This as it now appears has been intentionally mistranslated in order to simplify the requirements for such by over-zealous, proponents of certain faiths in their bid to enlist followers to their brand.

Penance also draws parallel meanings with the word "Hesychasm" which is an Orthodox term that focuses on re-establishing "a union with God" — or the uncreated Light — by inner or deep silent prayers. Such is called for in light of the fact that humans were sent out of "the Presence of God" after experiencing "the Forbidden".

This union is believed to be what is expected to take us back into "the Presence of God" if it is so desired by any human. This reunion can be achieved by withdrawal from regular daily activities in order to focus on "the Hesychastic aim", which  according to teachings of this faith, take a person to the final destination, one at which those who indulge seriously at such will arrive at a place where "a Knowledge of God" is experienced by them.

The Catholic faith similarly aims for corporal experiences of Divinity. "Divinity means the same as God". In Catholicism this aim for Divinity "or the Divine" is achieved by individuals subjecting themselves to a protocol of prayers and solitudes for God, such were the original intents and purposes for the priest and nuns lodged in monasteries.

Hesychasm is not so different to meditation because its literal translation means "Quietism", and like meditation it is about focusing with a clear mind on God in order to experience or interact with Him, such is emphasized in the Bible too.

The Jewish view of that word is expressed as descending into "the Merkabah", which is "the Throne of God" or "Throne Chariot of God". This is a place where "the Knowledge of God" is revealed to anyone who gets there. This phrase "the Knowledge of God" actually means and also depicts "a Discovery of God"; or "the Powers of God"; or "the Presence of God"; and that is what awaits or is encountered by those who seek to approach "the Throne of God".

From all my researches, I have come to one conclusion that all those who lace various religion with wrong doctrines contrary to this sole objective of reuniting humans with God, do so for the purpose of keeping humans away from "the Throne of God". This is because any human who approaches this place or zone becomes a prophet; servant; or son to God. One capable of manifesting God, His Will and Power among Humanity, and in my view, there certainly is a cloaked conspiracy against such manifestations on the Earth to be expounded further.

A second perspective of the problem which Humanity experienced from contact with "the Tree of good and evil" is that, because all energy can neither be created nor destroyed, but only transformed from one state into the other, whatever humans lost as "good-potential" a form of energy was immediately converted into "evil-potential" another form of energy to create or maintain a zero potential balance in obedience to the law of energy conservation.

The resulting balance somewhat looks like what is being described in the Yin Yang illustration of Asian origins, but it is not exactly accurate in my opinion. To me we are meant to be humans bearing one energy or potential form not humans having both energy forms in balance within our heart. Existing with both forms of energy "good and evil" is a recipe for chaos, and this was why humans were judged as unfit for living forever and sent away from the Garden of Eden.

*Genesis 3:22*
*And the LORD God said, Behold, the man is become as one of us, to know good and evil: and now, lest he put forth his hand, and take also of the tree of life, and eat, and live for ever:*

In such a state of this balance projected by the Yin Yang illustration, one where humans are presumed to bear freewill to do good or do evil, because their hearts became a dwelling place for both good and evil forces or spirits. Such a status is also considered as being "naked".

*Matthew 6:24*
*No man can serve two masters: for either he will hate the one, and love the other; or else he will hold to the one, and despise the other. Ye cannot serve God and mammon.*

*Mark 12:30*
*And thou shalt love the Lord thy God with all thy heart, and with all thy soul, and with all thy mind, and with all thy strength: this is the first commandment.*

However, I oppose that supposition of Yin Yang, because we are creations purposed only to do good, and this is possible only if our hearts are in a purely good state, and that can be done by reversing our heart's status back to a state where it was originally, with only "the Good Force" or "the Light" existing in it. It is only then that the human heart becomes a fit place for the LORD's Spirit to dwell. It is only then that we become clothed — the opposite to being naked — and bear its benefits, Eternal Life which we lost previously.

*2 Corinthians 5:3-4*
*If so be that being clothed we shall not be found naked. 4. For we that are in this tabernacle do groan, being burdened: not for that we would be unclothed, but clothed upon, that mortality might be swallowed up of life.*

*Luke 11:36*
*If thy whole body therefore be full of light, having no part dark, the whole shall be full of light, as when the bright shining of a candle doth give thee light.*

A righteous man is one whose heart and will is subject to being controlled by the entity that dwells in the environment of "the Good force" or "the Light" or "the Force of Love". Any creation with such a status is considered as "being good" and becomes the dwelling place of the entity called "the Spirit of God".

*Matthew 15:19-20*
*For out of the heart proceed evil thoughts, murders, adulteries, fornications, thefts, false witness, blasphemies: 20. These are the things which defile a man: but to eat with unwashen hands defileth not a man.*

Humans are considered to be unrighteous or demon possessed, when their behaviour is generally evil, and this is because their hearts are predominantly filled with the counter opposite environment to that of "the Good force".

That which is the "force of hatred" or "evil" or "that called darkness" and every such environment where these forces exist are cosy places for evil entities or spirits.

The religious notion of casting a demon out of a human is achieved by inviting sufficient Light "or the Good force", into a heart to expel any darkness, "or the evil force" that occupies such a heart. In verses below please note the word "eye" refers to or means "the human heart" and observe the relationship with "Light" being emphasized here.

*Luke 11:34-36*
*The light of the body is the eye: therefore when thine eye is single, thy whole body also is full of light; but when thine eye is evil, thy body also is full of darkness. 35. Take heed therefore that the light which is in thee be not darkness. 36. If thy whole body therefore be full of light, having no part dark, the whole shall be full of light, as when the bright shining of a candle doth give thee light.*

The whole body being full of light was exemplified in three instances in the Bible, by the lives of Moses, Jesus Christ and possibly Stephen. All these individuals had their faces shinning or glowing at various light intensities. In the case of Moses, he lost the glow on his face after a while, this may be because his heart was not totally "full of light", and that may perhaps explains why he was not totally submissive to the will of God and ultimately did things which displeased the LORD.

Jesus Christ on the other hand had his face shinning brighter than the Sun, and the LORD's voice was heard confirming him as one in whom He was well pleased when he achieved this status. Stephen too appeared to have been in the early stages of his heart being full of light. By observations it also appears there is an ability in such individuals to switch on and off this face shining phenomenon, because that was displayed in the life of Jesus Christ and it could be that this ability was also why Moses lost his facial glow as opposed to that suggested earlier.

> *Matthew 12:43-45*
> *When the unclean spirit is gone out of a man, he walketh through dry places, seeking rest, and findeth none. 44. Then he saith, I will return into my house from whence I came out; and when he is come, he findeth it empty, swept, and garnished.  45. Then goeth he, and taketh with himself seven other spirits more wicked than himself, and they enter in and dwell there: and the last state of that man is worse than the first. Even so shall it be also unto this wicked generation.*

Now all these factors have been laid out to help us understand why "the Spirit of LORD" was considered as dwelling in "the Ark of God" in those days. That was because the Ark was a fitting environment for "the Light" or "the Good force".  Ancient humans did not and could not understand that the state of their hearts were bi-polar. Thereby making it an unfit environment for "the Spirit of the LORD" to dwell in, neither did they understand the need for reversing the status of their heart, and considering that Jesus Christ had to say or express these views in parables, shows how hard it may have been to fathom or decipher, and things remain like that in our days too.

The human heart being bi-polar did not make it an expressly forbidden environment. It was still possible for "the Spirit of the LORD" to take over a human heart temporarily, such an event is described as "the Spirit of the LORD coming upon a person" in various instances in the scriptures.

Every time that occurred, the evil potential present in the human's heart and this realm will instantly begin to neutralize the power, effect or influence of "the Spirit of the LORD", just like closing the electric circuit discharges any potential or power within the battery. Several biblical accounts showed that whenever such occurred, the humans upon whom the LORD's Spirit comes were able to manifest exceptional abilities while "the Power of God" or "the Spirit of the LORD" was within or upon them. However, once that power drained out they all appear to default back to their original human or mortal status, and returned to creatures bearing the "good and evil" or "yin yang" status once again.

There is a recognizable pattern in scriptures that suggests or hints at such a human being marked to be destroyed by evil entities here on the Earth. Just like a rabid dog is put down, once it is discovered to bear the rabies virus. This marking for elimination of such humans, is in my view one of several attempts to keep out any manifestation of the LORD's Spirit in the midst of humans on the Earth. How else can we explain killing and persecution of prophets and apostles of God?

With human hearts in such an unstable state of shifting between good and evil, the best means by God to dispatch help via "His Spirit or Power" to humans was by placing "His Spirit" in a place where its effect could not be countervailed. Such as in a vessel or carrier that could not be put down like a rabid dog, and such a place was within the container now called "the Ark of God". Which was a conditioned container created as an environment for only "the Light" or "the Good Force" to dwell within. And from there this force also described as "the LORD's Spirit" was invoked whenever it was so desired as an aid to humans on the Earth.

The people who maintained the integrity of "the Ark" were named "Priest or sometimes Prophets of the God" dwelling within the Ark. These people were trained and educated by "the Spirit of the LORD" on what to do, and what not to do. Also they were taught how to maintain the integrity of the Ark. Scriptures shows they were told about how to approach the Ark, they were also warned not to open the Ark, because it appears that if that happened, it will lose its integrity and potency. This is similar to what occurred in the case of "the heart of humans" that initially were once with no duality or oppositional environment or force within it. In a case of it being opened, the Ark will also become filled with the counter or opposite of "the God force", which is "an evil force". Such will bring duality upon it, or transform the Ark into a dwelling place for evil forces also, just like the human heart was transformed bringing us — Humanity —to the state labelled as "sin".

The Ark was noted to have been opened after being captured by the Philistines from the Israelites during a war. Biblical records account of widespread sickness or tumours plaguing the people of the region, within which it was opened. Those accounts bear resemblance to the effects of exposure to radiation or the release of an atomic or biological weapon which may have been sealed up in a vessel initially. Such accounts suggest and lead us to safely opine that humans of biblical days were dealing with a force or entity more advanced than they were enlightened or had knowledge about, that force or entity is what we call by various names such as "God"; "the God force;" "the Spirit of the LORD"; "the true Light" and so on.

# PRE-REQUISITES FOR A NEW DOMAIN

As expressed in the section about King David building a temple for God, we observed that it appears that the LORD had waited patiently for "One human" within "the sea of Humanity", who would desire building Him a place to dwell amongst them, that trait or desire was discovered in and expressed by King David.

It's quite clear from scriptures that the LORD was searching for one among all humans, who will be willing to submit to His desires, to the extent that this person's submission would prompt a total expunging of all the residual evil inhabiting his or her heart. Such expurgation will come about by submission of both the heart and will of that human, following which the human's heart would wholly become a dwelling place of "the Spirit of the LORD" once again.

Such will happen simply because after the process of expurgating evil from this human's heart, there would be no room for the tiniest speck of "the evil force" or "darkness" within that human's heart anymore, such that this human's heart can be best described as being "full of Light" or "single" as phrased by Jesus Christ in his teachings.

It will only take a full submissions of one's free will to the LORD to achieve this objective, and if this submission level could be measured scientifically, perhaps in a metric or an imperial unit of measurement, it would be that amount of submission desired by the LORD from a human, in order for any human to become fully filled with "the Spirit of the LORD". It is also the amount of submission needed to fix the problem with the human heart, in order to reverse the effects of the phenomenon called "the Fall of man" also termed "Original sin of Humanity".

It should be understood that this level of submission was also what the devil desired of Jesus Christ in exchange for the kingdom of the whole world, when he offered to give it all to him, on the condition that Jesus Christ will simply bow down and worship the devil to gain that offered.

If indeed Jesus Christ had acceded to that request from the devil, his will would automatically become subjected towards doing whatever the devil required of him on the Earth. Thereby Jesus Christ will lose his own intrinsic freewill, even though there will still remain an illusion of possession of freewill within him. That illusion of freewill is the reason why most people indulging in evil acts or habits tend to perceive themselves as acting rightly, even though their ways are at variance and contrary to the voice within their heart or conscience. A full submission of a human's freewill is also desired by the LORD. And any human capable of this level of submission has been sought for amongst Humanity by the LORD for generations. "That One human" found with such a submissive heart (or will) is to be seen "as the Lamb who takes away the Original Sins of all humans" or "as a Scape goat for Humanity. Being the one upon whom the full weight of the human sin was to be placed, and that is done in other for humans to co-exist with the LORD God once again. Just as things were at the beginning of Creation before humans fell or were tempted to lose their "only good creation" status. Another way of expressing such perspective of "the Lamb" or "the Scape goat" role, is to consider the human who plays this role for Humanity as the first working prototype of a scientific invention. This prototype once tested to have worked successfully will then have its specifications reproduced in multiples, before being made available to others desiring its use. I opine that the comments by Jesus Christ of sending the Comforter or Holy Spirit, after he had left earth somehow relates with this view point in some perspectives.

Assuming from a scientific perspective, that this "One human" sought for who is capable of delivering what is desired was found. We can imagine that at some point down the line, the LORD's angels will need to take what I can at best describe as clinical records or medical observation and vital specifications of that human, all the way through the process he or she was subjected to, just as nurses would for a patient to be operated upon. During this "Scape goat ordeal", such will be done to monitor the human's body and mind's responses during the process of placing of "the weight of Humanities sins" on the person. Observations relating to how the human in question reacted throughout the process is needed for the creation and calibration of a benchmark dosage or a remedy fix, which will be applied as a solution for all other humans desiring such a curative procedure at their heart level. Just as clinical observations are taken in drug testing scenarios of medical science.

There is a verse in the bible that faintly hints at such a perspective where Jesus Christ didn't want to be touched by those he appeared to right after breaking free from "the powers of death". An event now religiously described as his "Resurrection from the death". From the context of that passage, we could perceive he did not want any contamination by or from any human contact until he had ascended first to the LORD as he expressed. It could be that during this "first ascension" was when all the respective records or specimens were retrieved or collated from his body for records and observational purposes to know what happened after He had been through the process of overcoming "death and the grave".

Such records will be these utilized to calibrate the next set of updates coming to humans, just as promised by Jesus Christ before his final ascension into Heaven. Such updates in my view were those to come via "the Spirit of God" interface also called "the Holy Spirit" or "Comforter" nowadays by Christians. An entity which was to be a companion assisting humans desirous to accomplish all which Jesus Christ had just accomplished. Miracles, overcoming the devil's temptations, "death and the grave" while he walked the Earth.

*John 20:16-17*
*Jesus saith unto her, Mary. She turned herself, and saith unto him, Rabboni; which is to say, Master.  17. Jesus saith unto her, Touch me not; for I am not yet ascended to my Father: but go to my brethren, and say unto them, I ascend unto my Father, and your Father; and to my God, and your God.*

*John 15:26*
*But when the Comforter is come, whom I will send unto you from the Father, even the Spirit of truth, which proceedeth from the Father, he shall testify of me:*

*John 16:7-8*
*Nevertheless I tell you the truth; It is expedient for you that I go away: for if I go not away, the Comforter will not come unto you; but if I depart, I will send him unto you.  8. And when he is come, he will reprove the world of sin, and of righteousness, and of judgment:*

Locating a place for "the Name of God" presently within "the Ark of God".

In addition to the need for a human fully submitted to the LORD's will, there was also a need for humans upon who "the Spirit of the LORD" could descend to make necessary interventions for Him, within the realm of Humanity. Such a need existed and was in place even before this fully submissive "One human" also  called "the Scape goat" who would bear the weight of our sins was found.

Some humans had fulfilled this requirement in the past; those humans, who met the criteria for such temporary descents of "the Spirit of God", were known as "Judges; Priest; or Prophets of God;" in those days. And these were trained to be Holy, being Holy is a requirement to keep their hearts in states of purity in order for them to be willing vessels suitable for use by the LORD to achieve His intervention purposes in the midst of Humanity.

The difference between a holy individual and one perceived as not holy, is related with the outstanding problem about "evil or the force of darkness", having access or control over the heart and will of a human. This problem came about since Humanity experienced that called "the Forbidden tree". Although, there were means to correct or minimize its deleterious effects on humans, such measures required discipline and dedication towards the purpose of re-establishing the holiness status in the heart.

Those humans through whom the LORD intervened by putting His Spirit upon them, were known as those manifesting "the Power, Glory, Finger, Hand, Word, Spirit or Name of the LORD" in various contexts.

There was a set of laid down procedures and protocols which had to be adhered to by humans in order to ensure a steady supply of willing vessels "or human hearts", suitable for use by the LORD among Humanity. These protocols are embedded in the Laws of God. Such were those practiced by priests of biblical days, upon willing vessels or human hearts, meeting the desired benchmarks set by these laws would the LORD place His Spirit, for the purposes of intervening in human affairs whenever they require His assistance to deliver Humanity from evil forces or trying circumstances on the Earth.

In such cases when there is no one or no human heart with status meeting the desired benchmark of being a willing vessel, conduit or proxy for the LORD's Power", or as a host for His Spirit" in the midst of Humanity. Then all humans are collectively considered as "being forsaken by the LORD God" or "bearing evil imaginations", and such happens only because the hearts of all humans existing in that generation have become totally corrupted or inaccessible to the LORD's Spirit.

We exist in a bi-polar universe of light and darkness, good and evil, as such when human hearts are shut to God, a posteriori it also means their hearts are fully accessible to or open to the opposing entity called evil. Technically human hearts can never be in a sitting-on-the-fence status or condition, and rarely does the LORD release His Power into a human heart upon which he has no control, because if He does He simply will have unwittingly empowered the devil or the evil entities in control of such a mind with His power, and it is surely going to be misused.

That expression about the heart of the people on the Earth being described as full of evil imagination as stated in narratives about the days of Noah, tells us that the hearts of all men were already somewhat fully under the control of the devil or other anti-God forces. Such circumstances are precursors to disaster or calamity for Humanity. This is simply because, the LORD has only one option in such situations, which is to wipe the slate clean and start all over again with Humanity.

The title of the LORD, "the Alpha and Omega" is one which is clearly accentuated in such context. He is the one who has a final say over when life on Earth starts, and when it ends or gets reset. Such a final say was decreed and executed when the floods of water killed all living on the Earth in Noah's days, and a similar thing happened when Sodom and Gomorrah was destroyed by fire and hail stones, likewise another of such is pencilled for the end times in our generation, as illustrated in the book of Revelations and various other prophecies. The same was also made reference to by Jesus Christ when he said; "it will be like in the days of Noah" when making comments about the end days, herein is wisdom.

In the case of Noah and the Land of Sodom, some humans escaped annihilation even though these ones were not considered perfect or bearing a righteous heart. These ones got an escape from destruction or calamity card purely because of the influences of Noah & Abraham who interceded with the LORD to spare their lives.

Some biblical scholars opine that all the eight people on Noah's ark were righteous people, and as stated earlier this is a view I really do not subscribe to. Furthermore, unimpeachable evidence to support that view comes by considering the actions of one of Noah's son towards his father when the left the ark after the flood ended. Such behaviour confirms he was not righteous. A righteous person is unlikely to do what he did. This leaps us to ponder why the LORD did not destroy all the bad ones and for sure put a permanent end to evil among Humanity?

The answer to that is simply that such can or will only happen when "the Messiah" or "the Perfect One" arrives amongst Humanity.

Noah was not the Messiah or perfect one sought by the LORD. But simply put, he was the best of the worst from "the sea of Humanity" of his generations. We all are also in our own pious ways best of the worst, but from that subset will the Messiah appear, he will be "the Perfect One" in the eyes of the LORD, and afterwards, the entire subset of imperfects one becomes Humanity's junk, herein lies wisdom.

> *1 Corinthians 13:9-10*
> *For we know in part, and we prophesy in part. 10.  But when that which is perfect is come, then that which is in part shall be done away.*

> *Ephesians 4:13*
> *Till we all come in the unity of the faith, and of the knowledge of the Son of God, unto a perfect man, unto the measure of the stature of the fulness of Christ:*

We must never forget that just as the Lord is searching for "the Perfect One" amongst Humanity for Him and to serve His purposes, the devil is also busy executing his agenda on the Earth, to ensure not one human is perfect in the eyes of the LORD. That is why he is sometimes called the accuser of all humans; he does this because if his aim gets accomplished. Meaning if he can makes us all imperfect in the LORD's eyes, the devil wins control over Humanity forever.

So just as the LORD's search continues for His Perfect One, that other entity called "the Serpent or Devil", the one that deceived the human race to experience "the Forbidden tree", that which made them imperfect, is also busy working, arranging and planning to prevent a situation where the LORD achieves His aim of finding one who will yield a full control over his human heart to Him.

This is so because once this happens, the devil loses all its control and domination over Humanity as a race forever, because we are all connected together in a way. Our being connected together is also symbolized by how the testimony of one human, Jesus Christ has helped the rest of Humanity.

This view may be better understood considering that Adam and Eve were one of many Humans walking the Earth when they were tempted, yet their errors affected the others.

The special thing about that couple was that they were custodians of "the Spirit of the LORD" and access route for Him into the world, they were some sort of central hub to Humanity. That should explain the origin of Cain's wife.

There is this context in Islamic text narratives that hints humans as "Kahlifa", a name from which the word "Islamic Caliphate" originates and this connotes that humans were representatives of God on Earth. Adam was called "the Kuhlifa" because he was the representative of God, by logic we should all understand that a person can't rule over anything if they are the only one there, they can only rule if they have subjects to rule over. If anyone really thinks that God created only one set of humans Adam and Eve, then I must say they missed it. Just ask yourself why God will create multiples of plants, animals etc., and when it gets to his best creation the Humans, He will choose to create only one. We are talking about the same entity that desired His people to exceed the stars in the sky. Ponder on that.

> *Genesis 5:1-2*
> *This is the book of the generations of Adam. In the day that God created man, in the likeness of God made he him; 2. Male and female created he them; and blessed them, and called their name Adam, in the day when they were created.*

Several methods have been deployed by the devil at accomplishing his objective of making Humanity imperfect. Such as making demanding of humans to be possessed by its own spirit too "also known as demons" through rituals and evil sacrifices. Following of which those who comply with such request are rewarded with things like fame, money or power, anything that will stop them looking or venturing in the direction of pleasing God's will.

We should recall the devil offered similar rewards to Jesus Christ when he requested of him to bow down and worship him in exchange for everything on the Earth. What the devil was asking Jesus Christ to do was to ignore all what God wants done and for looking the other way, Jesus Christ gets to co-rule over the world with him. Those humans who accept the devil's offer and bow to worship him are considered to have sold their soul to the devil, because by such actions he acquires their soul — or a piece of it — as a real estate asset and they are somewhat no longer available to be bought or acquired by the LORD unless a revocation of that given to the devil is executed.

A second subset of humans exists who will never consciously enter into any contract with the devil to sell their souls, because they have been warned about it, and are wise to take heed or listen. For such ones, the devil has other strategies, such as craftily bringing and using the cares of their flesh or the lures of life on Earth, greed, drugs, drinking, fornication, adultery, wickedness, or behaviours advanced by hatred of other individuals, those spurred by unexplainable prejudices etc. A lot of those who indulge in these habits are unaware that by indulging in such habits over and over again,

they sear into their souls, cavities of real estate immediately occupied by the devil and his demons. This is because for every time they fall for such temptations, they yield a portion of their free will or surrender a cavity in it to the evil one or force prompting such an act.

These cavities are small pockets of real estate taken over in the heart and over the will of such humans, a piecemeal acquisition strategy is deployed by the devil to take over their hearts or possess the will of such individuals. This is simply because he can't acquire such in a wholesale or block transaction. Gradually, such humans falling for this evil tactic will go from good to bad personalities over time. The devil will never yield back control of those cavities acquired in them or in any human without a fight, deliverance or an exorcism.

Such can only occur when the human in question truly craves and desires for a return of "the Spirit of the LORD" with a passion or dedication greater than that with which they had yielded to all the devil's temptations which they fell for, here again is a subtle overview of what the word "Penance" actually means or suggest. And it is open to all, even those who have made covenants with the devil concerning their soul in the past.

We must always remember that any grounds in a human heart gained by the devil is one lost to "the Spirit of the LORD", and any ground lost by the LORD's Spirit becomes gained and occupied by "the devil, or other evil forces also collectively called the darkness force". Likewise, the more of evil forces present in a human heart, the less there will be of "good forces; the force of Love; or Light;" every action and thought counts as stated by Jesus Christ in his teachings.

The Ark of God was for a period of time the only defacto point for the manifestation of "the Power or Presence of the LORD God" among Humanity. This is because back then humans could not understand or comply with the desired instructions of the LORD to aid His Presence being in their midst by keeping their hearts holy, mostly because of their cultures and lifestyle. Even in our days when you state these needs or requirements, it still sounds like garble to most people or appears pointless. In those days and for such reasons was the Ark made at the LORD's instruction in order to interface and deliver the LORD's Power or Presence within the realm of Humanity.

For the "attributes of God" it delivered the beholders, the Ark was always taken along with the military whenever the Israelites went to battle with their enemies, or when they were aiming at conquering territories, it represented and delivered on the battlefield the LORD's Glory needed to overwhelm the enemy in other to win their wars or battles.

Crucially, we have to note that the Ark does not represent where God dwells as presumed by humans back in biblical days, rather it represents a portal for delivery of the LORD's Presence, Power or Glory, just like a socket on the wall in a home does not represent the location of an electric power generation utility, but rather a point for accessing the electricity from that power station or utility which could be located thousands of kilometers away from that home.



*Exodus 25:21-22*
*And thou shalt put the mercy seat above upon the ark; and in the ark thou shalt put the testimony that I shall give thee. 22. And there I will meet with thee, and I will commune with thee from above the mercy seat, from between the two cherubims which are upon the ark of the testimony, of all things which I will give thee in commandment unto the children of Israel.*

Because the LORD's Glory or Power emanated from within the Ark, it may now be easy to understand how misconceptions about God's dwelling in the Ark came about in the mind of the unlearned or the clueless. Also in addition to that, certain protocols were commanded to the priests who were tasked to ensure the Ark's status was not compromised. Such must have been misconstrued as obligation towards the entity presumed to be dwelling within the Ark. In actual sense, those protocols were to preserve the Ark's wholesomeness, simply because replacing it was not easy. Some of those instructions are what we consider as religious ritual abounding and still practiced today by various faiths all over the globe.

I must stress here that although the Ark contained just stones which had been written on by the LORD's hands. These stones possessed certain attributes by virtue of their coming in contact with "the Presence of the LORD", and such attributes we can call or describe as "the Essence or Glory of God". In order to replace the Ark and its contents, another human must exist who develops a similar relationship to that which Moses had with the LORD. Such that he or she could also ascend or be allowed into "the Presence of God" with another set of ordinary stones from the Earth, just to capture a similar essence intrinsic to those stones brought down by Moses.

So in the case of the Ark's integrity being compromised, Humanity would need another human like Moses, one who must be capable of ascending up into "God's Throne" or "His Presence" just like Moses did to replace it. History tells us and we know such humans are rare to find. That realisation in itself is a sign to us all that we still suffer from the consequences of "the Original sin" of Humanity. One which separates us from the LORD and His Presence, and we all need repenting for this sin irrespective of lies peddled by a plethora of false religious doctrines abounding everywhere to suggest a contrary status. Quite sadly, "the Ark of God" did eventually become compromised when captured by the Philistines, and from the moment when this occurred, Humanity was thrown back into a state of absence of a conduit for the "LORD's Glory and His Power" in their midst.

This condition is also the same as an absence of "a place for God's Name on the Earth". A situation which was sometimes punctuated by appearances of those we call Prophets or Servants, but such a status persisted on Earth until the days of the man called Jesus Christ "an Anointed of God" and human host of "the Spirit of God".

Something crucial to note in Apostle Paul's New Testament teaching was that he mentioned death reigning from Adam to Moses. My interpretation of what he meant by those words, was "the separation of Humanity from the LORD" which is also termed as "death" in scriptural context. Moses was a human who put an end to that separation in his days, by reconnecting to God and that is why "the end of death", meaning "the separation of Humanity from the LORD" was pencilled to end in his — Moses' days.

> *Romans 5:12-14*
> *Wherefore, as by one man sin entered into the world, and death by sin; and so death passed upon all men, for that all have sinned: 13. (For until the law sin was in the world: but sin is not imputed when there is no law. 14. Nevertheless death reigned from Adam to Moses, even over them that had not sinned after the similitude of Adam's transgression, who is the figure of him that was to come.*

This "death" which was ended by Moses must not to be misconstrued as the one conquered by Jesus Christ, because there are two different contexts to death itself. The first is separation from the LORD, and the second the ability to transcend that which kills Humanity in the new realm (our Earth) which we occupy by still being separated from Him physically.

To overcome the death which kills us in our new realm, we need to first overcome our initial death. Also known as a state of "separation from the LORD", because without "His Presence or Spirit" being with us or we being connected to Him, we cannot accomplish the fore stated mission.

The man Jesus Christ did just that first, before bringing us the gift we now call "Eternal Life or Salvation by Grace", which in essence is ability to overcome the death "that kills our flesh" in this new realm. And by this gift we can now live like inhabitants of the old realm called "Paradise or Eden" — a place where nothing dies — even though we are existing in a new realm or frontier. This act by Jesus Christ also purifies our soul and transforms us into beings that are of no risk to the LORD, that is if we were to approach His Presence, and that is a context bringing clarity to the sin Jesus Christ took away for us or the gift of Eternal Life it depicts.

> *Rom 6:23*
> *For the wages of sin is death; but the gift of God is eternal life through Jesus Christ our Lord.*

Jesus Christ hinted about fearing One who is not only able to kill the flesh, but also able to kill the soul, in this context he expresses those two forms of death. Both sins of Humanity are "death". One of flesh while the other is of the soul, they have now been eliminated; "the death of the flesh" was vanquished by

Jesus Christ while "that of the soul" was vanquished by Moses. We all need to vanquish both "deaths" personally in order to establish our reunion with the LORD, by leveraging on the victories won for us by these great men of God.

It is a responsibility of our faith not a gift as wrongly peddled by some doctrines. The procedure to accomplish it has been perfected for us, we simply need to follow the rules and instructions of those who did it before us. That is the gift they give us, knowledge of how to do it. Just like someone who has been to a geographical location you haven't ever visited before, can tell you how to get there if you seek directions off them and follow it. But until you find your way to that destination, using their guidance, you have not made any use of the gift or knowledge they gave you about that location. By failing to utilize their guidance and directions to get you there, such gift is worthless.

Vanquishing of the plague of death existing in our nature was prophesied prior to Jesus Christ being born. This is symbolic of a problem that needed fixing in human beings.

> *Isaiah 25:7-8*
> *And he will destroy in this mountain the face of the covering cast over all people, and the vail that is spread over all nations.  8.  He will swallow up death in victory; and the Lord GOD will wipe away tears from off all faces; and the rebuke of his people shall he take away from off all the earth: for the LORD hath spoken it.*

> *Hosea 13:14*
> *I will ransom them from the power of the grave; I will redeem them from death: O death, I will be thy plagues; O grave, I will be thy destruction: repentance shall be hid from mine eyes.*

> *Isaiah 28:15-18*
> *Because ye have said, We have made a covenant with death, and with hell are we at agreement; when the overflowing scourge shall pass through, it shall not come unto us: for we have made lies our refuge, and under falsehood have we hid ourselves:16.  Therefore thus saith the Lord GOD, Behold, I lay in Zion for a foundation a stone, a tried stone, a precious corner stone, a sure foundation: he that believeth shall not make haste.  17.Judgment also will I lay to the line, and righteousness to the plummet: and the hail shall sweep away the refuge of lies, and the waters shall overflow the hiding place. 18. And your covenant with death shall be disannulled, and your agreement with hell shall not stand; when the overflowing scourge shall pass through, then ye shall be trodden down by it*

# A PLACE FOR "THE NAME OF GOD"

The Temple of Solomon was considered as the place for God's Name simply because "the Ark of God" was placed in that building. The Ark was "a source of the LORD's Power", which is also referred to as "the Name of God" in certain contexts.

What most people fail to understand was that from that point onwards at which the Ark became compromised, Solomon's temple in which the Ark was placed was now literally a place for God's Name, because "the Name of the LORD" or "the Name of God" had departed from it. Just as Humans lost their intrinsic good only attribute of God after experiencing "the Forbidden tree".

The message from the LORD to Solomon while he was about to build the temple he built reveals this clearly. The LORD highlights this in narrative, "I will come to dwell among your people if you walk in my statues". He did not say, I am already dwelling with you and your people as some may suppose. This physical dwelling place implied by the LORD, should not be confused with the notion of the LORD dwelling on the Earth side-by-side with Humanity.

He can do that even if no human provides a place for Him to dwell in their midst, by virtue of His Omnipresence attribute, so here again we can discern two perspectives of dwelling by the LORD that don't mix and each must be understood separately.

*1 Kings 6:11-13*
*And the word of the LORD came to Solomon, saying, 12. Concerning this house which thou art in building, if thou wilt walk in my statutes, and execute my judgments, and keep all my commandments to walk in them; then will I perform my word with thee, which I spake unto David thy father: 13. And I will dwell among the children of Israel, and will not forsake my people Israel.*

The LORD also stressed clearly to Solomon, that He had hallowed the house after the temple was commissioned and added, "I will fulfill my promise to David if you — Solomon — walk with me like your father did". But if not, the promise I made to your father, remains open to anyone who will fulfill it.

Though it was not expressed literally as stated here, that is what was implied. It should be understood that the person who will fulfill the requirements of God for a dwelling place with Humans, if such was not met by Solomon would be one of those to come after him, because this requirement will remain outstanding and its fulfillment likewise.

We also need to note that hallowing the house, was in no way a fulfillment of the promises the LORD made to King David. This in my view means; "a hallowed house of God" was not necessarily "a place for God's Name", but one that held such a potential which will become manifested, if the requirements for such manifestations are fulfilled by humans who walked the same path as King David.

It is like marking a piece of land and designating it, as proposed site for a state house, it doesn't become such or acquire the state house status, until the land is developed and the government building and apparatus of state power begins to occupy that land.

*1 Kings 9:3-8*
*And the LORD said unto him, I have heard thy prayer and thy supplication, that thou hast made before me: I have hallowed this house, which thou hast built, to put my name there for ever; and mine eyes and mine heart shall be there perpetually. 4. And if thou wilt walk before me, as David thy father walked, in integrity of heart, and in uprightness, to do according to all that I have commanded thee, and wilt keep my statutes and my judgments: 5. Then I will establish the throne of thy kingdom upon Israel for ever, as I promised to David thy father, saying, There shall not fail thee a man upon the throne of Israel. 6.But if ye shall at all turn from following me, ye or your children, and will not keep my commandments and my statutes which I have set before you, but go and serve other gods, and worship them: 7. Then will I cut off Israel out of the land which I have given them; and this house, which I have hallowed for my name, will I cast out of my sight; and Israel shall be a proverb and a byword among all people: 8. And at this house, which is high, every one that passeth by it shall be astonished, and shall hiss; and they shall say, Why hath the LORD done thus unto this land, and to this house?*

## What is "The Name of God"?

"The Name of God" is firstly: "the Presence of the LORD", and secondly: "the Glory of the LORD", which can then be further perceived as the Power, Might, Muscles, Hand or Finger by which the LORD does great works or performs wonders or things which we refer to as miracles, signs or wonders.

Over the ages, people seem to confuse the phrase, "The Name of the LORD" with the literal pronunciation of God's name. Jewish history reveals that in ages past, people dared not mention the name of God mindlessly, because it was considered as sacred.

Well in reality that which was considered sacred was "the manifested Power of God" which is also called "the Name of God". It is not the literal pronunciation of God's name as naturally may be presumed. Such cultural and religious presumptions are responsible for misinterpretations encircling the phrase "The Name of God". When considered, the commandment to the Israelites not to take the name of the LORD in vain may throw some light over that view.

The verses below indicate clearly that the name is more of an essence of the LORD's Presence, Glory, Might, Muscle and Power rather than something of literal pronunciation.

*Genesis 48:15-17*
*And he blessed Joseph, and said, God, before whom my fathers Abraham and Isaac did walk, the God which fed me all my life long unto this day, 16. The Angel which redeemed me from all evil, bless the lads; and let my name be named on them, and the name of my fathers Abraham and Isaac; and let them grow into a multitude in the midst of the earth.17. And when Joseph saw that his father laid his right hand upon the head of Ephraim, it displeased him: and he held up his father's hand, to remove it from Ephraim's head unto Manasseh's head.*

*Exodus 23:20-21*
*Behold, I send an Angel before thee, to keep thee in the way, and to bring thee into the place which I have prepared. 21. Beware of him, and obey his voice, provoke him not; for he will not pardon your transgressions: for my name is in him.*

*1 Samuel 17:45-47*
*Then said David to the Philistine, Thou comest to me with a sword, and with a spear, and with a shield: but I come to thee in the name of the LORD of hosts, the God of the armies of Israel, whom thou hast defied. 46. This day will the LORD deliver thee into mine hand; and I will smite thee, and take thine head from thee; and I will give the carcases of the host of the Philistines this day unto the fowls of the air, and to the wild beasts of the earth; that all the earth may know that there is a God in Israel. 47. And all this assembly shall know that the LORD saveth not with sword and spear: for the battle is the LORD'S, and he will give you into our hands.*

*Psalms 20:6-7*
*Now know I that the LORD saveth his anointed; he will hear him from his holy heaven with the saving strength of his right hand. 7. Some trust in chariots, and some in horses: but we will remember the name of the LORD our God.*

*Psalms 91:13-15*
*Thou shalt tread upon the lion and adder: the young lion and the dragon shalt thou trample under feet. 14. Because he hath set his love upon me, therefore will I deliver him: I will set him on high, because he hath known my name. 15. He shall call upon me, and I will answer him: I will be with him in trouble; I will deliver him, and honour him.*

*Jeremiah 3:16-17*
*And it shall come to pass, when ye be multiplied and increased in the land, in those days, saith the LORD, they shall say no more, The ark of the covenant of the LORD: neither shall it come to mind: neither shall they remember it; neither shall they visit it; neither shall that be done any more. 17. At that time they shall call Jerusalem the throne of the LORD; and all the nations shall be gathered unto it, to the name of the LORD, to Jerusalem: neither shall they walk any more after the imagination of their evil heart.*

We glean in the verse above that when the "the Name of God" is referenced; it points to His Presence, Glory or Power being with or within the subject of the context.

In the following verses the same phrase references the ability to perform great things or wonders. This come about as a result of the presence of "the Spirit of the LORD" also known as "the Name of God", such feats are what we call miracles. This context again shows us there is more than one perspective to this phrase "the Name of the LORD" or "the Name of God".

*2 Kings 2:22-24*
*So the waters were healed unto this day, according to the saying of Elisha which he spake. 23. And he went up from thence unto Bethel: and as he was going up by the way, there came forth little children out of the city, and mocked him, and said unto him, Go up, thou bald head; go up, thou bald head. 24. And he turned back, and looked on them, and cursed them in the name of the LORD. And there came forth two she bears out of the wood, and tare forty and two children of them.*

*Psalms 44:4-6*
*Thou art my King, O God: command deliverances for Jacob. 5. Through thee will we push down our enemies: through thy name will we tread them under that rise up against us. 6. For I will not trust in my bow, neither shall my sword save me.*

*Psalms 89:24-26*
*But my faithfulness and my mercy shall be with him: and in my name shall his horn be exalted. 25. I will set his hand also in the sea, and his right hand in the rivers. 26. He shall cry unto me, Thou art my father, my God, and the rock of my salvation.*

Misinterpretation about "the Name of God" and what it actually is or represents are still rife in our days. Such is perhaps one of the main folly of Christians who by faulty doctrine and teachings have turned "the Name of Jesus" into some sort of hocus-pocus mantra with which they expect to bring about their desires or petitions to God, provided such is appended to their prayers or supplications.

The "Name of Jesus Christ" actually points to the manifested power of "the Spirit of the LORD". Which was the miraculous power associated to Jesus Christ, and was that acquired by virtue of "the Spirit of the LORD" coming upon Him, after what is called his baptism at the Jordan river, and that power was the means by which He performed the miracles attributed to him and his overcoming "death and the grave".

This power is only available to those considered wise, because it takes great wisdom to seek and crave this power. It takes a sound ability of discernment to perceive what others can't see and to realize "the Hidden truth of all ages". Which is that there is a power, one greater in might than any other power existing in the Universe, which could become yours  by craving the companionship of its custodian, who is "the Spirit of the LORD" and His angels, just as Jesus Christ did while walking on the Earth, herein lies wisdom.



In the book of Acts, Peter is noted to be filled with "the Spirit of the LORD", when he was quizzed about the source of his ability to heal the crippled man. Those interviewing him asked him, "by what power or by what name have you done this". That phrase "by what name", indicates Peter bore an unknown authority, source or power in those days which prompted such a question and it was "the Name of God".

Jesus Christ when praying to LORD uttered these words to God, "I have manifested thy name". All biblical records show us that Jesus Christ manifested "the Powers of God" as a human and not a literal word or name. This is perhaps the most veritable proof that "the Name of God" is a reference to "the Powers of the LORD God". Jesus Christ did not use any hocus-pocus like statements to manifest God, all he used was "an Authority of God" availed him by "the Spirit of God" which rested upon him and which he was paired with at heart — also known as "the Name of God".

*John 17:6*
*I have manifested thy name unto the men which thou gavest me out of the world: thine they were, and thou gavest them me; and they have kept thy word.*

*John 17:25-26*
*O righteous Father, the world hath not known thee: but I have known thee, and these have known that thou hast sent me. 26. And I have declared unto them thy name, and will declare it: that the love wherewith thou hast loved me may be in them, and I in them.*

## Concept of equalization and re-assignment of values or meanings

Misinterpretations about "the Name of God" and what it refers to, does not only occur in this context all through the bible, it also occurs in several other instances which will be highlighted as we proceed. However, in order to help us understand whenever they are implied, I propose to use the phrase; "by equalization" and by "re-assignment" going forward to indicate that a value or meaning is given to a phrase or sentence because it equals the same as what another phrase or sentence suggests.

A good example would be when talking about Jesus Christ we could say he was "a Son of God", because "the Spirit of the LORD God" rested upon him. We could also say that by re-assignment, "the Son of God" was also "a Son of Man". Because Jesus Christ was born of a woman, like all humans are and principally, because the phrase "a Son of Man" also means or suggest a human being in certain context of scriptures.

Now, if Jesus Christ represents both "a Son of God" and "a Son of Man", whenever we spot a reference to Jesus Christ, we can automatically assume it also means or points to the one upon whom "the Spirit of God" came or rested, who was also someone born of a woman called Mary.

We can then reassign meanings and say:


Jesus Christ = Son of Man;
= Son of God;
= Son of Mary.

Now from the moment "the Spirit of the LORD" came upon Jesus Christ his body became a place where "the Presence of the LORD" dwelt, which is also a place where "the Name of God" was manifested from, which is the same as "the Power of God". Now we must recall that this power was also known to be manifested from "the Ark of God" in previous times.


We can then equalize and say:


Power of God dwelling within the Ark = "The name of God";

= "The name of Jesus Christ";

= "The Presence of God";

= "The spirit of the LORD's Presence".

### How the name "Emmanuel" means exactly what it suggested?

Emmanuel meant "God with us". If that was true, then the power dwelling within the Ark of God, or derived from it, which was that of the LORD God, is supposed to now reside with the son of Mary & Joseph.

If we examine all historical accounts regarding the life of Jesus Christ, we can easily conclude that this individual possessed some strange and unusual abilities, which perfectly dovetailed into the tree of all abilities, exhibited by previous servant or prophets of the LORD who were associated with "the Ark of God" and "the Spirit of God".

Elijah & Elisha raised up dead people, likewise did Jesus Christ. Elisha by blessing a limited resource of food fed many people and likewise did Jesus Christ. He also went further and did things that had not been done by any of the previous servants or prophets of God, such as walking on water. Although Elisha made an axe head that sunk into water refloat on the surface of the water, that feat bears some similarities in certain perspectives, but is not the same as walking on water.

Moses, a person with whom "the Name of God" was with too, is remembered to also have demonstrated abilities of controlling water masses, by splitting the sea into two halves, in order to allow passage for the Israelites on their way out of Egypt. Such a feat will have been impossible without access to some special power or ability to control or impact water molecules as demonstrated by Elisha and Jesus Christ simultaneously.

Jesus Christ is famously remembered for overcoming "the powers of death and that of the devil," before he ascended into Heaven. But before him Enoch, Elijah and Moses too had gone into this dimension, we call Heaven. Elijah went up into Heaven awake, but Moses' body was taken up by "an angel of God" while in deep sleep or in what may medically be described in our days as a state of coma. That is why no one knows where Moses' body was buried.

We'd all agree it is impossible for a human to die and for that human to bury them self or write about their death.

Strangely, that appears to be what was suggested for Moses by scriptural accounts. Additionally, since no one has any idea or recollection about where his body was buried, that sort of lays credence to the postulation that he was not buried, but rather that he ascended or was taken up into heaven like Elijah and Enoch.

Also, there is a passage in the book of Jude, saying his body was fought over in a battle between angels and the devil. Such clearly confirms he wasn't buried, but was taken up into Heaven. Angels as we know live in Heaven or within the Heavenly realm and not on the Earthly dimension. So if they took possession of something, it is likely that such is with them within their realm.

The presence of Moses & Elijah during the transfiguration of Jesus Christ also proves or suggests that Moses & Elijah came from the same realm and location namely Heaven. If Moses was dead and had gone into the grave where all dead people go, he could not have come out of that grave to rendezvous with Jesus Christ and Elijah, simply because the ability "or technology needed" to overcome "death or the grave" had not yet been tested or manifested for humans, prior to the transfiguration of Jesus Christ on the mount.

> *Deuteronomy 34:5-6*
> *So Moses the servant of the LORD died there in the land of Moab, according to the word of the LORD. 6. And he buried him in a valley in the land of Moab, over against Bethpeor: but no man knoweth of his sepulchre unto this day.*

> *Jude 1:9*
> *Yet Michael the archangel, when contending with the devil he disputed about the body of Moses, durst not bring against him a railing accusation, but said, The Lord rebuke thee.*

Returning back to our discourse about Emmanuel, if he was as expected "a Son of God", it should go without saying that he must have had knowledge or have discerned that God was with him. Well on several instances in his life he made claims to such effect. A notable one was when he went into the temple and sent out the traders and money-changers, because he felt they had turned a place he considered "His house" into a den of thieves. We have to recall that Solomon's Temple (the rebuilt edifice by the Romans) was supposed to be the house of the LORD with whom King David walked. Insight needed here, could it have been that the entity speaking those words about this temple and chasing people out of it was "the Spirit of the LORD"? Which now was resting upon Jesus Christ, and making him act and speak those words?

> *Luke 19:45-46*
> *And he went into the temple, and began to cast out them that sold therein,*

*and them that bought; 46. Saying unto them, It is written, My house is the
house of prayer: but ye have made it a den of thieves.*

The Temple as we know it was first built by Solomon, and rebuilt even before
Jesus Christ was born. So it should be of peculiar interest to consider that
someone who was not alive or around, when the temple was built, will lay
claim that it was his house?

Such a claim would be incredulous unless they were made by "the Spirit of
the LORD" and not by Jesus Christ to whom those statements are attributed.
Though he was the one who spoke, it does appears it was "the Spirit of God"
which had descended upon Him, prompting such speech and by such speech
he qualifies to be "a Prophet of God", because such are people through whom
the LORD speaks.

Let us look back and collate known knowns to assist our discernment here.
We know that the Temple was built as a place for "the Spirit of the LORD"
who was the God of Israel, by King David's son Solomon. We also know that
it was announced before Jesus Christ's birth, that the same one for whom the
temple was built was to be present with them — the nation of Israel — once
again via this son.

By stringing these known facts together, we can limn an influence or
presence in the background, one which suggests that it was not Jesus Christ
who was casting people out of the temple, rather it was that influence or
presence called "the Spirit of the LORD" casting people out of the temple,
being unpleased by what it had been turned it into by those humans now
occupying it.

This "Spirit of the LORD" dwelling within the body of Jesus Christ as his
name "Emmanuel" suggested, can clearly be observed here controlling his
will, thereby making Him execute the LORD's desires, concerning Solomon's
temple.

A logical question that follows to that suggestion is, how is it possible for a
spirit to take over a human's body and control the person, without the owner
of the body fighting or showing any signs of forceful resistance? This is where
the concept of submitting to the will of "the Spirit of LORD" becomes
emphasized and highlighted, because this is what the LORD desires from
every one of us, though we seldom deliver this or accede to this request
because of having our hearts hardened against Him and His will by gratifying
towards our fleshly desires.

Again in another instance bearing equal similarity, Jesus Christ went into
the temple one day, and announced to all who were there that "the Spirit of
the LORD" was upon Him. An announcement which suggests or shouts out
clearly, "Hey guys, I am a human-carrier or host for the LORD's Spirit" if
parsed correctly or interpreted clearly.

We know they did not believe His words nor take significant notice of
what he announced, though he was later crucified for making such or similar
comments. This instance again dovetails with the opinion that "the LORD was
actually with him" as his name Emmanuel suggested.

And since he was in Israel, it could be said that the LORD was present in Israel albeit via this son as pre-announced at His birth, though it appears the Israelites neither knew it nor accepted such a notion, because that was why he was persecuted and crucified.

> *Luke 4:18-20*
> *The Spirit of the Lord is upon me, because he hath anointed me to preach the gospel to the poor; he hath sent me to heal the brokenhearted, to preach deliverance to the captives, and recovering of sight to the blind, to set at liberty them that are bruised,  19.  To preach the acceptable year of the Lord. 20.  And he closed the book, and he gave it again to the minister, and sat down. And the eyes of all them that were in the synagogue were fastened on him.*

There exists several other instance that signify that the man Jesus Christ was not alone or bore multiple personalities, because several statements which he made were certainly not appropriate for someone of his age. A classic example occurs when he told the Jews that Abraham was happy to see him during his days on Earth. Such a statement about meeting Abraham personally from someone who was less than fifty years old could be adjudged as simply a silly utterance by a young lad. However, if it wasn't the young lad speaking, but "the Spirit of God", and by that I mean the same entity that interacted with Abraham in olden days.

Then, that statement makes perfect sense as voiced. The Jews or Pharisees did not clock on to that possibility, because they never expected God to bear human skin. Their doctrines told them God cannot be a man, and they held on to that view with a hook, line and sinker steadfastness and eventually persecuted Jesus Christ for these utterances. Although this utterance was another proof, that the name Emmanuel or "God with us", literally meant what it suggested. In this case God did not become a man, He simply took control of a human heart to speak as a man will speak to other men in order to communicate with humans. The same is what happened at all those instances when Jesus Christ was noted to have said to people that their sins were forgiven, it wasn't him forgiving sins but God, while he was the conduit through which God was speaking to the human whose sins were forgiven.

> *John 8:56-59*
> *Your father Abraham rejoiced to see my day: and he saw it, and was glad. 57.  Then said the Jews unto him, Thou art not yet fifty years old, and hast thou seen Abraham? 58. Jesus said unto them, Verily, verily, I say unto you, Before Abraham was, I am.  59.  Then took they up stones to cast at him: but Jesus hid himself, and went out of the temple, going through the midst of them, and so passed by.*

On another account Jesus Christ attempted to illustrate to the Jew or Pharisees their errors in understandings of the writings in the scriptures.

They all assumed that "the Messiah" was to be "a biological son of David's generation" and believed this as an unchangeable fact according to doctrines they were taught. However, Jesus Christ knowing better, tried to explain to them that "the Messiah" was only a son via a son-ship position to what was called "the bloodline of King David's inheritance", rather than one for being younger to David in human age or chronological birth order.

From these perspectives, we can glean that a spirit or entity was present with Jesus Christ when he was born that was far much older in age than David, Abraham; or the man Jesus Christ himself. That is the entity we call "the Spirit of the LORD". This entity had knowledge of events or things which occurred even before the lifetime of Jesus Christ, such knowledge and many others "the Spirit of the LORD" shares or reveals to those humans who draw closer to it, or are associated to it. Humanity has not yet scratched the surface if we consider what a union with this entity can bequeath to our race, herein lies wisdom.

*Matthew 22:42-46*
*Saying, What think ye of Christ? whose son is he? They say unto him, The Son of David.  43. He saith unto them, How then doth David in spirit call him Lord, saying, 44. The LORD said unto my Lord, Sit thou on my right hand, till I make thine enemies thy footstool?  45.  If David then call him Lord, how is he his son?  46.  And no man was able to answer him a word, neither durst any man from that day forth ask him any more questions.*

"The father" in this perspective in King David, because he was the first to seat on a throne backed by "the Spirit of God". The son in this perspective, who is also to seat on a throne backed by "the Spirit of God" is one who comes after King David "the father", hence this should bring clarity to why "the son of David" title only indicates that this is one successor to David inheritance. And as Jesus Christ aptly clarified, even David called this one considered his son, my Lord, showing that David was clear this person is my senior and my boss, even though he is regarded as my son by line of throne succession.

# ONE WITH THE FATHER

One question which we need to ask is, how could Jesus Christ be a man and also be or act as the entity we call "the LORD God" or "Spirit of the LORD" simultaneously without any clashes in personalities of both? It is obvious that humans do not think like God thinks, or speak like God speaks either. Neither do they act like Him.

The question is how then can a man be God? That is a paradigm almost all religions will tell you is impossible but was yet one manifested via Jesus Christ.

The truth is man can never be God, at least the real LORD God. However, man can become a proxy for the LORD God, and act on Earth as the LORD will act if He were present here. This is the role humans are meant to play as Khalifa according to Islamic teaching, and in such a circumstance, that human can be considered as being a de facto representative of the LORD God. Such circumstances only arise when there is "a harmonious DUET between that human and the Spirit of the LORD", herein lies wisdom.

In the verses below, we can discern that more than one entity or personality was speaking about the same issue. The first entity comments about doing things by another entity called "My Father". Then the second entity speaks about knowing who His sheep are and vows to give Eternal Life to these one. Then once again, the first entity talks about the greatness of the entity called "My Father", and finally states that both "himself and The Father" are One. Being one in this context means being united or joined together, in a duet or co-existing together.

If God was really the entity being referred to as "My Father", then it follows that this man speaking was joined or united with God by such definition of oneness, which again strikes a cord of relevance in context of the name "Emmanuel" which means "God with Us" given to the boy born by Mary and Joseph.

The secret behind being "One with God" is really knowing how to submit to every will of "the Spirit of the LORD", and most especially complying with His wills and desires. This was what the man Jesus Christ, did better than any other human who has ever lived or walked on the Earth. This submission was tested to the utmost, when Jesus Christ was made to face the crucifixion ordeal, comprising all the flogging, insults and torture which were all aimed at getting him to resist and renounce the LORD's will by snapping or fighting back at those who were hurting him. If he had succumbed to such actions, he would have violated the desire of "the Spirit of the LORD" paired to or resting with him, just as Moses struck the rock instead of speaking to it as the LORD desired

All through the ordeal Jesus Christ maintained a position of deferring or yielding to pleasing "the Spirit of the LORD's will", even unto a point where he was crucified and death of his human flesh overwhelmed his consciousness. This was described as him giving up the ghost by scriptural accounts.

If at any point in the ordeals of crucifixion he faced, he had overridden "the will of God" with his own human will, he would have failed at being "the unblemished Lamb of God". And by such failure, Humanity would have had to produce "another Lamb" suitable for the task, because the LORD will never lower his standards for excellence or submission. This view is also applicable to every standards set out for "the expected Messiah or Anointed One" that all faiths are awaiting, herein lies wisdom.

Remembering that "the Spirit of the LORD" was in Jesus Christ and by this fact he was also unified with God. The perfect union between himself and "the Spirit of the LORD", such that they operated in unison harmony with neither violating each others will is described as "being One with God". It is also the sort of union being referenced when a Man is expected to leave his father and mother, and become one (or perfectly united) with his Wife after a marriage ceremony where both become one flesh.

From such perspectives arise all the context of "Bride and Bridegroom" in the scriptures which hints or represents the plans and desires of the LORD for Humanity to those who may grasp it.

*Neither pray I for these alone, but for them also which shall believe on me through their word; 21. That they all may be one; as thou, Father, art in me, and I in thee, that they also may be one in us: that the world may believe that thou hast sent me. 22. And the glory which thou gavest me I have given them; that they may be one, even as we are one: 23. I in them, and thou in me, that they may be made perfect in one; and that the world may know that thou hast sent me, and hast loved them, as thou hast loved me.*

# THE ARK, THE TEMPLE AND JERUSALEM

The issue about "being One with God" gives us more insight into the nature of the LORD God, and His plans for dwelling with Humanity. It also give us more understanding of what Jesus Christ told the woman at the well, which was "forget about worshipping in a mountain or at Jerusalem, true worshippers must begin to worship God in spirit and in truth". A statement which he followed by saying clearly, "I am the Messiah also meaning the Anointed One".

> *John 4:21-26*
> *Jesus saith unto her, Woman, believe me, the hour cometh, when ye shall neither in this mountain, nor yet at Jerusalem, worship the Father. 22. Ye worship ye know not what: we know what we worship: for salvation is of the Jews. 23. But the hour cometh, and now is, when the true worshippers shall worship the Father in spirit and in truth: for the Father seeketh such to worship him. 24. God is a Spirit: and they that worship him must worship him in spirit and in truth. 25. The woman saith unto him, I know that Messias cometh, which is called Christ: when he is come, he will tell us all things. 26. Jesus saith unto her, I that speak unto thee am he.*

This statement was a pre-announcement about the body of a human, now becoming the real "Temple of the LORD", where His Spirit should dwell and must be worshipped by all humans. And these words are of vital significance that should never be overlooked or have its meaning undermined in any way, shape or form.

### There have been several "Anointed Ones"

When Jesus Christ affirmed that he was the Messiah to the woman at the well, he was simply confirming that he was "the One" upon who "the Spirit of the LORD" has rested in those days. This comment was perhaps one of those that made the Jews to completely disown Jesus Christ as their Messiah. It is also one of those comments that helps Christians rest their belief in Jesus Christ as their Messiah.

It is also the reason why they are awaiting His return back to earth in order to rule over the world. It is quite amazing how a simple and clear statement like this one, has developed into one with different meanings and interpretations to different individuals and various faiths.

The Moslems also expect the return of an awaited one, called the "Al Mahdi". He is expected to be guided by Allah and he appears like a saviour too, they believe he is expected to vanquish all their enemies principally the Jews because they are those occupying Jerusalem — the Promised Land — and in addition to them their Western backed supporters. Thereafter "Al Mahdi" will establish an Islamic world order over the Earth with Islam as the universal religion.

Zoroastrianism expects one called "the Saoshyant" who brings about the final renovation of the Universe, when evil will be destroyed and everything will come into unity with their God called Azura Mazda.

Buddhism expects "a Maitreya" or promised messenger. One who is expected to appear on Earth, achieve complete enlightenment and thereafter teach pure Dharma and guide Humanity to God.

The word "Messiah" means "the Anointed One". And that simply means the one upon whom "the Spirit of the LORD" rests or descended in scriptural context. The fact remains that there has been more than one individual, upon whom "the Spirit of the LORD" has rested or descended over the generations.

It rested upon Moses; Elijah; Saul; David; Cyrus; and Jesus Christ all for fulfilling different purposes of the LORD. All of these individuals were also referenced as "Anointed Ones".

Though some of them may be best described as "acting-Anointed Ones", and that is because we can see that the LORD's Spirit did not absolutely unite or settle within their hearts, to the extent of transforming them to the level of becoming "One with God" as it did with Jesus Christ, this was mostly due to their obstinacy in personal and free will issues.

Apart from those whom "the Spirit of LORD" rests on, there has also been another set of people upon whom "the Spirit of God" descends or comes upon momentarily, whenever such is desired to execute a certain or specific will of God on the Earth, and after such descent it returns back to the LORD. Such individuals are best known as Seers, Judges or Prophets.

It appears that these humans are like "Workers in the Kingdom of God", unlike the other set of people described earlier whom the spirit rests upon for extended periods. Those are the ones we call "the Anointed Ones" and are best perceived as "Royals in the Kingdom of God".

The worker subset of people also manifest "the Glory of the LORD" and "His Mighty Power" by virtue of the presence of "the Spirit of the LORD" with them, causing them to perform wonders momentarily. Individuals like Samuel; Gideon; Deborah; Samson; Isaiah; Jeremiah; Ezekiel etc., are captured in this subset, and also "the donkey" that spoke to Balaam fits perfectly into this category too.

Another crucial fact to note is that there are "fully Anointed Ones of the LORD"; and "acting-Anointed Ones". Just as there are also "full Prophets of the LORD" there are also "acting-Prophets of the LORD".

A possible reason for the suggestions about Jesus Christ being "the Jewish Messiah" by Christian doctrine is that there exist theological views that there was only "One Anointed of the LORD". A view that perhaps takes it roots in the fact that there is only one God, which is also a religious safeguard that may have been deployed to avoid any god-impostors by those controlling religion its doctrines and future expectations.

While that is an absolutely correct view, the error in that perception, is that it does not take into consideration that everyone upon whom "the Spirit of the LORD" descends or rest, is also fit to be called "an Anointed of the LORD".

Whether such is a full, acting or the expected Anointed One is a different matter entirely. Every anointed person is referenced in the scriptures as simply "an anointed of the LORD". The level of their anointment is not specified, calibrated or designated. If this were it would have dispelled all the ambiguities that prompted misinterpretations about titles such as "an Anointed of the LORD", a phrase which also means or is interpreted as "Messiah" or "Christos".


## Saul

In Saul's case, he became "an anointed of the LORD", albeit an acting one when "the Spirit of the LORD" came upon him. Prophet Samuel referred to him as "the anointed of the LORD", in several contexts and by such reference and the fact that he prophesied on his first encounter with "the Spirit of the LORD", all these show us clearly that he really did have God's Spirit resting on him at a point in his life.

> *1 Samuel 11:5-6*
> *And, behold, Saul came after the herd out of the field; and Saul said, What aileth the people that they weep? And they told him the tidings of the men of Jabesh. 6. And the Spirit of God came upon Saul when he heard those tidings, and his anger was kindled greatly.*

> *1 Samuel 12:1-3*
> *And Samuel said unto all Israel, Behold, I have hearkened unto your voice in all that ye said unto me, and have made a king over you. 2. And now, behold, the king walketh before you: and I am old and grayheaded; and, behold, my sons are with you: and I have walked before you from my childhood unto this day. 3. Behold, here I am: witness against me before the LORD, and before his anointed: whose ox have I taken? or whose ass have I taken? or whom have I defrauded? whom have I oppressed? or of whose hand have I received any bribe to blind mine eyes therewith? and I will restore it you.*

To prophesy means to break out speaking in tongues, under the influence of the spirit. And in my view is a sort of hand-shaking protocol that humans experience when they encounter the LORD's Spirit.

The same thing happened to those in the upper room on the day of Pentecost, and a similar reaction was noted when Moses laid hands on 70 elders who were to be anointed as his assistants during their sojourn in the wilderness.

> *Numbers 11:24-26*
> *And Moses went out, and told the people the words of the LORD, and gathered the seventy men of the elders of the people, and set them round about the tabernacle. 25. And the LORD came down in a cloud, and spake unto him, and took of the spirit that was upon him, and gave it unto the seventy elders: and it came to pass, that, when the spirit rested upon them, they prophesied, and did not cease. 26. But there remained two of the men in the camp, the name of the one was Eldad, and the name of the other Medad: and the spirit rested upon them; and they were of them that were written, but went not out unto the tabernacle: and they prophesied in the camp.*

King David was noted to in error consider King Saul as the LORD's anointed after he had been de-anointed by the LORD for his sins or misdeeds. This event shows or suggests in a way the fact that there can only be "One Anointed of the LORD" at any moment.

However, the Moses instance and the Pentecostal instance both shows that several individuals can have "the Spirit of the LORD" resting, interacting or placed on them simultaneously. Hence we can identify two categories of anointing or two perspectives about being anointed here, and both do not mix.

> *1 Samuel 24:5-6*
> *And it came to pass afterward, that David's heart smote him, because he had cut off Saul's skirt. 6. And he said unto his men, The LORD forbid that I should do this thing unto my master, the LORD'S anointed, to stretch forth mine hand against him, seeing he is the anointed of the LORD.*

> *1 Samuel 26:21-23*
> *Then said Saul, I have sinned: return, my son David: for I will no more do thee harm, because my soul was precious in thine eyes this day: behold, I have played the fool, and have erred exceedingly. 22. And David answered and said, Behold the king's spear! and let one of the young men come over and fetch it. 23. The LORD render to every man his righteousness and his faithfulness: for the LORD delivered thee into my hand to day, but I would not stretch forth mine hand against the LORD'S anointed.*

In the case of King David, he became an anointed of the LORD; right after the LORD rejected Saul for his concerns and heart desires, because these were set only to please the people of Israel, rather than to please the LORD God who had made him King over them.

From the moment David became anointed, as directed by the LORD and executed by Prophet Samuel, "the Spirit of the LORD" which previously rested upon Saul left him, and now rested upon King David. Just like the staff of office is always with or in possession of the incumbent Speaker in a Parliament, Senate or a congressional House of Representatives.

*1 Samuel 16:13-14*
*Then Samuel took the horn of oil, and anointed him in the midst of his brethren: and the Spirit of the LORD came upon David from that day forward. So Samuel rose up, and went to Ramah.  14. But the Spirit of the LORD departed from Saul, and an evil spirit from the LORD troubled him.*

This transfer of the LORD's Spirit unto King David, did not occur in full glare of the people, because it was a spiritual transaction not a physical one. And I presume it may not have been fully known to King David himself, who was the beneficiary until quite later in his life after he had realized it as confirmed it by his own words.

*2 Samuel 23:1-5*
*Now these be the last words of David. David the son of Jesse said, and the man who was raised up on high, the anointed of the God of Jacob, and the sweet psalmist of Israel, said,  2.  The Spirit of the LORD spake by me, and his word was in my tongue.  3  The God of Israel said, the Rock of Israel spake to me, He that ruleth over men must be just, ruling in the fear of God. 4. And he shall be as the light of the morning, when the sun riseth, even a morning without clouds; as the tender grass springing out of the earth by clear shining after rain. 5. Although my house be not so with God; yet he hath made with me an everlasting covenant, ordered in all things, and sure: for this is all my salvation, and all my desire, although he make it not to grow.*

King David saw "the real anointed of the LORD", the one also called "the expected Messiah". It was he who he referenced as the LORD's Anointed in context below.

It easy to come to that deduction because Jesus Christ confirmed by exposition, during a discussion with the Jews, that the personality brought to sit on a throne was senior to and older than King David who saw him by vision. Hence the reason why King David referenced this personality as "My LORD" in his writings, even though he was one to come after him and was presumed to be his bloodline son by the Pharisees' doctrine.

Concerning this passage, this view was contrary to the Jews opinions because they thought it made reference to "a son of David" or one to be borne of David's lineage. A crucial fact to be noted is that King David called this personality "an Anointed" and referred to him as "My LORD", simply because anyone whoever sits on "the Throne of the LORD" is both "LORD" and is also "an Anointed One of the LORD" contemporaneously.

That to me appears to be the origin of the phrase "Jesus Christ is LORD" for he sat on that Throne David saw too. David was also "an anointed of the LORD", an acting one in my view. Although he sat only on "a physical throne of the LORD", because "the LORD's Name or Presence" was not on the throne upon which he sat on as King in Israel. That does not in any way mean or suggest the LORD was not with him, because the LORD's presence was in "an Ark of God" in King David's possession; giving the throne authority or backing it needed to reign, and that association is in some ways "the Inheritance of King David" to which those called his seeds have a right, by that I mean the backing of their reign by the LORD's Presence or Power.

However, contrary to that setup, this person whom King David saw in a vision, was spotted seating on "a Physical and Spiritual Throne". One in which "the LORD's Name and Presence" was on and backed by, giving it absolute authority to rule and reign forever. Now going back to consider the promise the LORD made to King David about his seed, "one from his bowels sitting on a Throne lasting forever", we can observe that even though Prophet Nathan brought King David the words of this promise verbally, the LORD still revealed his plans to King David by prophetic vision later.

Such was to serve as a visual fulfillment of the words of the LORD brought to him by Nathan, the Prophet. By comparing the prophecy of Nathan with that King David's relayed via his prophetic perception, such will surely help us understand more about this promise, and fill up any missing gaps in each one or rendering, because they speak about the same subject, "the Anointed One" also " a Son of David" sitting on a Throne given by God.

*the order of Melchizedek.  5.  The Lord at thy right hand shall strike through kings in the day of his wrath. 6. He shall judge among the heathen, he shall fill the places with the dead bodies; he shall wound the heads over many countries.  7.  He shall drink of the brook in the way: therefore shall he lift up the head.*

*Psalms 2:1-7*
*Why do the heathen rage, and the people imagine a vain thing?  2. The kings of the earth set themselves, and the rulers take counsel together, against the LORD, and against his anointed, saying, 3. Let us break their bands asunder, and cast away their cords from us.  4.  He that sitteth in the heavens shall laugh: the Lord shall have them in derision.  5. Then shall he speak unto them in his wrath, and vex them in his sore displeasure.  6.  Yet have I set my king upon my holy hill of Zion.  7.  I will declare the decree: the LORD hath said unto me, Thou art my Son; this day have I begotten thee.*

## Cyrus (A Persian King)

For Cyrus being non-Jewish and Persian, his anointing appears quite controversial. Nevertheless the LORD placed His Spirit on this man, in order to fulfill His purposes. One of which was, rebuilding the temple at Jerusalem by those from exile. Cyrus knocks out all preconceived views, that you had to be a Jew or of Abraham's lineage to qualify for the status of "the LORD's Anointed One". Cyrus by origin was a Gentile, and also "an acting-Anointed of the LORD", in my view, because "the Spirit of the LORD" didn't rest upon him fully, but only partially.

Another individual who may have bore similarity to Cyrus would have to be Melchidezek, because he was not a Jew as well hence a Gentile by origin. Because by definition, the biblical Jews were sons descended through Abraham's lineage. Yet we know Abraham gave sacrifices to one who was not from his lineage. It should be noted that never did the LORD protest or condemn this action as worshipping of other gods by Abraham, herein lies wisdom for those recalcitrant doctrine promoters, Gentiles too have roles to play in the LORD's plans on Earth.

*Isaiah 45:1-7*
*Thus saith the LORD to his anointed, to Cyrus, whose right hand I have holden, to subdue nations before him; and I will loose the loins of kings, to open before him the two leaved gates; and the gates shall not be shut;  2.  I will go before thee, and make the crooked places straight: I will break in pieces the gates of brass, and cut in sunder the bars of iron:  3.  And I will give thee the treasures of darkness, and hidden riches of secret places, that thou mayest know that I, the LORD, which call thee by thy name, am the God of Israel.  4.  For Jacob my servant's sake, and Israel mine elect, I have even called thee by thy name: I have surnamed thee, though thou hast not known me.  5.  I am the LORD, and there is none else, there is no God beside*

*me: I girded thee, though thou hast not known me: 6. That they may know from the rising of the sun, and from the west, that there is none beside me. I am the LORD, and there is none else. 7. I form the light, and create darkness: I make peace, and create evil: I the LORD do all these things.*

*2 Chronicles 36:22-23*
*Now in the first year of Cyrus king of Persia, that the word of the LORD spoken by the mouth of Jeremiah might be accomplished, the LORD stirred up the spirit of Cyrus king of Persia, that he made a proclamation throughout all his kingdom, and put it also in writing, saying, 23. Thus saith Cyrus king of Persia, All the kingdoms of the earth hath the LORD God of heaven given me; and he hath charged me to build him an house in Jerusalem, which is in Judah. Who is there among you of all his people? The LORD his God be with him, and let him go up.*

## Nebuchadnezzar (A Babylonian King)

King Nebuchadnezzar was simply raised up or assisted by the LORD, to knock some sense into the heads of the people of Israel and other nations like Egypt. This was so because they had all displeased the LORD in their ways, and needed correction. Nebuchadnezzar was the one chosen suitable for executing the desired task, thereafter the authority to execute such was handed over to him as an anointment.

*Jeremiah 27:5-8*
*I have made the earth, the man and the beast that are upon the ground, by my great power and by my outstretched arm, and have given it unto whom it seemed meet unto me. 6. And now have I given all these lands into the hand of Nebuchadnezzar the king of Babylon, my servant; and the beasts of the field have I given him also to serve him. 7. And all nations shall serve him, and his son, and his son's son, until the very time of his land come: and then many nations and great kings shall serve themselves of him. 8. And it shall come to pass, that the nation and kingdom which will not serve the same Nebuchadnezzar the king of Babylon, and that will not put their neck under the yoke of the king of Babylon, that nation will I punish, saith the LORD, with the sword, and with the famine, and with the pestilence, until I have consumed them by his hand.*

Nebuchadnezzar was not holy, righteous or pious in anyway desirable to the LORD. In fact his nation was no better than those he was conquering, by assistance of "the Presence of the LORD's Spirit" being with him. Considering that the LORD may allow an even more vile character to oppress His people, so they will hearken on to His words ultimately in their misery, is a signal to all of Humanity to fear Him. For that is the only path to peace and wellbeing for Humanity. Simply that of fulfilling and pleasing the LORD's desires. It should be noted that although Nebuchadnezzar was anointed too, albeit "an acting-Anointed of the LORD" in my view, he was also judged by the LORD for all his misdeeds after the LORD was done using him. The desired purpose of Nebuchadnezzar was whipping the people of Israel into desired shape.

> *Jeremiah 25:11-12*
> *And this whole land shall be a desolation, and an astonishment; and these nations shall serve the king of Babylon seventy years. 12. And it shall come to pass, when seventy years are accomplished, that I will punish the king of Babylon, and that nation, saith the LORD, for their iniquity, and the land of the Chaldeans, and will make it perpetual desolations.*

> *Isaiah 14:4-6*
> *That thou shalt take up this proverb against the king of Babylon, and say, How hath the oppressor ceased! the golden city ceased! 5. The LORD hath broken the staff of the wicked, and the sceptre of the rulers. 6. He who smote the people in wrath with a continual stroke, he that ruled the nations in anger, is persecuted, and none hindereth.*

## Jesus Christ

In the case of Jesus Christ, what we perceive as his baptism at the river Jordan was actually his "Anointing ceremony". Namely the point, when "the Spirit of the LORD" rested fully on him. From that moment onwards, He began to sit on the throne; described figuratively, as "the Throne of David". A point at which all that had been foretold in prophecies began to manifest literally.

> *Matthew 3:16-17*
> *And Jesus, when he was baptized, went up straightway out of the water: and, lo, the heavens were opened unto him, and he saw the Spirit of God descending like a dove, and lighting upon him: 17. And lo a voice from heaven, saying, This is my beloved Son, in whom I am well pleased.*

Sitting on King David's Throne is a pointer-phrase for identifying the human hosting "the Spirit of the LORD" or the One whom "the Presence of the LORD" was with on the Earth. Just as it was in the days of King David — a period at which — the nation of Israel achieved its peak of civilization.

Scriptures show us that when Jesus Christ went into the synagogue and announced the presence of "the Spirit of the LORD", being with him to the congregation there, they either took no notice of the announcement or simply denounced Him as a deranged individual. What we need to grasp is that when Jesus Christ was saying to the lady at Jacob's well that, "I am the Messiah", what he was really saying was, "I am the One upon who the Spirit of the LORD" is resting presently on the Earth — in this — generation. And he made those comment to let the lady know, he was one qualified to give her sound advice regarding how to worship the LORD. For in her thoughts the lady was expecting one to come or appear, who was able to issue such guidance to people of the Nation of Israel, such a person was called "the expected Messiah", we should also note that such expectations were found in other faiths and cultures worldwide.

> *Luke 4:18-21*
> *The Spirit of the Lord is upon me, because he hath anointed me to preach the gospel to the poor; he hath sent me to heal the brokenhearted, to preach deliverance to the captives, and recovering of sight to the blind, to set at liberty them that are bruised, 19. To preach the acceptable year of the Lord. 20. And he closed the book, and he gave it again to the minister, and sat down. And the eyes of all them that were in the synagogue were fastened on him. 21. And he began to say unto them, This day is this scripture fulfilled in your ears.*

Again we need to realize that being the one upon whom "the Spirit of God" rest, does not mean others cannot bear minute portion of that spirit operating within them contemporaneously. A clear example is when Jesus Christ gave his disciples anointing power to preach about the Kingdom of God, that power was portions of anointing dished out to them by the main host of "the Spirit of God", the same applied to Moses and the seventy elders, and also Peter and the early church. In both circumstances Jesus Christ and Moses remained the custodian of "the Spirit of God" on Earth, just as intended for Adam or the Khalifa as he was called in Islamic text.

> *Matthew 10:1-7*
> *And when he had called unto him his twelve disciples, he gave them power against unclean spirits, to cast them out, and to heal all manner of sickness and all manner of disease. 2. Now the names of the twelve apostles are these; The first, Simon, who is called Peter, and Andrew his brother; James the son of Zebedee, and John his brother; 3. Philip, and Bartholomew; Thomas, and Matthew the publican; James the son of Alphaeus, and Lebbaeus, whose surname was Thaddaeus; 4. Simon the Canaanite, and Judas Iscariot, who also betrayed him. 5. These twelve Jesus sent forth, and commanded them, saying, Go not into the way of the Gentiles, and into any city of the Samaritans enter ye not: 6. But go rather to the lost sheep of the house of Israel. 7. And as ye go, preach, saying, The kingdom of heaven is at hand.*

"The Messiah" is the one who is prophesied to have the answers to all of Humanity's problems, and that was why the Samarian woman said, "we are awaiting our Messiah, and he will give us right guidance and counselling" and since he will be sent by the LORD, he will eliminate their ignorance, take their miseries away and also help them overcome all their sufferings.

The fact that Jesus Christ confirms to this lady that he is the Messiah, provides a direct linkage between the word "Messiah" and the one upon who "the Spirit of the LORD" rest or "the one sent by God to assist Humanity". It also shows by contextual interpretation that the word "Christ" actually called "Christos" is another word for "Messiah".

A word which means the one who will appear bearing "the Spirit of the LORD", and this also means "the Anointed of the LORD", and by that definition is "the awaited or expected Anointed One" also identified in various faiths and expected likewise.

*John 4:25-26*
*The woman saith unto him, I know that Messias cometh, which is called Christ: when he is come, he will tell us all things. 26. Jesus saith unto her, I that speak unto thee am he.*

*John 1:41*
*He first findeth his own brother Simon, and saith unto him, We have found the Messias, which is, being interpreted, the Christ.*

*Mark 14:61-62*
*But he held his peace, and answered nothing. Again the high priest asked him, and said unto him, Art thou the Christ, the Son of the Blessed? 62. And Jesus said, I am: and ye shall see the Son of man sitting on the right hand of power, and coming in the clouds of heaven.*

*Luke 9:18-22*
*And it came to pass, as he was alone praying, his disciples were with him: and he asked them, saying, Whom say the people that I am? 19. They answering said, John the Baptist; but some say, Elias; and others say, that one of the old prophets is risen again. 20. He said unto them, But whom say ye that I am? Peter answering said, The Christ of God. 21. And he straitly charged them, and commanded them to tell no man that thing; 22.Saying, The Son of man must suffer many things, and be rejected of the elders and chief priests and scribes, and be slain, and be raised the third day.*

In another instance, it was noted that an unclean spirit or a demon, also signified publicly that this human in this case referring to Jesus Christ is "the Holy One of God". An announcement which should have broken His cover and also revealed to everyone within that vicinity, the identity of their generation's Messiah. It appears they all did not clocked in on that announcement meant at indicating that this is not an ordinary human as you may assume, but rather one paired or in a duet with the entity called "the Holy One".

This disclosure happened because the unclean spirit was able to discern things regular humans couldn't because such knowledge are not available within the realm of human consciousness.

"The Holy One" is a name for "the Spirit of the LORD" or "the Spirit of God". And so when an evil spirit bursts out saying, this is the LORD's representative or proxy, everyone needs to pay close attention, because such comments are not mere or flippantly uttered words but an announcement of the presence of the messenger of "a Great One or Entity". The one we call "the LORD God" being present in the midst of Humanity.

*Mark 1:23-28*
*And there was in their synagogue a man with an unclean spirit; and he cried out, 24. Saying, Let us alone; what have we to do with thee, thou Jesus of Nazareth? art thou come to destroy us? I know thee who thou art, the Holy One of God. 25. And Jesus rebuked him, saying, Hold thy peace, and come out of him. 26. And when the unclean spirit had torn him, and cried with a loud voice, he came out of him. 27. And they were all amazed, insomuch that they questioned among themselves, saying, What thing is this? what new doctrine is this? for with authority commandeth he even the unclean spirits, and they do obey him.28. And immediately his fame spread abroad throughout all the region round about Galilee.*

*Isaiah 43:3*
*For I am the LORD thy God, the Holy One of Israel, thy Saviour: I gave Egypt for thy ransom, Ethiopia and Seba for thee.*

*2 Kings 19:21-23*
*This is the word that the LORD hath spoken concerning him; The virgin the daughter of Zion hath despised thee, and laughed thee to scorn; the daughter of Jerusalem hath shaken her head at thee. 22. Whom hast thou reproached and blasphemed? and against whom hast thou exalted thy voice, and lifted up thine eyes on high? even against the Holy One of Israel. 23. By thy messengers thou hast reproached the Lord, and hast said, With the multitude of my chariots I am come up to the height of the mountains, to the sides of Lebanon, and will cut down the tall cedar trees thereof, and the choice fir trees thereof: and I will enter into the lodgings of his borders, and into the forest of his Carmel.*

An equally significant description was that made by Bartholomew, the blind man, when he referred to Jesus Christ as, "the Son of David". It is crucial to discern here, that what this blind man was expressing was a higher level of insight. A perception about "a son of David" who was to be born in Israel, who will sit or have access to his father's throne, or presumed biological inheritance called "the Throne of David". This inheritance was an established connection to the entity we call the LORD God, who made David King in Israel and backed his reign by His Presence in the Ark.

*Mark 10:47-52*
*And when he heard that it was Jesus of Nazareth, he began to cry out, and say, Jesus, thou Son of David, have mercy on me. 48. And many charged him that he should hold his peace: but he cried the more a great deal, Thou Son of David, have mercy on me. 49. And Jesus stood still, and commanded him to be called. And they call the blind man, saying unto him, Be of good comfort, rise; he calleth thee. 50. And he, casting away his garment, rose, and came to Jesus. 51. And Jesus answered and said unto him, What wilt thou that I should do unto thee? The blind man said unto him, Lord, that I might receive my sight. 52. And Jesus said unto him, Go thy way; thy faith*

*hath made thee whole. And immediately he received his sight, and followed Jesus in the way.*

All these descriptions could be equalized thus:

The One upon whom "the Spirit of the LORD" rested is :
> = Jesus Christ;
> = the Messiah (or the Anointed one);
> = The Holy One of God;
> = A Son of God;
> = The Son of the Blessed One;
> = The prophesied "Son of David";
> = One Seating on David's Throne.

### Moses

Moses was anointed by the LORD, to deliver the Israelites from the bondage of the Egyptians. In order to achieve this mission, the LORD invested "His Authority or Spirit" also called "His Name" upon Moses, thereby transforming him into "a representative of God", just like Jesus Christ was identified as a representative of "the Holy One of God" by the unclean spirit.

> *Exodus 3:10-12*
> *Come now therefore, and I will send thee unto Pharaoh, that thou mayest bring forth my people the children of Israel out of Egypt. 11. And Moses said unto God, Who am I, that I should go unto Pharaoh, and that I should bring forth the children of Israel out of Egypt? 12. And he said, Certainly I will be with thee; and this shall be a token unto thee, that I have sent thee: When thou hast brought forth the people out of Egypt, ye shall serve God upon this mountain.*

> *Exodus 7:1-2*
> *And the LORD said unto Moses, See, I have made thee a god to Pharaoh: and Aaron thy brother shall be thy prophet. 2. Thou shalt speak all that I command thee: and Aaron thy brother shall speak unto Pharaoh, that he send the children of Israel out of his land.*

This investiture of the authority of the LORD, came to Moses by the LORD placing His Spirit upon Moses. An act which changed the status of Moses from a mere human into that of "the LORD's Anointed or representative", or "the Holy One of God" as in the case of Jesus Christ or better still, "the God of the Earth". Although this last view is not chronicled within scriptures in that perspective, rather scriptures depict he was made "a god to Pharaoh" that appears to me as a deliberate misinterpretation or mistranslation of the actual status or position Moses played on the Earth in those days. If Pharaoh was the world ruler in those days, and Moses became a god to the world ruler, by the

LORD God's appointment, does that not make Moses a representative of the LORD God or "God of the Earth"?

It is obvious from the text, that Moses was actually representing the LORD on the Earth and in all confrontations with Pharaoh, while Aaron deputized as his Prophet. Just as Jesus Christ did represent the LORD in his days although he played the role of being a prophet too, depicting an evolutionary upward trend in manifesting God on Earth by Humans.

In my view and for doctrinal reasons, I presume that those who canonized the bible, chose a depiction of small "god" for Moses, because of the need to have only "one Anointed of the LORD". Jesus Christ who is chiefly promoted and described also as "the only Begotten Son of God", by Christianity and its doctrine. This in my view was either an uninformed or evil ploy, hatched to dissuade any other human from attempting to become "a Son of God" too.

A lot of such misrepresentations abound and are featured in the bible. Simply for the purposes of making scriptures dovetail with the doctrine of Christianity. In my view these are desperate intentions of keeping Humanity away from seeking the LORD, in the way He truly desires of Humans, and for the purposes He wants. Most of these misrepresentations, can only be spotted by anyone who studies the bible clearly, deeply and intensely while keeping an open mind searching for all truths about the LORD God.

Anyone who falls for the classic "if it is not written in the bible then its not true gospel mantra" regularly spewed out by Christian apologists to validate dominance for their doctrine, is bound to be misled and lost. By not investing ones own time into research towards finding out what the truth is, because bibles are usually scripted to support doctrinal views and not to conflict them. And by saying that, I will like to draw attention to the fact that people like Noah, Abraham, Moses and others did not read any bible, they did not attend a church services every Sunday, or listen to a pastor's sermon on television, they were not regular payers of tithes on their income and most importantly all these individuals including Jesus Christ did not pray to God in Jesus' name as Christians do nowadays. Yet they all were able to discover and develop an intimate relationship with the LORD, herein is wisdom.

Moses is quite significant because he was brought up as an Egyptian prince. As a youth, he worshipped the gods of Egypt, and in spite of that he was still able to encounter the real God of Israel. Abraham was also a pagan worshipper and an Amorite until he encountered the LORD God. I will simply say here to those who will listen, that beware of people with their pre-set conditions and doctrine, as a criterion for your Salvation. Such people are no better than the Pharisees who Jesus Christ cursed for similar actions, simply because their doctrine was wrong still yet they refused any corrections to it.

*Matthew 23:13-29*
*But woe unto you, scribes and Pharisees, hypocrites! for ye shut up the kingdom of heaven against men: for ye neither go in yourselves, neither suffer ye them that are entering to go in. 14. Woe unto you, scribes and Pharisees, hypocrites! for ye devour widows' houses, and for a pretence make*

*long prayer: therefore ye shall receive the greater damnation. 15. Woe unto you, scribes and Pharisees, hypocrites! for ye compass sea and land to make one proselyte, and when he is made, ye make him twofold more the child of hell than yourselves. 16. Woe unto you, ye blind guides, which say, Whosoever shall swear by the temple, it is nothing; but whosoever shall swear by the gold of the temple, he is a debtor! 17. Ye fools and blind: for whether is greater, the gold, or the temple that sanctifieth the gold? 18. And, Whosoever shall swear by the altar, it is nothing; but whosoever sweareth by the gift that is upon it, he is guilty. 19. Ye fools and blind: for whether is greater, the gift, or the altar that sanctifieth the gift? 20. Whoso therefore shall swear by the altar, sweareth by it, and by all things thereon. 21. And whoso shall swear by the temple, sweareth by it, and by him that dwelleth therein. 22. And he that shall swear by heaven, sweareth by the throne of God, and by him that sitteth thereon. 23. Woe unto you, scribes and Pharisees, hypocrites! for ye pay tithe of mint and anise and cummin, and have omitted the weightier matters of the law, judgment, mercy, and faith: these ought ye to have done, and not to leave the other undone. 24. Ye blind guides, which strain at a gnat, and swallow a camel. 25. Woe unto you, scribes and Pharisees, hypocrites! for ye make clean the outside of the cup and of the platter, but within they are full of extortion and excess. 26. Thou blind Pharisee, cleanse first that which is within the cup and platter, that the outside of them may be clean also. 27. Woe unto you, scribes and Pharisees, hypocrites! for ye are like unto whited sepulchres, which indeed appear beautiful outward, but are within full of dead men's bones, and of all uncleanness. 28. Even so ye also outwardly appear righteous unto men, but within ye are full of hypocrisy and iniquity. 29. Woe unto you, scribes and Pharisees, hypocrites! because ye build the tombs of the prophets, and garnish the sepulchres of the righteous,*

There are accounts in a Jewish book, called "the Golden Haggada" about an old man, who was asking Moses to come up to him and sit on his throne. It is hinted that Moses did not complete the journey to sit with the old man on the Throne by other writings, faiths or beliefs. This is a view symbolized by the fact that the LORD forbad him entry into the Promised Land "Jerusalem" for his offences or misconducts by some faiths. This old man's invitation anecdote bears striking similarity to that featured in the book of Revelations. One which depicts a personality or entity sitting on "the Throne of God", inviting others to come and join Him on it. Some believe it was Jesus Christ sitting on "the Throne of God" depicted in Revelations, as opposed to it being the LORD God Himself as we all would have naturally expected. Thereby, equating Jesus Christ as LORD God by doctrinal interpretation. That view is both correct and incorrect in various contexts. This is because if we consider that Prophet Ezekiel and Isaiah saw visions of "the Throne of God" also and there was always someone sitting on it, in all such visions prior to the birth of Jesus Christ. It is likely that the person or entity sitting there wasn't Jesus Christ but actually the LORD God Himself in duet with whomever played the role of LORD's Servant at such a time or era. It is equally possible that there exists an arrangement of humans, sitting on the Throne or joined to the LORD on His Throne, in an arrangement similar to that of hollow wooden dolls called Matryoshka or Russian dolls. This a perspective that chimes with various prophets of God sent by Him to accomplish specific missions and one which may buttress and give insight for understanding those 24 elders sitting around "the Throne of God" conundrum.

Another such similar play of events centering on the Throne occurs in the accounts of Daniel's vision. This was when a human "one like a Son of Man", is brought up to "the Throne of God", by the angels. Again some opine this person is Jesus Christ but I have differing views which are expounded later in this writing.

*Daniel 7:13-14*
*I saw in the night visions, and, behold, one like the Son of man came with the clouds of heaven, and came to the Ancient of days, and they brought him near before him. 14. And there was given him dominion, and glory, and a kingdom, that all people, nations, and languages, should serve him: his dominion is an everlasting dominion, which shall not pass away, and his kingdom that which shall not be destroyed.*

I will now provide another example to support my thesis about biblical text misinterpretations and misrepresentations. This one occurs when the LORD introduces himself to Moses, as the "I AM that I AM" in the book of Exodus.

*Exo 3:14*
*And God said unto Moses, I AM THAT I AM: and he said, Thus shalt thou say unto the children of Israel, I AM hath sent me unto you.*

What is recorded in the Jewish Torah/Bible is that the LORD told Moses that His name is "I AM" which when interpreted correctly means "That Great One".

Jesus Christ also restated his identity as "I AM" when the High Priest asked Jesus Christ who he was, but because it was misinterpreted or translated, the ability to realize that he was saying "I AM, meaning That Great One" get blurred out. Which if really this was what was being communicated again suggests that the entity we call the LORD God, was the one speaking those words, by virtue of being united or being one with Jesus Christ.

*Mark 14:62*
*And Jesus said, I am: and ye shall see the Son of man sitting on the right hand of power, and coming in the clouds of heaven.*

There are possible explanations to how such misinterpretations occur. In my understanding of cultures of those days, we know there were various gods worshipped by people for different reasons. Such as for having a good harvest, for being prosperous and so on. Then there was knowledge of one deity referred to as "the Great One" or "I AM" as contained by scriptures.

It appears in my view that the lesser gods and their prophets or priests, seem to have made humans believe that, He "the Great One" does not communicate or interact with human beings. Because it appears that the "I AM" was known to only converse with gods-like beings or lesser gods, which humans worshipped for their various reasons. And so if humans had anything they wished to discuss with him, they would have to relay it to these lesser gods (or their priests) for onward transmission to "The Great One" here to fore known as "I AM" and that gave room for relaying of false messages from Him to clueless humans.

With benefits of hindsight, it becomes acutely clear to me, that this view was apparently a contorted lie or fabrication, to keep Humanity from pursuing any direct encounter with "The Great One". A phenomenon called coming into "The knowledge of God" when such happens, and sadly it appears that various religions, including Christianity all still have doctrines that present "The Great One", as an entity with which humans cannot interact with directly, without a mediator or go in between.

Such is because the promoters of these faiths create hierarchies and lofty perceptions of themselves as representatives of the LORD, "or I AM" on the Earth. And as go betweens for humans seeking help, contact, answers or blessing from the LORD. Contrary to that, is the fact that all humans are expected to interact directly with the LORD, a crucial essence of the message to the lady at Jacob's well. Several humans have done this in the past and are considered or treated as special humans by religious doctrines. Such treatment creates a flawed perception, which hinders or precludes other humans from attempting to establish similar or direct contact or union with "the LORD God" or "The Great One".

Jesus Christ represented the LORD as a human, and transfigured with his face shining brighter than the Sun after establishing a direct contact with "the Spirit of the LORD". Moses also represented the LORD likewise and was also recorded to have exhibited similar traits in his days. These similarities are not to be ignored or overlooked, because they are essentially a manifestation of the effects of contact with the same entity at differing levels of human interaction. In my understanding, such shows they were united with the entity dwelling within what is called "the Light of God".

The "Spirit of the LORD", was placed upon Moses just like it came or rested upon Jesus Christ. And it was by virtue of its presence with Moses, that he did or achieved all the things that are recorded about him. Just as it was by virtue of its presence with Jesus Christ, that he was able to do all that he did also, in both cases these individuals had their faces shine as brightly as the Sun, a pointer to manifesting "the Light" nature or attribute of God.

The verses below highlights this view by attributing to the LORD (or His Spirit or His Name or His Power) the wonders attributed to Moses. Just as we accept that the miracles performed by Jesus Christ were by virtue of the LORD's Presence (or His Spirit or His Name or His Power) being with him.

To clearly understand this view, we have to remember that without "the Presence of the Spirit of the LORD", being with these individuals there would never have been either a Moses or a Jesus Christ, recorded doing those great works or wonders, the same presence is what anyone who seeks such manifestations must pursue.

*Numbers 11:16-17*
*And the LORD said unto Moses, Gather unto me seventy men of the elders of Israel, whom thou knowest to be the elders of the people, and officers over them; and bring them unto the tabernacle of the congregation, that they may stand there with thee. 17. And I will come down and talk with thee there: and I will take of the spirit which is upon thee, and will put it upon them; and they shall bear the burden of the people with thee, that thou bear it not thyself alone.*

*Psalms 66:3-7*
*Say unto God, How terrible art thou in thy works! through the greatness of thy power shall thine enemies submit themselves unto thee. 4. All the earth shall worship thee, and shall sing unto thee; they shall sing to thy name. Selah. 5. Come and see the works of God: he is terrible in his doing toward the children of men. 6. He turned the sea into dry land: they went through the flood on foot: there did we rejoice in him. 7. He ruleth by his power for ever; his eyes behold the nations: let not the rebellious exalt themselves. Selah.*

*Psalms 68:6-9*
*God setteth the solitary in families: he bringeth out those which are bound with chains: but the rebellious dwell in a dry land. 7. O God, when thou wentest forth before thy people, when thou didst march through the wilderness; Selah: 8. The earth shook, the heavens also dropped at the presence of God: even Sinai itself was moved at the presence of God, the God of Israel. 9. Thou, O God, didst send a plentiful rain, whereby thou didst confirm thine inheritance, when it was weary.*

*Psalms 77:11-20*
*I will remember the works of the LORD: surely I will remember thy wonders of old. 12. I will meditate also of all thy work, and talk of thy doings. 13. Thy way, O God, is in the sanctuary: who is so great a God as our God? 14. Thou art the God that doest wonders: thou hast declared thy strength among the people. 15. Thou hast with thine arm redeemed thy people, the sons of Jacob and Joseph. Selah. 16. The waters saw thee, O God, the waters saw thee; they were afraid: the depths also were troubled. 17. The clouds poured out water: the skies sent out a sound: thine arrows also went abroad. 18. The voice of thy thunder was in the heaven: the lightnings lightened the world: the earth trembled and shook. 19. Thy way is in the sea, and thy path in the great waters, and thy footsteps are not known. 20. Thou leddest thy people like a flock by the hand of Moses and Aaron.*

*Psalms 78:12-16*
*Marvellous things did he in the sight of their fathers, in the land of Egypt, in the field of Zoan.  13.  He divided the sea, and caused them to pass through; and he made the waters to stand as an heap.  14.  In the daytime also he led them with a cloud, and all the night with a light of fire.  15.  He clave the rocks in the wilderness, and gave them drink as out of the great depths.  16. He brought streams also out of the rock, and caused waters to run down like rivers.*

# THE HOUSEKEEPER PERSPECTIVE

The intention for this chapter is to use the role of a housekeeper employed in a private home, to help us understand how several prophecies dovetail with each other. And to dispel any ambiguities that could arise in our interpretations of scriptures or various prophetic depictions by applying such a perspective.

Our housekeeper named Dora, does the following things for my family, she cleans the house; maintains the lawn and our garden; does all our laundry; feeds and walks the dogs; she cleans out their kennels and washes them too; she purchases all items we put on our groceries list; and picks up any deliveries to our home whilst we are out.

Now, if I was recounting to a co-worker about how the stains on my shirt were gotten rid of, I'll simply say to him that the lady who does my laundry is incredible. She found a substance that took off all those stains on my shirt, from our last factory inspection without any damage to the fabric or prints of my shirts. Anyone who is close to my family would immediately realise I was referring to "my housekeeper Dora" when I made those comments. But my work colleague being someone not so close to my family, would reference her as "my laundry lady", if he were to make any references to her in the future. This is because even though I did not define lifting stains off my shirts as her core job specification, it is a role Dora now plays in my life by being employed as my housekeeper and by doing my laundry.

If during a cocktail party chit-chat, my wife tells her girlfriends about how green her lawn now looks, just a week after her "gardening lady" applied a new soil treatment solution, which made the grass grow verdantly.

Anyone of them, who is close to my family would figure out she was referring to "our housekeeper Dora". However, anyone not close or familiar with my family would assume my wife was talking about a lady whose profession is manicuring private lawns and garden, or "a gardening specialist" and is bound to refer to her as such in future.

My daughter could also say to her friends at school, Lady Dora has taught me to always use different brushes for different effects when painting to avoid smearing the canvas. Any of her friends close to my family will know she was referring to "our housekeeper Dora". Now imagine my daughter's classmate's mother asking my wife for a contact number of the "oil painting tutor" who was giving my daughter oil painting lessons. Initially, my wife may get startled by such a request, because she has no recollection of employing the services of an "oil painting tutor" for my daughter. But after pausing to think about it, the answer would be the contact details of "our housekeeper Dora", who is now renamed as an "oil painting tutor", by a third party unaware of the role she actually plays in my household that of a housekeeper.

The delivery man leaves a parcel for my neighbour with my housekeeper, and she leaves it on the kitchen table, the delivery man drops a note in my neighbour's mailbox that his parcel has been left with a lady called Dora next door. Later in the evening, my neighbour comes knocking on our door and says to me. "Hi, Dora signed for a delivery on my behalf, I'm here to collect it, kindly let her know I'm here?" It is rational for my neighbour to assume Dora is a member of my household who resides in my home, because they have no inkling that she is our housekeeper, and is only at my home during the day. However, since the parcel is on the kitchen table I am able to pass it on to my neighbour, who unless I tell him otherwise, will still assume a lady called Dora leaves next door to him and may in the future request for missed deliveries to be drop with his neighbour Dora.

Now if we look back at all the interventions of Dora in my family, she has been addressed as the laundry lady, the gardening lady, the oil painting tutor and my housemate or a member of my family, and this is because she played multiple other roles leading people to assume those were who she was. In all cases though, those appellations fitted the additional roles she played, but these aspects were not in her original job description as our housekeeper.

The only role she played in my family, by her job description was that of a Housekeeper. It is a role which if she did not play, by virtue of not playing it, she would never have had access to my laundry items. If she did not accept the job of being my housekeeper, she would never have had access to my daughter or any opportunity to teach her more about oil painting. If she did not play the role of my housekeeper by which she had access to my home, she would never have been in a position to take a delivery for my neighbour or become someone presumed to live in my house.

All these are stated to help us understand that a person, place or location could be referenced, by several different appellations because of the various other roles, characteristics or associations connected to the main roles they play. Such is so stated to bring an insight into how "the expected Messiah" or "the Anointed One" and "the Throne of God" all have various other descriptions, roles, characteristics and functions associated with them which all dovetails together when examined with precision and care.

# VESSELS FOR "THE SPIRIT OF GOD"

The branch of Sciences called "Physics" will aid in expressing some perspectives, and I must add that such theoretical perspectives are needed for explaining things that have influenced my reasoning since my first physics class in secondary school.

The "Spirit of the LORD" is an entity without mass, (and all other spirits are mass-less too) and for it to become active in our dimension or reality it has to occupy some space within this dimension, and it is from this space occupied, that it can influence or control whatsoever it desires to manipulate in our world.

The need to occupy space is just as important to "the Spirit of the LORD" as learning to space-walk is to cosmonauts planning a journey into outer space. Because the outer space environment is a place where there are no active forces of gravity to keep them grounded as astronauts are used to on Earth.

In order to occupy space on the Earth, "the Spirit of the LORD" must be placed within something that already has "Mass and Space attributes", which are locale to the Earth or our dimension and reality. Once it is within such a container, "the Spirit" could then share "the Mass and Space attribute" of the container or vessel, within which it is in order to acquire mass and space attributes needed to operate in our dimension or world. This could also be described as acquiring locality in this dimension, and could best be perceived as those benefits an aircraft-carrier could give a fighter jet in the middle of an ocean where no land-based airports are available. Such requirements as a landing & taking off runway, refuelling, engineering maintenances, weapons or armament reloading and so on could be handle by the aircraft-carrier for a fighter jet in high seas.

As humans, we are all expected to create a landing space and dwelling space for "the Spirit of the LORD" within our hearts on Earth. The LORD previously placed in humans "His Spirit" and by so doing they became potential "Images of God". An attribute which if fully activated and enhanced could transform them into beings that become "One with God". That is because provided the pre-requisites are fulfilled, "the LORD" also shares with them, in this case I mean those who allow Him to do so by yielding their hearts; His Glory, Power and Authority, just as they have shared with Him their locality attributes as dwellers on the Earth.

In actuality, any human within whom "the Spirit of the LORD" dwells is also a host to that spirit. But unlike other parasitic organisms, most of which tend to kill off their host by sucking the life out of them, "the Spirit of the LORD" on the contrary, injects life into its host by diffusing its hosts matter with what is called "the Eternal Attribute of God". This is "a force of Life" and a very powerful force I must add. One which gives what we call "Eternal Life" as put forward by religious societies, in mundane expressions. It is also termed as "the elixir of eternal youthfulness", by alchemists or "the nectar of Immortality" as referenced by philosophers or some other faiths and esoteric professions.

This "Eternal Attribute of God" is also in my view the attribute that Jesus Christ must have acquired sufficiently enough of, to overcome the effects of "the force of death" as played out in an event which we now describe as his rising up or resurrection from the dead or grave.

The "Spirit of the LORD" was ported temporarily into a device called "the Ark of God" for the simple reasons that a part of our human body which was its official domain or landing-space called (the Human Heart), became compromised by the deceptions of "the serpent". In an event which is called, "the fall of Man" or "the Original Sin of Humanity" or "the act of consuming of the Forbidden fruit".

One made for a purpose

There are crucial requirements for any domain or vessel that is to hold "the Spirit of the LORD" within it. From studying the bible, I can conclude that such vessels could either be "a human container" or "a non-human container", such as the one called "the Ark of God".

In the case of a non-human container such a vessel must meet certain physical conditions suiting to "the Spirit of the LORD". For a non-human container, it must be made of certain types of materials, which are to keep "the Spirit of the LORD" at prescribed physical conditions of stability in this realm. While for a human heart, certain level of internal cleanliness is desired which we term as "Holiness or Righteousness", in order for such a person to be a vessel fitting for "the Spirit of the LORD", able to host, hold or anchor it to this realm.

*Exodus 25:10-13*
*And they shall make an ark of shittim wood: two cubits and a half shall be the length thereof, and a cubit and a half the breadth thereof, and a cubit and a*

Once again let us use the perspective of a cosmonaut, going into space to help understand this view about "the Spirit of the LORD" and the human container requirements. Human astronauts can't operate in an environment without air, and for this reason before humans ever launch out into space, they are duly kitted with spacesuits designed to certain specifications, which aim to provide them with unlimited air supply, needed for respiration in that vacuum of space bereft of atmospheric oxygen.

Substituting the astronaut with the "Spirit of the LORD", and then the space suit with the human body in the earlier depiction, would help us understand the concept about the vessel characteristics and its need to fulfill certain criteria desired to serve certain purposes. If an astronaut's suit is not sturdy enough and as such it accidentally gets torn or violated during a spacewalk, the human in it is likely to die of asphyxiation, if not immediately rescued from the outer space environment after the damage occurs.

There is a somewhat similar relationship between the human body and the human spirit, similar to that between a spacesuit and an astronaut. This is because the human body anchors the human soul to the Earth. And whenever a person dies, their human soul departs from the body, which then begins to decompose. That is simply because the soul which kept the human alive here has departed from that body. The crucial thing to note here is that if the human body is not in a good state of health, one which is usually regulated by the soul of the person in my view, such a person dies ultimately as a result of such irregularities too, so in many ways the soul regulates life for a human.

The human body is however not designed to anchor only the human soul that keeps us alive to the Earth. It was also designed to be a vessel that anchors "the Spirit of the LORD" onto the Earth, and if the conditions needed for such are met by any human body, "the Spirit of the LORD" will come to dwell in it. And by that I mean anchor itself to that body aided by its human's soul. And while dwelling in such a body, if it happens that the human's body becomes violated or unfit, as was the case at the Garden of Eden, "the Spirit of the LORD" simply returns back to its source from which it originated. And that is the death highlighted by what is called the wages of "the Original Sin".

That process of the LORD's Spirit returning back to the LORD after the human soul was compromised is what happened to Adam and Eve, that which is called "the first Death" or "the Original sin of Humanity". It was the loss of the "Spirit of the LORD" as a companion to humans on the Earth. As a result of that we all became like children in a public park whose parents disappeared, and guess what? The other entities in the park took full advantage of our parents' absence. That sort of explains how the domination of the Human race, by evil entities; the counter opposite of "the force of Light or Good" emerged, it also accentuates what is termed as nakedness in Humans.

Scriptural views that the LORD kicked Humans out from His Presence may be slightly inaccurate, when considered in perspective of actions and their consequences. Because facing reality, humans wilfully compromised their soul, which was the vessel that should be a container or anchor for "the Spirit of the LORD" in this realm. Trying to suggest the LORD kicked humans out of His Presence is like trying to suggest that a lady is responsible for sending her husband packing after she found out he just had unprotected sexual intercourse with another female known to be human immunouvirus positive.

## Locality is crucial

Everything that is made up of matter in our dimension or reality must occupy space here, and must also be located somewhere or positioned at someplace within this realm. Such a characteristic is best considered as its locality.

Therefore "the Human body" or "the Ark of God" as vessels that were to house "the Spirit of the LORD" also possessed such attributes, which were super essential for the LORD God to operate or dwell in our dimension or world or perhaps in any other one.

The attempt to prevent Humanity from understanding that they need "the Spirit of the LORD" dwelling in their hearts and acquiring its locality here, is mainly a clever strategy of "the serpent" or devil, to keep Humanity from re-establishing our lost connection with the LORD. An event which he knows that when it occurs, such will ultimately bring "the Kingdom of Heaven"; or "the Kingdom of God"; and re-establish "the Knowledge of God"; back onto the Earth. Which is what we lack in our world or dimension, and its absence is currently heavily exploited by the devil and his cohorts to rule or reign over humans.

To further accentuate this locality perspective, let us imagine we have a longing for a delicious Chinese meal, there are two options for us at getting such. The first is we get on an airplane and go to China, where for sure Chinese meals are a staple diet.

The alternative is we search for a Chinese restaurant located in our town to purchase or have prepared for us the Chinese meal we desire.

The Chinese chef or restaurant in our town brings to us all the delicacies of the Chinese food as it is prepared and consumed in China, by the Chinese citizens, with all their traditional spices.

And this is made available to us only because our local government, town or city authorities provided a space for this Chinese restaurant to operate and prepare Chinese dishes within our town or city. We call this space, where we go to eat such meals "the Chinese Restaurant". Or in some cites where there is an aggregation of this and other Chinese cultures or services, we call such a location where the restaurant is situated "China town".

Now in the case of "the Ark or God", we call the space or place where we go to encounter the essence of the Presence or Power of God by the name "the Temple of God". Such a Temple is where people go to experience or interact with the LORD God, because that is where He can be invoked or worshipped on the Earth, because His Spirit is domiciled or present in such a place, which is usually located at some sacred location.

And that location was known to be at a place traditionally called Jerusalem by virtue of King David declaring its name as such. This location has also been referenced by various other names, such as "the Holy Hill; the Top of Mountain; the Holy City; Throne of David; The City of the Lord; and The Zion of the Holy One".

As in the case of the restaurant, whenever someone says "I am going to the Chinese restaurant", or "I am going for a meal at China town", they will convey the same meanings to someone who understands that the Chinese restaurant is a place located in China town. Hence both statements are essentially stating the same purpose, although expressed in various perspectives similar to that of "my Housekeeper Dora". In the case of the human body, whenever "the Spirit of the LORD" comes to dwell with a person, such a body automatically becomes "the Temple of God" too, because every encounter or experience that could be derived from visiting or contact with "an Ark of God", which was usually located in "a Temple of God" could also be derived from such a human's body once it has acquired that new status.

The space and location attributes pertaining to such a body serving as "a Temple of God", has also been referenced by several other appellations or titles.

All through the bible, humans in whose body "the Spirit of the LORD" has dwelt or rested, including those of the future, have been known as either a Prophet; a Priest; an Anointed of God; the Branch; the Messiah; the Holy One of God; Offspring of David; The Seed of David; The Inheritor of Abraham, Jacob or Judah; The Messenger of the Lord; Beloved Servant; The Bridegroom; The First Born; The Judge; My servant David; The First Born of Death, The One who Overcomes and sits on the Throne.

This location of the Temple where "the Ark of God" was situated in the past was called Jerusalem. There are however several other identifiers or references for Jerusalem. Such identifiers are in various context, such as of a name for "the Temple of God", or in context of a name for where "the Spirit of the LORD" resides, or in context of a place from where "the LORD's Power comes", or in context of a place from "where the LORD's Throne is located".

The verses following express some of such several titles, definitions or meanings for Jerusalem stating the same thing, but in different words or context as expressed under the housekeeper perspective.

Jerusalem is where "the Temple of God is located"

The most favoured name for where the LORD's temple is located is Jerusalem

*Psalms 68:26-29*
*Bless ye God in the congregations, even the Lord, from the fountain of Israel. 27. There is little Benjamin with their ruler, the princes of Judah and their council, the princes of Zebulun, and the princes of Naphtali. 28. Thy God hath commanded thy strength: strengthen, O God, that which thou hast wrought for us. 29. Because of thy temple at Jerusalem shall kings bring presents unto thee.*

## Jerusalem is also called "the Holy City"

The LORD's people also call or refer to Jerusalem as a Holy City. This is a characteristic to emphasize a crucial requirement of the LORD which is utmost Holiness.

*Nehemiah 11:1*
*And the rulers of the people dwelt at Jerusalem: the rest of the people also cast lots, to bring one of ten to dwell in Jerusalem the holy city, and nine parts to dwell in other cities.*

*Isaiah 52:1*
*Awake, awake; put on thy strength, O Zion; put on thy beautiful garments, O Jerusalem, the holy city: for henceforth there shall no more come into thee the uncircumcised and the unclean.*

*Revelation 21:2*
*And I John saw the holy city, new Jerusalem, coming down from God out of heaven, prepared as a bride adorned for her husband.*

## Jerusalem is also called "the Holy Mountain"

The LORD Himself calls Jerusalem "His Holy Mountain" because the word mountain or certain references to such are associated with spirituality or domain, occupied by spiritual entities in biblical days.

*Zechariah 8:3*
*Thus saith the LORD; I am returned unto Zion, and will dwell in the midst of Jerusalem: and Jerusalem shall be called a city of truth; and the mountain of the LORD of hosts the holy mountain.*

*Isaiah 65:23-25*
*They shall not labour in vain, nor bring forth for trouble; for they are the seed of the blessed of the LORD, and their offspring with them. 24. And it shall come to pass, that before they call, I will answer; and while they are yet speaking, I will hear. 25. The wolf and the lamb shall feed together, and the lion shall eat straw like the bullock: and dust shall be the serpent's meat. They shall not hurt nor destroy in all my holy mountain, saith the LORD.*

*Daniel 9:16*
*O Lord, according to all thy righteousness, I beseech thee, let thine anger and thy fury be turned away from thy city Jerusalem, thy holy mountain: because for our sins, and for the iniquities of our fathers, Jerusalem and thy people are become a reproach to all that are about us.*

*Isaiah 66:20*
*And they shall bring all your brethren for an offering unto the LORD out of all nations upon horses, and in chariots, and in litters, and upon mules, and upon swift beasts, to my holy mountain Jerusalem, saith the LORD, as the children of Israel bring an offering in a clean vessel into the house of the LORD.*

## Jerusalem is also called "the City descending from God" unto the Earth

The LORD's Presence and any domain it occupies becomes the LORD's city, since the LORD's city is where His Presence occupies also called Jerusalem. It is figuratively prophesied that whenever this Presence returns into our world, the domain of its impact with the Earth should automatically be renamed as Jerusalem.

In this context, it is the New Jerusalem because it is a new version of an old phenomenon experienced on the Earth thousand of years ago. It is worthy to note that suggestions about it descending highlights the views about the mountains as high altitude positions which are ascribed to spiritual entities, and the coming down symbolises coming to a lower altitude level as the Earth is considered in such perspectives.

*Revelation 21:1-2*
*And I saw a new heaven and a new earth: for the first heaven and the first earth were passed away; and there was no more sea. 2. And I John saw the holy city, new Jerusalem, coming down from God out of heaven, prepared as a bride adorned for her husband.*

*Revelation 21:10-12*
*And he carried me away in the spirit to a great and high mountain, and shewed me that great city, the holy Jerusalem, descending out of heaven from God, 11. Having the glory of God: and her light was like unto a stone most precious, even like a jasper stone, clear as crystal; 12. And had a wall great and high, and had twelve gates, and at the gates twelve angels, and names written thereon, which are the names of the twelve tribes of the children of Israel:*

## Jerusalem is also called the Holy Hill

There are close relationships between a hill and mountain and these appear in perspective of where the LORD's Presence rests or occupies in scriptures. It appears both terms are used to express the same idea or opinion in relation to some destination or realm considered as above the standard reach of humans.

*Psalms 3:3-4*
*But thou, O LORD, art a shield for me; my glory, and the lifter up of mine head. 4. I cried unto the LORD with my voice, and he heard me out of his holy hill. Selah.*



## Jerusalem is also called "the Holy Heaven"

Heaven traditionally is where most people believe The LORD dwells, some individuals or interpreters affix the prefix Holy to it, and this is to suggest or emphasize an essential attribute or characteristic required for access into such a zone by Humans.

*Psalms 20:5-6*
*We will rejoice in thy salvation, and in the name of our God we will set up our banners: the LORD fulfil all thy petitions. 6. Now know I that the LORD saveth his anointed; he will hear him from his holy heaven with the saving strength of his right hand.*

## Jerusalem is "the place where the Lord's fire dwells, the place of His furnace"

The LORD's furnace is an attribute of His Strength and Power. It is only rational to opine that such is present wherever He dwells. Just as the command centre of a nation's or country's military might are known or perceived to be domiciled, wherever the head of such a nation dwells or is presently located.

*Isaiah 31:5-9*
*As birds flying, so will the LORD of hosts defend Jerusalem; defending also he will deliver it; and passing over he will preserve it. 6. Turn ye unto him from whom the children of Israel have deeply revolted. 7. For in that day every man shall cast away his idols of silver, and his idols of gold, which your own hands have made unto you for a sin. 8. Then shall the Assyrian fall with the sword, not of a mighty man; and the sword, not of a mean man, shall devour him: but he shall flee from the sword, and his young men shall be discomfited. 9. And he shall pass over to his strong hold for fear, and his princes shall be afraid of the ensign, saith the LORD, whose fire is in Zion, and his furnace in Jerusalem.*

## Jerusalem is "the Holy dwelling place of the LORD" also known as "Heaven"

The LORD is "the Holiest of all entities" in the Universe, the "Holy" attribute of His dwelling place is implied by the characteristic virtue of Holiness that He bears one which is unique to only Him.

*2 Chronicles 30:26-27*
*So there was great joy in Jerusalem: for since the time of Solomon the son of*

*David king of Israel there was not the like in Jerusalem. 27. Then the priests the Levites arose and blessed the people: and their voice was heard, and their prayer came up to his holy dwelling place, even unto heaven.*

## The Throne of God

The Throne of the LORD is simply where He lives and it is also the place from which He operates, it should be considered also as His office and from where He conducts all His affairs, and because the LORD lives forever and cannot die this Throne is one that also exists forever by virtue of such an attribute of God.

Just as Jerusalem has various appellations, the LORD's Throne has also over the time been defined, described and expressed by various words and phrases some of which are:

### The Throne of God is in a location called Heaven

Over the ages "The Throne of God" has also acquired various descriptions used at liberty as the choice of those making a reference to it. It is sometimes called "Heaven" another name which is one that encompasses references to the location where it is known to exist presently. Just as "the White House" could be automatically assumed to mean or suggest "the Office of the President of the United States" in some context or even as "Washington" in other contexts of interpretation.

*Isaiah 66:1*
*Thus saith the LORD, The heaven is my throne, and the earth is my footstool: where is the house that ye build unto me? and where is the place of my rest?*

*Psalms 11:4*
*The LORD is in his holy temple, the LORD'S throne is in heaven: his eyes behold, his eyelids try, the children of men.*

*Psalms 2:4-6*
*He that sitteth in the heavens shall laugh: the Lord shall have them in derision. 5. Then shall he speak unto them in his wrath, and vex them in his sore displeasure. 6. Yet have I set my king upon my holy hill of Zion.*

### The Throne of God as a place prepared for a human to sit upon, is "the Hill of the Lord"

Strangely the LORD's Throne bears some descriptions suggesting it is prepared for humans bearing a certain set of qualities. In addition various promises or benefits are expected to be given to those found meeting such requirements; a clear understanding of this perspective throws insight into God's plans for Humanity.

*Psalms 24:1-5*
*A Psalm of David. The earth is the LORD'S, and the fulness thereof; the world, and they that dwell therein. 2. For he hath founded it upon the seas, and established it upon the floods. 3. Who shall ascend into the hill of the LORD? or who shall stand in his holy place? 4. He that hath clean hands, and a pure heart; who hath not lifted up his soul unto vanity, nor sworn deceitfully. 5. He shall receive the blessing from the LORD, and righteousness from the God of his salvation.*

*Psalms 2:1-6*
*Why do the heathen rage, and the people imagine a vain thing? 2. The kings of the earth set themselves, and the rulers take counsel together, against the LORD, and against his anointed, saying, 3. Let us break their bands asunder, and cast away their cords from us. 4. He that sitteth in the heavens shall laugh: the Lord shall have them in derision. 5. Then shall he speak unto them in his wrath, and vex them in his sore displeasure. 6. Yet have I set my king upon my holy hill of Zion.*

*Psalms 103:17-19*
*But the mercy of the LORD is from everlasting to everlasting upon them that fear him, and his righteousness unto children's children; 18. To such as keep his covenant, and to those that remember his commandments to do them. 19. The LORD hath prepared his throne in the heavens; and his kingdom ruleth over all.*

## The Throne of God is "The Top of the Mountains"

The word "Mountains" as explained earlier are descriptions for domains occupied by entities bearing no mass attributes. Those we humans call spirits or gods. "The Top of the Mountains" is a figurative description that implies an opinion validating the LORD as "the Most High God or Spirit", because it conveys that His Mountain (Spirit) or domain is the summit of all other mountains — or those of other gods — that exist in the Universe. Interchangeably "the Mountain of the LORD" is also a phrase that represents the entity occupying that location, which is the LORD God Himself or His Spirit. It is He who occupies the place sometimes referenced as "Top of the Mountain".

*Isaiah 2:2-3*
*And it shall come to pass in the last days, that the mountain of the LORD'S house shall be established in the top of the mountains, and shall be exalted above the hills; and all nations shall flow unto it. 3. And many people shall go and say, Come ye, and let us go up to the mountain of the LORD, to the house of the God of Jacob; and he will teach us of his ways, and we will walk in his paths: for out of Zion shall go forth the law, and the word of the LORD from Jerusalem.*

*Micah 4:1-3*

*But in the last days it shall come to pass, that the mountain of the house of the LORD shall be established in the top of the mountains, and it shall be exalted above the hills; and people shall flow unto it.  2.  And many nations shall come, and say, Come, and let us go up to the mountain of the LORD, and to the house of the God of Jacob; and he will teach us of his ways, and we will walk in his paths: for the law shall go forth of Zion, and the word of the LORD from Jerusalem.  3.  And he shall judge among many people, and rebuke strong nations afar off; and they shall beat their swords into plowshares, and their spears into pruning hooks: nation shall not lift up a sword against nation, neither shall they learn war any more.*

# THE THRONE OF "DAVID'S or GOD'S"

The Throne promised to King David's seed was one which will be established forever, this is because "the Son of David" who will sit on it and occupy it must have acquired "the Eternal Attributes of the LORD". Such could only be obtained by intimacy with Him, because this is a requisite for seating on it. This person who fulfills the requirements for it would become "The First One" or "First Human" to reacquire the "Image of God" that all of Humanity lost ages ago. The knowledge for other humans to reacquire such attributes will be imparted into "The First One" for other humans with a desire to do likewise to learn about it from him or her, just as a map drawn by someone who has visited a location could give direction to the same destination for others who study it and use it as a guide to arrive at the same location.  This perspective also syncs with the expectations of the lady at Jacob's well awaiting the Messiah who will tell or reveal things to their generation about worshiping God. Let us imagine for a moment how ridiculous it would be to have a God who also dies like humans die every other day, if such were real only a fool would consider such a deity as a true God. Simply because one of the crucial meanings behind the word "GOD" is supposed to be one who is greater, mightier or more powerful than every other force, power or entity that exists in the Universe. So in essence a God that dies doesn't match the description of the real GOD, this is simply because another entity called "the death force" overcomes such a deity. Any possibility of such a misconception about the LORD God's attributes was put to rest when Jesus Christ over came death in duet with His Spirit as a Human, we know he vanquished "death & the grave".

Understanding such perspectives can explain why the LORD has placed the requirement to become like him before all humans, such that anyone who desires to be like me, also expressed as "sit with me on my Throne" in scriptural context, must fulfill certain criteria, and then, after fulfillment of these shall that person be availed entry or access "by the angels who are gatekeepers into the LORD's Presence or Throne".

Such access is given for the purpose of approaching, merging and or diffusing into God or as certain scriptures state "to become One with God" and this is in order to share all the LORD's Attributes with Him as a Human or "sit on His Throne" as "His Son or Seed" forever.

Biblical records tell us "the Throne of Solomon" wasn't automatically established forever as promised; it doesn't exist even physically or politically anymore. In addition to that when the LORD visited Solomon, He outlined to him certain conditions which were needed to be satisfied in order for Solomon to become "The One" entitled to the rights of a promise made by the LORD to King David for one of "his seeds".

*2 Samuel 7:5-13*
*Go and tell my servant David, Thus saith the LORD, Shalt thou build me an house for me to dwell in? 6. Whereas I have not dwelt in any house since the time that I brought up the children of Israel out of Egypt, even to this day, but have walked in a tent and in a tabernacle. 7. In all the places wherein I have walked with all the children of Israel spake I a word with any of the tribes of Israel, whom I commanded to feed my people Israel, saying, Why build ye not me an house of cedar? 8. Now therefore so shalt thou say unto my servant David, Thus saith the LORD of hosts, I took thee from the sheepcote, from following the sheep, to be ruler over my people, over Israel: 9. And I was with thee whithersoever thou wentest, and have cut off all thine enemies out of thy sight, and have made thee a great name, like unto the name of the great men that are in the earth. 10. Moreover I will appoint a place for my people Israel, and will plant them, that they may dwell in a place of their own, and move no more; neither shall the children of wickedness afflict them any more, as beforetime, 11. And as since the time that I commanded judges to be over my people Israel, and have caused thee to rest from all thine enemies. Also the LORD telleth thee that he will make thee an house. 12. And when thy days be fulfilled, and thou shalt sleep with thy fathers, I will set up thy seed after thee, which shall proceed out of thy bowels, and I will establish his kingdom. 13. He shall build an house for my name, and I will stablish the throne of his kingdom for ever.*

*1 Kings 6:11-14*
*And the word of the LORD came to Solomon, saying, 12. Concerning this house which thou art in building, if thou wilt walk in my statutes, and execute my judgments, and keep all my commandments to walk in them; then will I perform my word with thee, which I spake unto David thy father: 13. And I will dwell among the children of Israel, and will not forsake my people Israel. 14. So Solomon built the house, and finished it.*

*1 Kings 9:1-5*
*And it came to pass, when Solomon had finished the building of the house of the LORD, and the king's house, and all Solomon's desire which he was pleased to do, 2. That the LORD appeared to Solomon the second time, as he had appeared unto him at Gibeon. 3. And the LORD said unto him, I have*

It should be noted that "the Throne of God" and "the Throne of David" are not ALWAYS the same, although they appear as the same figuratively in most perspectives, that is if no attention is paid to details about them. This is so because both are sometimes referenced to as "the Throne of David" in biblical context most of which suggests unification between God and Humans a pace set by King David.

Various scriptures shows there are several instances when one of these two Thrones can exist without the other being joined to it or in alliance with it, whenever they exist or are merged together, such an alliance is determined by the heart condition of the human seating on or occupying the physical portion of "the Throne of David".

There are several instances in the history of the biblical nation of Israel when wicked and evil men were appointed as kings in Israel. These kings sat on "the Throne of David" too, albeit the physical portion only, and they were all know to exhibit conducts displeasing to the LORD. In all such instances "the Throne of God" became temporarily separated from "the Throne of David" because the spirit dwelling or controlling the hearts of such kings was not the same spirit as the one that dwelt in King David's heart or controlled it when he sat on that Throne as a king.

Back then whenever an evil kings reigns or sits on "the Throne of David", the LORD simply distances Himself from such individuals or we could say He pushes them away from His own portion of the Throne so their reign is not in any alliance with His Spirit's or Power's influence. The inverse of that happens if it were a good king sitting on "the Throne of David", both King Hezekiah and Josiah's reign provide faint evidences to such a suggestion.

All those kings who are drawn closer to "the Throne of the LORD" by "the Spirit of the LORD" during their reign must bear certain characteristics. The bible is full of prophecies about "One who is Righteous"; and who will be "One with God"; "One who is also expected to sit on the Throne of David"; sometime in the future. This one will conquer and defeat all of God's enemies, just like King David did in his days, and this is because the Spirit that was upon or with King David during his earthly reign will be upon and with this one too, in its fullest ever manifestation since human existence.

This manifestation of "the Spirit of the LORD" on this person is in my view going to exceed the manifestation of "the Spirit of the LORD" in the life of Jesus Christ because he hinted about it to those who have a hear to hear it, herein is wisdom.

*John 14:12*
*Verily, verily, I say unto you, He that believeth on me, the works that I do shall he do also; and greater works than these shall he do; because I go unto my Father.*

That is why any person who heeds to that message from Jesus Christ and works hard at making it true is in my view "potentially a Messiah", or the one who will take the manifestations of "the Presence, Power and Spirit of the LORD" on the Earth to a higher level not yet achieved by Humanity.

It should be realized that such a person who is expected to do greater works than Jesus Christ in my view will also have to tick all the other boxes of unfulfilled prophecies about "the expected Messiah", those which Jesus Christ didn't. This person is also called or considered "the Anointed One of God" in prophecies and goes by various other description and several other titles enumerated in next section.

The "Throne of God" is where the LORD's Presence is, so anyone who secures access to this Throne is automatically said to be in or dwell in "the Presence of the LORD", and by virtue of being in the LORD's Presence, some of "the Eternal Attributes of the LORD" which could also be described as "the Spirit of the LORD", gets deposited on the person, just like if a person was in a night club where smoking and alcohol are consumed without any discretion they would come out with their clothes reeking of such vices.

These Eternal Attributes are what are also described as "the Glories of God" and whenever the one who accessed "the Presence of God" departs or descends back to the realm where mortal men dwell, such glories become visible. A typical example of such was visible on Prophet Moses' face after he ascended up to God at Mount Horeb, upon his descent he was noted to have a face which glowed.

We can confirm that by virtue of the undisputable fact that God dwells in light, some of such light attributes were what Moses picked up when he visited the LORD God at Mount Horeb. The stone placed in the ark was also known to contain similar essence and attributes captured as a result of that visit to the LORD by Moses.

*Exodus 34:29-30*
*And it came to pass, when Moses came down from mount Sinai with the two tables of testimony in Moses' hand, when he came down from the mount, that Moses wist not that the skin of his face shone while he talked with him. 30. And when Aaron and all the children of Israel saw Moses, behold, the skin of his face shone; and they were afraid to come nigh him*

.

# "A SEED OF DAVID & A SEED OF JACOB"

The "Seed" prefix has been used in several instances in various books of the bible. Its first usage occurs when the LORD said to the serpent that a seed of the woman will bruise its head, and this prophecy has been misinterpreted as fulfilled by Jesus Christ by him conquering "death", because death is construed as the serpent's head by those making such erroneous interpretations.

Jesus Christ, "The seed of man" who is presumed to fulfill this prophecy was a distant relative of the first human, "Adam & Eve". They were the original possessors of "the Human attributes" which they passed down the generations to all humans. This attribute also known as "the Adam & Eve attribute" became a sacred attribute, from the moment that pronouncement was made, because it was needed to fulfill what the LORD said to the serpent concerning how its end or reign will occur. It is for such reasons that Jesus Christ had to bear human flesh similar to that borne by Adam & Eve.

In addition to that we should also remember that Humans were created as vessels to ultimately bear "the Image of God", a purpose which also makes "the Human attributes" borne by "Adam & Eve" a sacred one. From those perspectives or viewpoints we may understand the reason why the genealogy of Jesus Christ was traced back to Adam in certain New Testament books of the bible, such was simply to prove that he was actually "a seed of Adam & Eve" or "a bearer of "the Human attribute" which they also bore.

King David was a man precious to the LORD simply because he loved God with all his heart and desired to dwell with God. These attributes of King David was one which the LORD had been seeking for amongst the midst of Humanity since our existence. And I also believe this attribute was quite an essential attribute for the progress of the Human race, because most of those who possessed it in scant traces, were the ones preserved in the midst of calamities befalling the Earth, such as during the flood in Noah's days.

Perhaps to explain further I could use this analogy. A woman will search for a man who truly loves her for herself from a bunch of suitors seeking marital union with her before making a decision to get married to such a person fitting her preference. I am fully aware that such is not the only criteria considered by the female specie of our generation for selecting a marriage partner, but please allow my patchy focus on love for the purposes of stating my point because it relates to a marriage of which love is essential.

As stated earlier, I firmly believe the LORD had waited and patiently searched for "a human" with such love as King David had for Him before proceeding to sanction a marriage between God and Humanity. One followed by His promised to dwell with humans forever. It would be right for us to consider why the LORD would want a human with true love for Him?

Taking a glimpse back into what happened at the beginning of Creation, will aid our understanding or help us locate the answer to that question. From one perspective, it appears obvious that Adam and Eve fell for the deceptions of the serpent because they did not really love the LORD. It is right to imagine they really wanted to be better than the LORD God in actuality. Such a view could explain why they acted as they did after that proposal was put to them. Perhaps they thought the LORD was old fashioned and antiquated. Perhaps they saw the serpent revelling in what we call sin and likewise craved for such experiences too. That explains why once the opportunity came to abandon the LORD by a consumption of "the Forbidden tree" as we are told by the narrative, they jumped at it thoughtlessly and that action triggered "the Fall of Adam & Eve" or humans and their separation from the LORD's Presence, and also their right to residence in the location called "Eden or Paradise". By their actions they abandoned the ship of certainty and jumped into the sea of uncertainty wilfully, surely such an act was part of the triggers for a search for humans better in judgment and loyalty than "Adam & Eve".

The desired higher loyalty attribute and sound judgment characteristics is encumbered in the word "LOVE" which we are enjoined to have for the LORD with all our heart.

If we recall, Jesus Christ made a comment about "the Kingdom of Heaven" being likened to that of a rich man whose son opted to leave him under the famous prodigal son parable. This is one that portrays an anecdote of what happened to Humanity at the earlier stages of our existence. Though the father gave his son a worthy portion of inheritance — in our case the Image and Gory of God —and did let this son go as desired, — the Fall of man or our separation from God by the actions of "Adam and Eve" — fits here perfectly, but then like a smouldering ember, the prodigal son burnt out all the inheritance given to him by his rich father.

"The loss of inheritance in humans is equivalent to the loss of "the Glory of God" which they bore previously as "Images of God" before their fall".

From the moment this lad's inheritance ran out, he became a prey to those in the new environment he found himself, and likewise in Humanity's case, once "the Glory of God" we bore ran out, we also became prey to those called "the children of wickedness". Such were those in the lad's case who owned the pigs who he had to feed as a labourer, making him a servant to those owning an estate or kingdom separate to that of his father's.

Similarly, all the miseries of Humanity fit here because we now serve strange gods or entities ruling over our race, that explains evil being present in or world. But one day, the prodigal son got back to his senses, and realized that his father was far richer and kinder and was one who treated his servants better that he had been treated in this place of his sojourn, after such realization he made the decision to return back to his father, because he was sure that even as a servant in his father's kingdom, life for him would be of a better quality.

Such a realization is what all humans collectively or one among our race is expected to come to, it is also termed as "Salvation", an act preceded by that called "Repentance" which is the decision to return back to the LORD God.

That parable to me clearly depicts our story as humans "seeds of Adam & Eve", who by our fore bearers' genes have also forsaken "the Presence of the LORD and His Glory" by a freewill decision they made. Which is the sin we all need to repent of, and it is also the reason why we are preyed on by the devil and other evil entities present in this world. We became preys because we all lost our union to the LORD, that which connects us with Him and allows sharing with us of His Glory, which was the source of our strength and shield and bore capability to defend and protect us from all peril or danger. To presume that there is no danger to our race or deny the existence of one which seeks to annihilate our race us is great folly.

There are two contexts to Salvation, the personal one and the collective one for Humanity, the second can be best expressed by considering that by one human's act, Humanity separated its race from the LORD. A reverse of that is desired and all provisions for it are already in place by means of roles played by Jesus Christ. The choice to re-establish the lost union with the LORD, who can protect us is ours to make and accomplish both for ourselves and for future generations of our race. Such is desired in order that Humanity can once again experience peace and a cessation of all evils on the Earth, it is the personal one to be made by another one human too, because only when one human activates it will Humanity enjoy its benefits.

Once Humanity succeeds at accomplishing these expectations of Salvation, "the Kingdom of God" is then known to have come back upon the Earth, because "the Presence of God" will return back to the Earth and be in our midst. This comes about by virtue of the fact that Humanity becomes reunited with Him once again and from then onwards only the LORD's will shall be done on the Earth, through his conduit who triggers the awaited Salvation.

*Luke 11:2*
*And he said unto them, When ye pray, say, Our Father which art in heaven,*
*Hallowed be thy name. Thy kingdom come. Thy will be done, as in heaven, so*
*in earth.*

For those who may presume that the LORD's will is presently done on the Earth, I will simply ask them to ponder upon and try to explain why Jesus Christ taught people to pray for God's kingdom to come upon the Earth and for His will to be done here. Do we really think Jesus Christ will ask us to pray for what we already have? If anyone can accept that which is being suggested here, then they should go further and wonder, if really the LORD's kingdom is not on the Earth, and if the LORD's will is not being done on the Earth presently, then whose will is being done here now, and whose kingdom is upon the Earth? Well, my hint to that is, it is that of the same entity who offered Jesus Christ the whole world, only if he would bow and worship him, he who has an ear let him hear this.

To further emphasize that opinion, I will draw attention to a prophecy uttered by Prophet Amos stating that the LORD God will one day cut off or wipe off a kingdom called "the sinful kingdom" from the face of the Earth. Those words should give a clear insight into reasons for the prayers Jesus Christ taught his disciples about which was praying for "the Kingdom of God" coming upon the Earth. In my view "the Kingdom of God" will only come after "the sinful kingdom" is wiped off the Earth. We should also recall that Jesus Christ stressed on several occasions about not being subject to the earthly kingdom or the one on the Earth, in addition to that by considering that he was crucified, the question on our mind should be who really issued the command to execute such an action? It surely wasn't the LORD.

*Amos 9:8*
*Behold, the eyes of the Lord GOD are upon the sinful kingdom, and I will destroy it from off the face of the earth; saving that I will not utterly destroy the house of Jacob, saith the LORD.*

Concerning the word of the LORD, that "a Seed of the Woman" will bruise the serpent's head, we must discern that pronunciation as raison d'être why the whole human race is loathed and enslaved by the devil. It should also explain why he oppresses us and constantly attempts to wipe off the pure human gene entirely. We should be rest assured that the devil will do everything possible to ensure that the truth about reclaiming "the lost Glory of God" or returning of Humanity back into "the LORD's Presence" is concealed from humans, because this is needed in order for "a seed of the Woman" to gain power to successfully bruise the serpent's head, a vital component of "the Messianic Enigma" or destruction of the sinful kingdom on Earth.

Ceaselessly, conspiracy theorists howl and cry about human gene manipulation, cross-breeding of Humanity, human abductions and poisoning of the human race with chemicals and genetically modified substances or food. All of which are parts of the serpent's attempts to ensure not one human is found fit for the purpose of being reinvested with "the Glory of God" or allowed back into "the LORD's Presence". Such attempts by evil entities are also to reconfigure the human structural makeup into one that fits with their kind, just like a bandit who snatches a car from the owner at gun point will busy himself with adjusting the seat position, rear and wing mirror settings etc to suit his driving style.

If anyone really presumes that the devil will sit back, do nothing and just wait for one considered righteous among Humanity to rise up. One who is expected to be fit for the LORD's purposes to appear and by such qualifications acquire the capability to destroy the devil's hegemony over Humanity and our world, then I'll have to say to anyone with such thoughts, please think about that once again. This time, in the concept of "an incumbent and the opposition", in order to understand clearly what is at stake.

The devil was the same entity that made Cain to slay his brother because it thought Abel was the one to unseat his control over the world, similar strategies played out in the days of Moses' birth in Egypt when all male children were decreed to be killed at birth, and quite similar attempts were made to kill baby Jesus Christ by King Herod after his birth.

Let it be clear, that the serpent via its human puppets will do everything possible to prevent and preclude those humans desiring to bring back Humanity's lost union with the LORD. Including concealment or effacing all truths or any knowledge that will allow "the Kingdom of God" to come upon or return to the Earth. Simply because it knows that upon such returning, "the sinful kingdom" it rules over here on the Earth comes to its end.

The moment the LORD spotted this desired attributes of true love for Him in King David's heart, an attribute which is one of the pre-requisites for His kingdom returning to the Earth. It should be noted that He acted on that discovery and made a vow to King David, that all humans who possesses such attribute best described as "the David-like attribute" will be precious to Him forever, such humans in my view are those referenced as "the sons of David" in certain other context and perspectives.

From that moment onwards any human bearing those attributes — or similar ones to it — were sought of by the LORD in the midst of all Humanity, because the LORD knew they had some good traits in them fitting for His Purpose. Which is an ability to love Him the way King David did, such was that which He had desired from Humanity ever since the beginning of their fall away from Him after consuming the Forbidden fruit.

In my view, I presume that on the LORD's side, the process of looking for humans with this attribute will work similarly like we humans searching for a person with a particular blood type or gene trait for a certain scientific purpose. Another view is that it is also possible that the LORD may have even taken specimens of "the David-like attributes" or traits of such from his body and may have grafted it into the sea of unborn humans. I hold that view because it was surely from this "subset of unborn humans" that the ones who will be called the "sons of David" will arise, these are those who are expected to fulfill future prophecies. Such appearing in Humanity's midst can either be as a result of chance or purposeful breeding.

This view is arrived at because while exploring the bible, great excitement can be observed in the LORD's voice when he found another human with the same attribute as King David. From His speech, as captured in the verses of Psalm 89 which was a prophetic outburst. For those who think this person called David in that passage was "David the King of Israel", I would say you have to realize it couldn't be him because the real David had been personally known to the LORD prior to this prophetic word or psalm was composed.

It makes no sense announcing the discovery of what was already discovered. It will be like a man saying I have found the woman I will marry despite the fact that he had already married her several years ago. We have to take into consideration that this psalm and prophecy was composed after or most likely during King David's lifetime, suggesting he was already the King of Israel. Such should cause us to wonder why the LORD will be talking about making a human king, if he had already done so as detailed in the narrative, that aim seems pointless if we consider David was already King of Israel. It is right to presume that the real King David may have died and was already safe in Abraham's bosom waiting for resurrection at the final judgment day of all Humanity, at that point when the one who was found was being announced and the LORD's plans and intentions for him were being stated.

> *Psalms 89:20-28*
> *I have found David my servant; with my holy oil have I anointed him:  21. With whom my hand shall be established: mine arm also shall strengthen him.  22.  The enemy shall not exact upon him; nor the son of wickedness afflict him.  23.  And I will beat down his foes before his face, and plague them that hate him.  24.  But my faithfulness and my mercy shall be with him: and in my name shall his horn be exalted.  25.  I will set his hand also in the sea, and his right hand in the rivers.  26.  He shall cry unto me, Thou art my father, my God, and the rock of my salvation.  27.  Also I will make him my firstborn, higher than the kings of the earth.  28.  My mercy will I keep for him for evermore, and my covenant shall stand fast with him.*

There could however be another more logical explanation for the excitement in the LORD's utterance about finding "David His servant" as gleaned in the verses above, and in my view it could be that King David after his death also disappeared from "the Presence of the LORD" into "the realm of death", like all humans do when they die.

But because King David possessed minute traces of the "Eternal attributes of God", such attributes acquired by his love and intimacy with the LORD during his lifetime would have bequeathed upon him the ability to overcomes and vanquish all the forces of "the realm of death", this is possible, once we remember that God cannot die and such attributes of Him — the Eternal attributes — are also transferrable to those who draw closer to Him.

It is possible that this attribute, "the Eternal attributes of God" empowered King David to somehow fight his way back, into the land of the living from the realm of the dead, just like a drowning man who clutches firmly onto a floating log of dry wood in the sea could overcome all the perils of the waves and currents at sea until he is thrown back onto the shores by a sea wave that splashes him upon the beach.

In King David's case, the log of dry wood would have to be "the Eternal attributes of God" acquired during his lifetime of intimacy with the LORD God, such attributes we should all crave and strive to acquire in order to accomplish greater feats than King David.

*Psalms 71:19-22*
*Thy righteousness also, O God, is very high, who hast done great things: O God, who is like unto thee! 20. Thou, which hast shewed me great and sore troubles, shalt quicken me again, and shalt bring me up again from the depths of the earth. 21. Thou shalt increase my greatness, and comfort me on every side. 22. I will also praise thee with the psaltery, even thy truth, O my God: unto thee will I sing with the harp, O thou Holy One of Israel.*

It is right to wonder, if really it was King David that was brought up from "the depths of the Earth" as expressed in the verses above or if it was a prophecy referencing to Jesus Christ.  If it was indeed him then, it could have been that after several days in the jaws of death, King David — "the True Warrior" — fought his way to resurface back into the land of the living from "the depths of the earth".

Which seems a fitting description for "the land or realm of the dead", the place where humans go after dying? Could that have been the first resurrection from death? Could that have been the much awaited breakthrough for Humanity even though the one who made it came back in a battered and roughened state? The following verses suggest so in my view.

*Psalms 89:47-49*
*Remember how short my time is: wherefore hast thou made all men in vain? 48. What man is he that liveth, and shall not see death? shall he deliver his soul from the hand of the grave? Selah.  49.  Lord, where are thy former lovingkindnesses, which thou swarest unto David in thy truth?*

If it was so, then finding "David the LORD's Servant" was the discovery of a new potential in Humanity, one first borne by King David, an ability which was later to be perfected for the Human race by Jesus Christ when he totally overcame Death for us all and by that act he settled "the plague of Death" upon Humanity finally.

I must admit that I personally feel more at ease leaning on the view that the pronouncements in Psalm 89 couldn't be about the King David already known to the LORD, because of hints of about his discovery, which suggest it was another person possibly one with a genetic makeup similar to him, who as expressed above also possessed "David-like attributes". Making him "a son of David", with that said I cannot discard the other view expressed suggesting the found one was perhaps a re-incarnation of the real King David of Israel, hence I leave all options on the table.

The person who was referenced in Psalm 89 as "David my Servant" also sounds by description more like Jesus Christ to me because he also loved the LORD with all his heart even to a greater degree than King David did, and perhaps that is one of the meanings connoted by calling him "a Son of David", a phrase that could also be assumed to equalize or mean another one bearing "David-like attributes". The LORD's plans for this person called David also fit those for "the expected Messiah" if we consider its entire context.

I am conscious of the fact that there exist a possible third meaning to that phrase "David my Servant", which is being one with filial links to King David, and this appears to be the view prevalently adopted by Christianity. But then we should consider if that view was religious doctrine and its proponents simply trying to prove or make valid their suppositions about what the phrase "a Son of David" and "David my Servant" meant, in their bid to keep Humanity craving religious attachments rather than pursuing "a True Knowledge of God".

I say that because if anyone perceives Jesus Christ as a biological "son of David" and also a "son of God" as taught by Christian doctrine, they become bound to reserve that status for only him, and by such resignation they automatically bar themselves from every trying to be like Jesus Christ or achieving the status of "a son of God". The next best option available to anyone holding such beliefs or views is obeying and serving those who impose themselves as representatives of "King David's God", because by doing so and by that I mean complying to the dictated decrees of such religious edicts put forward as the laws or requirements of serving King David's God, which guarantees those in compliance passage into heaven after dying as taught by Christian and other doctrines.

That again in my view is a contorted representation of "the Truth" because the path to heaven is not in dying, but rather in overcoming "the forces of death" like Jesus Christ did, or likewise Moses, Enoch and Elijah before him. Our God is not that who promises goodies to those who die or kill themselves. Jesus Christ expressed such clearly as stated below, herein lies wisdom and let he who has an ear hear it, let him with an eye see clearly and him with a nose smell the essence of this truth, same caveat applies to she who reads this.

> *Matthew 22:31-32*
> *But as touching the resurrection of the dead, have ye not read that which was spoken unto you by God, saying, 32. I am the God of Abraham, and the God of Isaac, and the God of Jacob? God is not the God of the dead, but of the living.*

Imagine if we found a Zebra with pink stripes instead of the usual black stripes somewhere on the Earth. It would surely attract human attention and we would probably name it "the pink Zebra" after its discovery. If some years later in some remote part of the world another Zebra with pink stripes is found, we will simply refer to it as "another pink Zebra" or a specie relative of "the first pink Zebra" rather than give it another name. It is possible that when the LORD God announced finding "David His servant" he could have been saying, I have found "another David" or one with "David-like Attributes".

> *Psalms 18:49-50*
> *Therefore will I give thanks unto thee, O LORD, among the heathen, and sing praises unto thy name. 50. Great deliverance giveth he to his king; and sheweth mercy to his anointed, to David, and to his seed for evermore.*

The bible is littered with a lot of instances where the LORD makes reference to an individual — "David their King" — a phrase which in my view and in those contexts suggest that the person is to be a future King reigning just like King David reigned. Also noted is that this person possesses "David-like attributes", which quite simply is a heart with great love for the LORD.

The most crucial thing to note is that this person is expected to "bear seeds" as can be gleaned in verses above which is an indication of more than one of them existing in the future of time.

*Hosea 3:5*
*Afterward shall the children of Israel return, and seek the LORD their God, and David their king; and shall fear the LORD and his goodness in the latter days.*

*Jeremiah 30:9*
*But they shall serve the LORD their God, and David their king, whom I will raise up unto them.*

Also to note is that in all such references there exist the depictions of a duet, one where both the LORD and "a David their King" are reigning over Israel at a time in the future. In my view, I believe what is being suggested is a reign on the Earth where both the LORD and a human, obviously one with "David-like attributes" is ruling over the whole earth, and this view is also depicted in the dreams of King Nebuchadnezzar which Daniel interpreted for him.

In the Nebuchadnezzar perspective, the everlasting attribute of that reign is something that is parallel with other prophecies concerning the return of the Kingdom of God upon the Earth, such are similarities that cannot be discarded easily, including the fact that it overcomes other kingdoms existing on Earth.

Considering the Khalifa perspective in Islam, where a caliph who heads a caliphate is expected to be a political and religious ruler on Earth, one chosen by Allah to reign. We can spot clear similarities in such depictions which could equate "the Caliphate's authority" to "the Throne of David's authority", that is if the characteristics bequeathed each perspective by religious doctrines or cultural expressions are differentiated.

*Daniel 2:42-44*
*And as the toes of the feet were part of iron, and part of clay, so the kingdom shall be partly strong, and partly broken. 43. And whereas thou sawest iron mixed with miry clay, they shall mingle themselves with the seed of men: but they shall not cleave one to another, even as iron is not mixed with clay. 44. And in the days of these kings shall the God of heaven set up a kingdom, which shall never be destroyed: and the kingdom shall not be left to other people, but it shall break in pieces and consume all these kingdoms, and it shall stand for ever.*

I am aware that leagues of biblical scholars like to perceive or interpret all such future prophecies as indicating that the old King David, who reigned over the nation of Israel, will arise or be raised up by God once again to reign over the nation of Israel.

In my view such a misunderstanding comes from assuming that Israel will be a nation among many nations when "the Spirit of the LORD" returns to the Earth. Contrary to that, Israel will be the only nation and other nations will become sub-nations to it. The nation called Israel then will be the political capital of the world and the city called Jerusalem will be where "the Glory of the LORD" goes out from within this nation called Israel, not one of geographical situation on a map as we may automatically presume.

Such a similar misinterpretation concerning Israel or what it connotes is encountered by the phrase "raise up" which is embedded in some prophecies too.

Phrases like "I will send you Elijah", also created similar confusions about another one who was expected to return, presumed to be "Elijah the Prophet" at the last days.

It is crucial to note that Jesus Christ told his disciples that the expected Elijah has come as expected of him and as foretold by prophecies, yet at that time there was no visual sighting of him in their midst. That should indicate something to the discerning about interpreting prophecies in context of names or personalities.

> *Matthew 11:13-15*
> *For all the prophets and the law prophesied until John. 14. And if ye will receive it, this is Elias, which was for to come. 15. He that hath ears to hear, let him hear.*

In my view what was meant to return or appear prefixed as "Elijah the prophet" by the prophecies was a human with "Elijah-like attributes". One of its poignant characteristics was zeal for the LORD's Kingdom. Such attribute's criteria were fulfilled and manifested by John the Baptist and even confirmed by his own words, though it appears everyone paid no notice to his utterances as typical of religious people who remain fixated on what they read and are told or taught by the promoters of their respective religion's doctrines, because they are too lazy to be autodidacts.

> *John 1:19-23*
> *And this is the record of John, when the Jews sent priests and Levites from Jerusalem to ask him, Who art thou? 20. And he confessed, and denied not; but confessed, I am not the Christ. 21. And they asked him, What then? Art thou Elias? And he saith, I am not. Art thou that prophet? And he answered, No. 22. Then said they unto him, Who art thou? that we may give an answer to them that sent us. What sayest thou of thyself? 23. He said, I am the voice of one crying in the wilderness, Make straight the way of the Lord, as said the prophet Esaias.*

From preceding text we can clearly glean that John the Baptist was stressing to them that he was that human whose voice played the role prophesied by Prophet Isaiah. That role was about a voice which would be heard in the wilderness of Israel.

A voice which was to pre-announce the upcoming revelation of "the Glory of the LORD" on Earth; such Glories were manifested by Jesus Christ in those days, and will be repeated in the future.

There is undisputable fact that John the Baptist spent most of his days in the wilderness, and quite strangely records show people in the city left to listen to his wilderness teachings. His sermons must have been deeply anointed for people to make such sacrifices to attend them in those days in my opinion. John the Baptist's announcement about the revelation of the LORD's Glory could come to be only when there appeared one human bearing "the Spirit of the LORD" walking the Earth capable of manifesting such glories as fulfilled by Jesus Christ, likewise it is for future revelations.

To confirm that there was actually one bearing "the Spirit of the LORD" on the Earth, let us look back at what happened when Mary the mother of Jesus Christ visited Elizabeth her cousin. It was observed that Elizabeth snapped into a prophetic outburst spurred by the spirit within the baby that she had in her womb, this baby was John the Baptist. What he did then was to announce the presence of one greater than him in the womb of Mary, that one was the human to bear the LORD's Spirit and reveal His Glories upon the Earth during that period.

*Luke 1:39-46*
*And Mary arose in those days, and went into the hill country with haste, into a city of Juda; 40. And entered into the house of Zacharias, and saluted Elisabeth. 41. And it came to pass, that, when Elisabeth heard the salutation of Mary, the babe leaped in her womb; and Elisabeth was filled with the Holy Ghost: 42. And she spake out with a loud voice, and said, Blessed art thou among women, and blessed is the fruit of thy womb. 43. And whence is this to me, that the mother of my Lord should come to me? 44. For, lo, as soon as the voice of thy salutation sounded in mine ears, the babe leaped in my womb for joy. 45. And blessed is she that believed: for there shall be a performance of those things which were told her from the Lord. 46. And Mary said, My soul doth magnify the Lord,*

*Isaiah 40:2-5*
*Speak ye comfortably to Jerusalem, and cry unto her, that her warfare is accomplished, that her iniquity is pardoned: for she hath received of the LORD'S hand double for all her sins. 3. The voice of him that crieth in the wilderness, Prepare ye the way of the LORD, make straight in the desert a highway for our God. 4. Every valley shall be exalted, and every mountain and hill shall be made low: and the crooked shall be made straight, and the rough places plain: 5. And the glory of the LORD shall be revealed, and all flesh shall see it together: for the mouth of the LORD hath spoken it.*

That view about John the Baptist being "the expected Elijah" was put forward by Jesus Christ even to the extent of him stressing to his disciples, "you need to pay close attention to prophetic facts and correlate them with what was happening in your times". Most especially, stop being literal in all your scriptural interpretations, if you really want to discern the truths about God and the sign of times. That is advice all humans of our times also need to take heed off, in order to discern the plans and ways of the LORD.

*Matthew 17:10-12*
*And his disciples asked him, saying, Why then say the scribes that Elias must first come? 11. And Jesus answered and said unto them, Elias truly shall first come, and restore all things. 12. But I say unto you, That Elias is come already, and they knew him not, but have done unto him whatsoever they listed. Likewise shall also the Son of man suffer of them.*

It is also essential to state, that Elijah was simply a human upon who "the Spirit of the LORD" rested, while he walked on the Earth. Just before he was taken into Heaven, he passed this spirit resting with him on to Elisha as instructed by the LORD. That transfer of the spirit, which could also be called the anointing of Elisha, is stated here to indicate that Elijah was not the only one who passed on "the Spirit of the LORD" resting with him on to another person on the Earth. Several others did the same thing such as, Moses who passed it on to Joshua and John the Baptist who passed it on to Jesus Christ.

John the Baptist was a fore-runner for Jesus Christ, in the sense that the LORD's Spirit was upon him right until the moment John passed "the Spirit of the LORD" on to Jesus Christ that is what happened at what we call the baptism at the river Jordan. It also explains why John the Baptist made comments to the effect that, he must decrease while the one destined to bear "the Spirit of God", and also called "the Bridegroom" or "the Christ" must increase. It also explains why John was stressing and almost begging that he needed to be baptised by Jesus Christ as opposed to him baptising Jesus Christ when they met. It should be noted clearly that Jesus Christ did impressed upon John the Baptist to do the baptising, because he knew that there was something in the possession of John the Baptist that he needed to be anointed or blessed with before he could bear all the potentials foreseen by John the Baptist. Isn't it curiously strange that at the river Jordan, both individual were eager to increase in what they possessed portions of? What is a better definition for a zeal for the LORD but such desires?

*John 3:27-31*
*John answered and said, A man can receive nothing, except it be given him from heaven. 28. Ye yourselves bear me witness, that I said, I am not the Christ, but that I am sent before him. 29. He that hath the bride is the bridegroom: but the friend of the bridegroom, which standeth and heareth him, rejoiceth greatly because of the bridegroom's voice: this my joy therefore is fulfilled. 30. He must increase, but I must decrease. 31. He that cometh*

*from above is above all: he that is of the earth is earthly, and speaketh of the earth: he that cometh from heaven is above all.*

*Matthew 3:13-16*
*Then cometh Jesus from Galilee to Jordan unto John, to be baptized of him. 14. But John forbad him, saying, I have need to be baptized of thee, and comest thou to me? 15. And Jesus answering said unto him, Suffer it to be so now: for thus it becometh us to fulfil all righteousness. Then he suffered him. 16. And Jesus, when he was baptized, went up straightway out of the water: and, lo, the heavens were opened unto him, and he saw the Spirit of God descending like a dove, and lighting upon him:*

From his mother's womb, John the Baptist knew he was to pass the Spirit onto Jesus Christ as ordained and that was what the prophetic outburst he made as a baby was all about. Though it appears he may have forgotten such when he met Jesus Christ, the spirit resting within him was not as senile as he was, despite saying that it is clearly visible that he also bore within him a fervent desire to manifest "the Glory of God" on Earth.

Now with all that stated, we may begin to discern how it was that the expected Elijah had already come, even though those awaiting his appearance seem to have missed all signs of his return or appearance. The expected Elijah was simply one human bearing "the Spirit of the LORD" with "an Elijah-like zeal for God's Kingdom", this was fulfilled by John the Baptist.

Curiously it appears that at that appearance of one bearing the LORD's Spirit according to prophecy, two individuals appeared to fulfill the stated prophecy. That would prompt me to conclude in my opinion, that actually "two Elijahs" had appeared instead of one yet both were not recognized. And that means two bearers of the LORD's Spirit appeared fitting such descriptions. The first one was "John the Baptist" who decreased by giving what he bore or was anointed with to the second one "Jesus Christ" who increased in it because it was ordained to be like this from above.

Both of them exhibited "Elijah-like attributes" during the course of their lives, they equally demonstrated intense zeal for the LORD and His purposes, just as Prophet Elijah had in his days.

Though it is recorded in scriptures that people visited John in the wilderness to hear his teachings, I opine even despite that there isn't concrete biblical records or citations to support my presumptions other than a scant linkage, from a comment made by King Herod, which in some ways suggests that John may also have manifested signs and miracles too in the wilderness. That may have been the reason why people went to listen to him in such an out of town location. I really can't fathom why people will bother or venture after a prophet of God, if there wasn't something special or exceptional to be benefitted from him out there in the wilderness. I must point out also that it is also stated that John did no miracles in the bible but somehow I lean in the direction that he did because there is evidence suggesting something of such in the bible and my reasoning inclines me towards such a conclusion.

Both Elijahs' who appeared were like athletes in a two-lap relay, where the one starting the sprint will be expected to pass on the baton. This will be a portion of their anointing of "the Spirit of God", unto the other Elijah for him to finish his lap of the race they both ran.

Their individual payload or portions of the LORD's anointing to manifest God's power must have been broken down into two tranches to avoid detection by the enemy until it was activated. This activation will be what happens by connecting both payloads or uniting them together and that happened at river Jordan. We must recall that it wasn't until John the Baptist passed his payload or portion of the LORD's anointing on to Jesus Christ that the devil spotted him, and afterwards tempted him in the wilderness.  Before such an event Jesus Christ was no threat to the devil or on his radar at all and there was no need to tempt him, or offer him any deal which may have prompted him to abandon his God sent mission. But the moment he acquired a potential perceived as a threat to "the kingdom upon the Earth", he was offered bribes also perceived as being tempted to abandon his mission.

To consider that the devil was prepared to allow Jesus Christ hold a position of second in command to him on Earth, if he had fallen for the temptation and opted to abandon his mission by bowing down, such should suggest clearly that the potential which Jesus Christ's anointing now bore by merging his with that of John the Baptist, was one that would make him ruler of the whole world if activated. I say that because in the high stakes game of power, no one offers another individual the opportunity to be their second in command if such a person does not bear the potential to be number one.

This perspective about the anointing and payload above, re-emphasizes my earlier suggestions about how everything Humanity needs to reclaim the Earth from evil forces controlling it, as expressed in the first chapter must be concealed and hidden from the enemy's  purview until the time to strike with it is right. The phrase "go before him in spirit and power of Elias" in the verses below highlights my view about two portions or payload of the anointing of God clearly. The spirit and power of Elias in context below is simply "the Spirit of God" or His anointing.

*and power of Elias, to turn the hearts of the fathers to the children, and the
disobedient to the wisdom of the just; to make ready a people prepared for the
Lord.*

Now applying "the Elijah spirit and power return" concept to expectations of
Jesus Christ returning as prophesied, we may now realise that what we await
is really one upon whom the same spirit that rested upon Jesus Christ, which is
"the Spirit of the LORD" also previously know as "the spirit and power of
Elijah" will rest. And not a return of "Jesus Christ the personality" as Christian
doctrines have put forward in error. Such makes clear sense with all
expectations for "the Messiah" which Jesus Christ did not fulfill at his
appearance, and also syncs perfectly with all expectations for a Messiah
expected by other faiths awaiting one.

This perspective should be applied at discerning all prophetic references to
"the Son of Man" or "the Anointed One" also called "the Messiah", unless or
otherwise the text we are reading is referring to a prophecy already fulfilled.
Also to be noted is a striking similarity between the pattern of the two bearers
of Elijah's anointing, and the expected appearance of the two witnesses of the
God at end times. These personalities or witnesses overcame death too as
prophesied in the book of Revelations; they are two individuals bearing
"Christ-like attributes".  They were also "anointed with the LORD's Spirit"
bearing abilities to overcome death just as Jesus Christ had done before them. If
other humans can later in the future of Humanity do what Jesus Christ did in
the past, does that not suggest clearly that other humans too can be "sons of
God" or acquire attributes and abilities borne and manifested by Jesus Christ?
Such are those Christian doctrine desperately attempts to restrict to only him.
In some cases, these prophecies could be manifested by more than one
anointed servant of God — or those whose ways are pleasing to Him.

Jacob "often referenced as Israel" was a person just like King David. A man
also precious to the LORD, he unlike his brother Esau was keenly interested in
what was known as "The Birth-right". Which was actually the most precious
asset in the world, what we call or reference as "The Birth-right" in Jacob and
Esau's story, was simply a presence of "the Spirit of the LORD" being with
who ever had or possessed right to it as such can be clearly discerned from the
verses below.

*1 Chronicles 5:1-2*
*Now the sons of Reuben the firstborn of Israel, (for he was the firstborn; but,
forasmuch as he defiled his father's bed, his birthright was given unto the
sons of Joseph the son of Israel: and the genealogy is not to be reckoned after
the birthright.  2.  For Judah prevailed above his brethren, and of him came
the chief ruler; but the birthright was Joseph's:)*

Having "The Birth-right" meant the bearer was conferred a title of being
"anointed by the LORD". This is because "the Spirit of the LORD" would be
known as dwelling with the bearer rather than with others in the family, who it

should have been with according to the order of firstborn.

We can see in the verse above that "the Anointed One" or "the one who prevailed", in this case King David came from the tribe of Judah, rather than from the tribes of Reuben or Joseph to which this privilege should have been passed on to from their father Jacob. Since it can't be disputed that King David was anointed by God, and made leader of the twelve tribes that proposition of mine is fact.

In the case of Isaac he inherited "the Birth-right" from Abraham, because he was the promised child from the LORD through Sarah, unlike Ishmael his step-brother. Who though was firstborn son of Abraham came forth from another woman's womb in this case Hagar. In this instance "the Birth-right" did not rest with Ishmael who was actually Abraham's firstborn son because he did not fulfill the criteria of coming forth from Sarah's womb, which was what the LORD stated to Abraham concerning his seed's promise. In the verses below there is an inter correlation between the word "seed" and "he that shall come forth from thy bowel" this connection must not be glossed over to understand what transpired.

> *Genesis 15:3-4*
> *And Abram said, Behold, to me thou hast given no seed: and, lo, one born in my house is mine heir. 4. And, behold, the word of the LORD came unto him, saying, This shall not be thine heir; but he that shall come forth out of thine own bowels shall be thine heir.*

> *Genesis 12:7*
> *And the LORD appeared unto Abram, and said, Unto thy seed will I give this land: and there builded he an altar unto the LORD, who appeared unto him.*

> *Genesis 17:8-21*
> *And I will give unto thee, and to thy seed after thee, the land wherein thou art a stranger, all the land of Canaan, for an everlasting possession; and I will be their God. 9. And God said unto Abraham, Thou shalt keep my covenant therefore, thou, and thy seed after thee in their generations. 10. This is my covenant, which ye shall keep, between me and you and thy seed after thee; Every man child among you shall be circumcised. 11. And ye shall circumcise the flesh of your foreskin; and it shall be a token of the covenant betwixt me and you. 12. And he that is eight days old shall be circumcised among you, every man child in your generations, he that is born in the house, or bought with money of any stranger, which is not of thy seed. 13. He that is born in thy house, and he that is bought with thy money, must needs be circumcised: and my covenant shall be in your flesh for an everlasting covenant. 14. And the uncircumcised man child whose flesh of his foreskin is not circumcised, that soul shall be cut off from his people; he hath broken my covenant. 15. And God said unto Abraham, As for Sarai thy wife, thou shalt not call her name Sarai, but Sarah shall her name be. 16. And I will bless her, and give thee a son also of her: yea, I will bless her, and she shall be*

It is wise to take a cautious note of this position taken by the LORD concerning who the heir will be in Abraham's instance. Because both Ishmael and his servants were rejected as heirs fit for the everlasting Covenant of God's fulfillment. We need to pay attention to this because when people start to assert that Jesus Christ was "the Messiah" and considered him as "Humanity's heir" in some context. There is cautious need to remember he was not a pure human and was not made of pure human seed.

Such an attribute remains a crucial pre-requisite of Messianic prophecies. Just like Ishmael was not a son born by Abraham and Sarah, but one borne by Abraham and Hagar. I state the preceding by virtue of the wildly promoted status of being half-human given to Jesus Christ by Christian doctrine, by such he does not fulfill the criteria of being "a pure breed human", just like in Abraham's precedence. The LORD said "a pure human seed" not "a mixed breed or half-human" will bruise the head of the serpent after "the Fall of man" at the Garden of Eden.

Isaac for being a son of both Abraham and Sarah was the one fulfilling that criteria set by the LORD's promise, and by such he had "the Presence of the LORD" also referenced as "my Covenant by the LORD" resting with him.

This was despite the fact that he was the second son of Abraham not his firstborn son, a similar pattern plays out with Jesus Christ and "the expected Messiah". This Presence or Covenant resting with Isaac, would also automatically pass onto Esau because he was Isaac's firstborn son. It usually passes on to the firstborn son unless other issues come up that disqualify that firstborn offspring from inheriting it.

We should recall from Rebekah their mother's pregnancy accounts, that there was a struggle in her womb by both babies. I do presume that struggle must have been about who will come out as firstborn son, because to the one with such birth accomplishment amongst the two babies was a great prize awaiting, the prize was "the Presence of the LORD" or "the Birthright" or "Covenant of the LORD" promised their father's father.

Whenever I read through that part of the bible which narrates the Birth-right transaction, in my mind I visualise Jacob longing to play with his twin brother's "Birth-right Companion", which is "the Spirit of LORD" when they were toddlers. I seem to perceive Jacob crying and longing to be the host or friend of this companion which his brother had and he didn't have.

I can see Jacob feeling lonely "or naked" all because he did not have such a companion which his brother Esau had, and by the way, the real meaning of the nakedness "Adam and Eve" felt after experiencing "the Forbidden tree" was a separation from "the Spirit of God", and other consequential events spurred by its departure that all humans suffer even in our days.

*2 Corinthians 5:1-3*
*For we know that if our earthly house of this tabernacle were dissolved, we have a building of God, an house not made with hands, eternal in the heavens. 2. For in this we groan, earnestly desiring to be clothed upon with our house which is from heaven: 3. If so be that being clothed we shall not be found naked.*

Esau, the one with "the Birth-right" would like all young toddlers remain territorial with his Birthright inheritance and surely not let his twin brother come close to "the Birth-right Companion", even if he wasn't playing or interacting with it. We see toddlers do this all the time with their toys or anything they know belongs to them, such shouldn't be that hard to imagine happening back then.

With all that laid out, one could understand why Jacob would be given to scheming or doing anything that will avail him access to something he had longed for or been denied all his life.

Once it was within his power to grasp by prompting his brother to sell it off to him in exchange for a meal of porridge. That desire manifested by Jacob, in one perspective is a stronger love and desire for "the Birth-right Companion" which was "the Spirit or Presence of the LORD" than his brother Esau who owned it had for it. Stupid Esau you goofed I would say to him if we ever met.

*Genesis 25:31-34*
*And Jacob said, Sell me this day thy birthright. 32. And Esau said, Behold, I am at the point to die: and what profit shall this birthright do to me? 33. And Jacob said, Swear to me this day; and he sware unto him: and he sold his birthright unto Jacob. 34. Then Jacob gave Esau bread and pottage of lentiles; and he did eat and drink, and rose up, and went his way: thus Esau despised his birthright.*

Jacob's insight into Esau's Birth-right potentials may have been what pushed him to act cunningly and cadge his brother into selling it to him for a bowl of pottage. Something strange and shocking which we should observe, was that right after that transaction took place, even though both brothers did not swear any oath or sign any documents to such effect, neither did they have anyone bear them witness to the exchange, it came to be as they had bargained, strange indeed.

Well what we may fail to note was that "the Presence or the Spirit of LORD", also called "the Birth-right Companion" was with Esau during the negotiations, and the moment Esau rejected "the Spirit of the LORD" or his "Birth-right Companion" for a bowl of food, the Spirit or Presence moved away from him. And from that moment onwards, it began to dwell with Jacob, the benefactor of the ensuing transaction and that is why he got Isaac's blessings.

This departure is quite similar to what happened at the consuming of "the Forbidden tree" episode with Adam and Eve in perspective, and such was once again a demonstration of scant love for the LORD's Spirit by humans hoping to exchange His companionship and presence for something lesser in value.

I often hear people making statements to the effect that Esau was destined to serve Jacob, and his actions were somewhat pre-ordained. In my view, that is really not the case, and such comments are infantile. It is true that while in pregnancy their mother enquired of the LORD, and was told that the younger child will rule over the older of the brothers. However, what we must never fail to take cognisance of was that, Esau had a personal choice (or free-will) with which he chose to sell out on his Birth-right Companion — "the Spirit of the LORD" — for a bowl of pottage.

If he never exercised that choice or made such a decision, he would have been the stronger of both brothers. It was a similar choice of free-will that Adam and Eve used to fall away from the LORD's Presence by opting to experience "the Forbidden tree"; thereby throwing away a good state of existence for a miserable one we all exist in.

The LORD God in both cases retained the right stop these decisions, yet He didn't exercised it. It is clearly observable fact, that when it comes to choosing over Him or something else, He simply stands backs and waits for human choice same applied with Solomon, herein lies wisdom.

*Malachi 1:2-3*
*I have loved you, saith the LORD. Yet ye say, Wherein hast thou loved us? Was not Esau Jacob's brother? saith the LORD: yet I loved Jacob, 3. And I hated Esau, and laid his mountains and his heritage waste for the dragons of the wilderness.*

Though the verse above may seem a harsh one, voiced by the LORD's Prophet, but truly whom among us wouldn't hate a friend, partner or workmate, who sells you out, in order to satisfy their hunger, personal or self-interest? In my view, that could explain why certain verses in the bible voice the LORD's hatred for Esau. Such is justifiable and we shouldn't have a hard time understanding it, because just like us, "the Spirit of the LORD" has feelings too. We get our feelings from Him; our atavistic traits can only be traced back to the Creator. We have to be careful not to hurt His feelings in any way to avoid incurring His wrath similar to that upon Esau, and every time we chose to reject His will or desire, we are in some way walking similar paths to that which Esau walked too herein is wisdom.

In my view, I presume that what actually took place when Rebekah their mother consulted the LORD during her pregnancy was most likely a case of the LORD speaking to their mother in future perspective about the babies' lives. Because He knows all things, He can see past, present and future simultaneously and not interfere with any of the outcomes. So those words did not violate or foreclose upon the free-will of Esau to act contrary just like in the case of Adam and Eve His warnings did not interfere with their freewill tendencies, because if His words did they will not have consumed of "the Forbidden tree". The LORD often-times speaks to humans in present or future perspective devoid of his authority. However what I have noticed is that how things pan out in our lives or future seem to be always connected to the free-will or choices made by the person.

This is also how it applies to Prophet Eli, Saul, and Solomon, to name a few from the scriptures. We should note that both Jacob and King David demonstrated free-will attributes which endeared "the Spirit of the LORD" towards them.

Their off-spring are tagged "the seeds of Israel (or Jacob)", and "the seed of Judah (or David)", and to all those bearing such attributes of their fathers or fore-fathers as the case may be, was the potential of inheriting promises made by the LORD God to their fathers.

> *Jeremiah 33:14-16*
> *Behold, the days come, saith the LORD, that I will perform that good thing which I have promised unto the house of Israel and to the house of Judah. 15. In those days, and at that time, will I cause the Branch of righteousness to grow up unto David; and he shall execute judgment and righteousness in the land. 16. In those days shall Judah be saved, and Jerusalem shall dwell safely: and this is the name wherewith she shall be called, The LORD our righteousness.*

It is my opinion, that not all off-spring or sons birthed by King David or Jacob had the required attribute for being the sought seeds or sons. Because historical accounts reveal to us that they both had many children who did not love the LORD in the way their fathers did. Just as not all a man's offspring look like him. Perhaps that explains the great delight in the LORD's heart when he spotted "another David", or another one with "David-like attributes" as prophesied in Psalm 89 and explained earlier.

Referencing to that verse once again, it does appear to me, that all of the LORD's plans have been finished and settled, and all we simply await are manifestations of such by fitting or appropriate human candidates who will execute such for Him, herein lies wisdom.

A close similarity to that opinion expressed, would be that in our times, scientists also do likewise. By announcing to the world a significant scientific breakthrough or discovery once it is discovered, verified and authenticated. Like the cure for cancer, or some other disease. But we all know that it still takes the passage of time, before such break-throughs becomes available to everyone on the street, or the regular Joe Public.

Likewise, it appears to be with the LORD's prophecies, time gaps always exist between the moment a prophecy is declared, and its fulfillment realised. It should be known, that either King David's and Jacob's seeds (or traits or attributes bearer) have eternally unbreakable covenant with the LORD, we should covet such and strive to do better than they did to secure such covenants or better ones. Because I do not think the LORD has run out of such bountiful blessings for those who wow His heart, herein lies wisdom.

> *Jeremiah 33:23-26*
> *Moreover the word of the LORD came to Jeremiah, saying, 24. Considerest thou not what this people have spoken, saying, The two families which the LORD hath chosen, he hath even cast them off? thus they have despised my people, that they should be no more a nation before them. 25. Thus saith the LORD; If my covenant be not with day and night, and if I have not appointed the ordinances of heaven and earth; 26. Then will I cast away the seed of Jacob, and David my servant, so that I will not take any of his seed to be rulers over the seed of Abraham, Isaac, and Jacob: for I will cause their captivity to return, and have mercy on them.*

Individuals who bear these traits first spotted in Jacob and David have what can be best described as a right to "the Throne of the LORD", and they were promised to be taken care of in a way that will cause their offspring to be multiplied. This equates to planting more seeds of a crop or fruit that taste pleasantly by a farmer so he has many more of such at the next harvest time.

> *Jeremiah 33:19-22*
> *And the word of the LORD came unto Jeremiah, saying, 20. Thus saith the LORD; If ye can break my covenant of the day, and my covenant of the night, and that there should not be day and night in their season; 21. Then may also my covenant be broken with David my servant, that he should not have a son to reign upon his throne; and with the Levites the priests, my ministers. 22. As the host of heaven cannot be numbered, neither the sand of the sea measured: so will I multiply the seed of David my servant, and the Levites that minister unto me.*

> *Ezekiel 34:23-24*
> *And I will set up one shepherd over them, and he shall feed them, even my servant David; he shall feed them, and he shall be their shepherd. 24. And I the LORD will be their God, and my servant David a prince among them; I the LORD have spoken it.*

# A TITLE WITH MANY CHARACTERISTICS

### The Anointed is "The Branch"

There are several references to "a Branch". One springing up in the last days, and in some prophetic instances, the same springs from "the stem of Jesse", while in others "from David". These two phrases by equalisation mean essentially the same thing. It is like saying an off-spring of the Jones family will do such and such in one context or saying Tom's son (whose surname is also Jones) will be the one doing such and such in another context.

"The Branch" is supposed to be a human upon whom "the Spirit of the LORD" will rest, and this human is expected to execute judgment and righteousness on behalf of the LORD as desired by Him. All that can be accomplished simply because he will have "the spoken Word of the LORD" in his mouth, an attribute also called "the Rod of his mouth" and referenced as such in other perspectives. It is by this investiture that he is expected to judge righteously, wipe out the wicked, or evil seed planted amongst Humanity, by the serpent and restore peace to the Earth upon his appearance.

By such accomplishments, this individual called "the Branch", seems more like the one the Jews were expecting as their Messiah. Because he will simply have reformed the Earth or restored it back to its original status, the Garden of Eden status. This person is supposed to have roots in David or be "a son of David" and this in my view means he will possess "David-like attributes" as explained in the preceding chapter.

"The Branch's" association with King David, could be best explained by considering that David was the last human, and by that I mean pure human upon whom "the LORD's Spirit" rested, prior to all the prophecies about "the Branch" were uttered. At such a period, King David was the one holding the record for having the best "human and God relationship".

And such remained until his records were subsequently shattered by Jesus Christ, taking human and God relationship to a higher level. That to me explains reasons why King David was made the poster-child of all the LORD's prophecies back then.

> *Isaiah 11:1-4*
> *And there shall come forth a rod out of the stem of Jesse, and a Branch shall grow out of his roots: 2. And the spirit of the LORD shall rest upon him, the spirit of wisdom and understanding, the spirit of counsel and might, the spirit of knowledge and of the fear of the LORD; 3. And shall make him of quick understanding in the fear of the LORD: and he shall not judge after the sight of his eyes, neither reprove after the hearing of his ears: 4.But with righteousness shall he judge the poor, and reprove with equity for the meek of the earth: and he shall smite the earth with the rod of his mouth, and with the breath of his lips shall he slay the wicked.*

> *Jeremiah 33:15*
> *In those days, and at that time, will I cause the Branch of righteousness to grow up unto David; and he shall execute judgment and righteousness in the land.*

> *Zechariah 3:8-9*
> *Hear now, O Joshua the high priest, thou, and thy fellows that sit before thee: for they are men wondered at: for, behold, I will bring forth my servant the BRANCH. 9. For behold the stone that I have laid before Joshua; upon one stone shall be seven eyes: behold, I will engrave the graving thereof, saith the LORD of hosts, and I will remove the iniquity of that land in one day.*

> *Zechariah 6:12-13*
> *And speak unto him, saying, Thus speaketh the LORD of hosts, saying, Behold the man whose name is The BRANCH; and he shall grow up out of his place, and he shall build the temple of the LORD: 13. Even he shall build the temple of the LORD; and he shall bear the glory, and shall sit and rule upon his throne; and he shall be a priest upon his throne: and the counsel of peace shall be between them both.*

It is essential to note that "The Branch" appears to be a personality that is in duet with the LORD, as a priest for Him, as a King who bears the LORD's Glory and also as one who rules on His Throne as can be gleaned in Zech 6. That is in no way different to expressions of a Caliph to rule a Caliphate put forward in Islam.

We must also not forget that it is possible for a human to prophecy for the LORD God or on His behalf without "the Spirit of the LORD" actually resting upon or dwelling with the person prophesying, that is restated to prevent any assumptions that all those prophets after King David were anointed ones or played the roles of the Branch. Because such criteria does not necessarily need fulfillment before prophesying for the LORD can take place. "The Anointed one" referenced under the context of "The Branch" must fulfill all those roles simultaneously as specified; any individual who doesn't fulfill all is not fitting to be considered as "the Branch".

Perhaps one of the more crystal perspectives of "The Branch" being a human could be gleaned from references made in other prophecies to the subset called "the branch of my planting", a subset which refers to humans dwelling on the Earth for the LORD's purposes as clearly depicted below.

> *Isaiah 60:20-21*
> *Thy sun shall no more go down; neither shall thy moon withdraw itself: for the LORD shall be thine everlasting light, and the days of thy mourning shall be ended.  21.  Thy people also shall be all righteous: they shall inherit the land for ever, the branch of my planting, the work of my hands, that I may be glorified.*

In another perspective "the Branch" is depicted as "a fruit of the Earth". A description which chimes with the vineyard and seed sower perspectives of other prophecies and parables, where he who sows or plants, expects to reap fruits. During the days of "the Branch" the Earth is also expected to be purified to such a state where all those dwelling in it are holy or righteous. But prior to achieving such a status there will be a purging of it, by what is considered a judgment process or separation of the weeds from the chaff during the harvest, and those who survive such will be the ones who are considered holy or righteous by the LORD God.

Quite jaw-dropping is a prophecy stating that the Earth will experience a similar phenomenon of a cloud over-shadowing it, by day to prevent those dwelling there from being scorched by the heat of the sun, whilst the cloud also serves as a light to them at night, just as it was recorded to happen in the days of Moses when "the Presence of the LORD" was recorded to be on the Earth.

> *Isaiah 4:2-6*
> *In that day shall the branch of the LORD be beautiful and glorious, and the fruit of the earth shall be excellent and comely for them that are escaped of Israel.  3.  And it shall come to pass, that he that is left in Zion, and he that remaineth in Jerusalem, shall be called holy, even every one that is written among the living in Jerusalem:  4.  When the Lord shall have washed away the filth of the daughters of Zion, and shall have purged the blood of Jerusalem from the midst thereof by the spirit of judgment, and by the spirit of burning.  5.  And the LORD will create upon every dwelling place of mount Zion, and upon her assemblies, a cloud and smoke by day, and the shining of a flaming fire by night: for upon all the glory shall be a defence.  6. And there shall be a tabernacle for a shadow in the daytime from the heat, and for a place of refuge, and for a covert from storm and from rain.*

Crucially we must observe that "the Branch " is depicted in several instances as a human, never is this personality depicted to be "a Son of God" or one borne by virgin birth, or one who comes down from Heaven according to Christian doctrine which propose and presents Jesus Christ as the one referenced by such prophecies.



To sit on "The Throne of God" in my view as interpreted from scriptures means to be positioned so close to the LORD God, or side by side with Him, also referred to as being on His Right hand, or His Right arm in certain scriptural perspectives.

Some may wonder why there is a need for such juxtaposition. That can be understood by looking back into biblical history and observing that closeness to the LORD is a sine-qua-non for all great men of God to fulfill His Heart desires, and manifest His Glory. That perspective should dispel any curiosity about the need to be close to God, herein lies wisdom.

The closest to the LORD that Humanity will ever experience will be accomplished by having their representative, "a human" or "a son of man", brought closer into "the Presence of the LORD God" or "the Throne of God". And afterwards, this human representative will then acquire the ability to manifest "the Love, Glory, Power, Righteousness and Judgment of God" to fellow humans on Earth, just as Moses, Elijah, and Jesus Christ, did after securing such proximity to the LORD's Spirit, Throne or Presence in their days.

> *Revelation 12:3-5*
> *And there appeared another wonder in heaven; and behold a great red dragon, having seven heads and ten horns, and seven crowns upon his heads. 4. And his tail drew the third part of the stars of heaven, and did cast them to the earth: and the dragon stood before the woman which was ready to be delivered, for to devour her child as soon as it was born. 5. And she brought forth a man child, who was to rule all nations with a rod of iron: and her child was caught up unto God, and to his throne.*

Despite that King David saw "One human" being brought to sit upon "the Throne of God", we know that person was not him because he called the person in question my LORD. It couldn't be him because he was himself in that dream or vision. History also tells us that King David did not rule over the world or nations with "a rod of iron", as promised or expected of this person depicted by the verses of Psalm 2. Jesus Christ made a faint reference to that personality while trying to tell the Pharisees they did not clearly understand scriptures by virtue of their wrong interpretations.

In addition to that we must realise that an outstanding invitation exists. One issued by Jesus Christ in Revelations, stating that whoever overcomes will sit on "the Throne of God". Such a call made out to the person who will overcome (also called a Son of David because he will be like him at heart) is also a call to the person who will be raised up in the last days of our generation on the Earth, to fulfill all the prophecies about "a servant David" sitting on "the

Throne of God". Anyone of us who answers or takes up the open invitations thrust upon the world by Jesus Christ while he too was sat on "the Throne of God", is potentially the one to reap the specified rewards of such an invitation, herein is wisdom. Crucially we must observe that this invitation is an open one and was not addressed to King David of old, as some other prophecies may mislead us to interpret. It was for whoever answers the call, invalidating any suppositions it was meant specifically for King David or Jesus Christ as may be erroneously presumed. Surely this person will be the one "to keep the LORD's works unto the end", as is required by him. That phrase in my view suggests doing what the LORD had expected of Humanity long ago including some set of plans He has laid out for our world. Such include raising up a human fitting for the LORD's Purpose and meeting the LORD's standards in order that such a person will represent Humanity — a race created by the LORD — to fully bear His Image and manifest His Purposes and Glory.

> *Revelation 2:26-29*
> *And he that overcometh, and keepeth my works unto the end, to him will I give power over the nations:  27.  And he shall rule them with a rod of iron; as the vessels of a potter shall they be broken to shivers: even as I received of my Father.  28. And I will give him the morning star. 29. He that hath an ear, let him hear what the Spirit saith unto the churches.*

> *Psalms 2:7-9*
> *I will declare the decree: the LORD hath said unto me, Thou art my Son; this day have I begotten thee.  8. Ask of me, and I shall give thee the heathen for thine inheritance, and the uttermost parts of the earth for thy possession.  9. Thou shalt break them with a rod of iron; thou shalt dash them in pieces like a potter's vessel.*

> *Micah 6:9*
> *The LORD'S voice crieth unto the city, and the man of wisdom shall see thy name: hear ye the rod, and who hath appointed it.*

We need to pay attention to the fact that sitting upon "the Throne of God" and what ever it figuratively depicts must all be accomplished before judgment starts, and "a New Age" begins on Earth.

> *Isaiah 16:5*
> *And in mercy shall the throne be established: and he shall sit upon it in truth in the tabernacle of David, judging, and seeking judgment, and hasting righteousness.*

The Anointed is the one "who Judges on behalf of the LORD God"

The Anointed One will be the one brought to sit on "the Throne of God", and will then become saddled with the responsibility of interfacing between humans for God. Judging in righteousness is a task which involves making just wars against all evil or unrighteousness on the Earth, on the LORD's behalf. All this will be done by him, as "the LORD's Servant or Representative for Humans", a status acquired by God's Spirit resting on this person.

Judging on behalf of the LORD also involves" treading of the wine-press of His fury" and making those giving to acts displeasing the LORD in the midst of Humanity to pay for their sins and misdeeds. All of such will be killed, wiped-off or gotten rid of, unless they change their ways before "the Judgment Day of the LORD" also known as "the Day of the LORD" in other scriptural perspectives.

It is very sad to consider that even the LORD God can't make the world a better place without killing off the bad ones in Humanity's midst.

*Jeremiah 33:15-17*
*In those days, and at that time, will I cause the Branch of righteousness to grow up unto David; and he shall execute judgment and righteousness in the land. 16. In those days shall Judah be saved, and Jerusalem shall dwell safely: and this is the name wherewith she shall be called, The LORD our righteousness. 17. For thus saith the LORD; David shall never want a man to sit upon the throne of the house of Israel;*

*Revelation 19:11-16*
*And I saw heaven opened, and behold a white horse; and he that sat upon him was called Faithful and True, and in righteousness he doth judge and make war. 12. His eyes were as a flame of fire, and on his head were many crowns; and he had a name written, that no man knew, but he himself. 13. And he was clothed with a vesture dipped in blood: and his name is called The Word of God. 14. And the armies which were in heaven followed him upon white horses, clothed in fine linen, white and clean. 15. And out of his mouth goeth a sharp sword, that with it he should smite the nations: and he shall rule them with a rod of iron: and he treadeth the winepress of the fierceness and wrath of Almighty God. 16. And he hath on his vesture and on his thigh a name written, KING OF KINGS, AND LORD OF LORDS.*

*Isaiah 63:1-7*
*Who is this that cometh from Edom, with dyed garments from Bozrah? this that is glorious in his apparel, travelling in the greatness of his strength? I that speak in righteousness, mighty to save. 2. Wherefore art thou red in thine apparel, and thy garments like him that treadeth in the winefat? 3. I have trodden the winepress alone; and of the people there was none with me: for I will tread them in mine anger, and trample them in my fury; and their blood shall be sprinkled upon my garments, and I will stain all my raiment. 4. For the day of vengeance is in mine heart, and the year of my redeemed is come. 5. And I looked, and there was none to help; and I wondered that there was none to uphold: therefore mine own arm brought salvation unto me; and my fury, it upheld me. 6. And I will tread down the people in mine anger, and make them drunk in my fury, and I will bring down their strength to the earth. 7. I will mention the lovingkindnesses of the LORD, and the praises*

### The Anointed is the one like "the Son of Man"

The trait or attribute of "a Son of man" appears to convey several different meanings, depending on the context of its usage in scriptures. Sometimes it depicts a pure human, sometimes an Anointed human, at other instances a cross-breed human.

In my opinion, for any individual to merit such a nomenclature they must be of pure human kind first or bear such attributes, rather than being of any other race or life form existing in the Universe.

In several instances, Jesus Christ referred to himself as a Son of Man (and also as a Son of God). I can glean clearly that he was making reference to himself as "the Anointed One" or one bearing "the Spirit of God" when making such comments.

We should note that when Shadrach, Meshach and Abednego, were thrown into the fiery furnace for refusing to worship the Babylonian gods, a fourth being was spotted to be walking in the fire with them, looking like "a Son of God", but also appearing to look like a human by description. I think we can safely assume that this entity spotted in the furnace had traits or attributes tagged "a Son of God attributes", similar to those Jesus Christ also possessed, just as the entity equally possessed human traits which we label as "a Son of Man attribute".

The "Son of Man attributes" possessed by Jesus Christ availed him the "seed of Adam attributes", this attribute is a requirement needed in order to access "the Throne of God", which is the place where he obtained power to become the one who overcame "death and the grave".

This attribute is also the reason why humans are cross-breed with other entities in the Universe because of what privileges such attributes bequeaths.

Jesus Christ needed the "Son of Man attributes" to fulfill this requirement too, because without being "a Son of Man" or "Human in some form" he could not have had access to "the Throne of God".

This Throne is the exclusive preserve of Humanity, the only creatures created to bear "the Image of God". In addition to that we must realise that Jesus Christ could not have died as a human, unless he was a human first or "a son of man", also from both expressions exist perspectives about both ends of the problems plaguing Humanity, namely the "Original Sin" and its consequence "Death" suffered by Humanity. The fact that only "a son of man", or a human is permitted to access "the Throne of God", again validates the view that Humanity is a special and a purposeful creation of the LORD.

Though it appears we do not know what powers or privileges we have been given or what great inheritance is laid out for us in the Universe. If we consider why and how the enemies of God, or evil oppress the human race it should give us a bit of insight that can trail out thoughts in such directions.

Additionally, if we consider that the devil is always ready to trade wealth, fame and power for a human soul, which simply is something, that bears the human image, "Adam & Eve's" likeness or its attributes including abilities to manifest the supernatural or God, that should light up a curiosity about how special humans and what their souls are worth in this Universe to the discerning.

The "Son of Man" is also the one expected to come and rule over the world, bringing a new kingdom upon the Earth judging every man and manifesting "the Glory of God", his Father. These are essentially the same things we expect "the Branch" to do as stated in the prophecies.

> *Matthew 16:27-28*
> *For the Son of man shall come in the glory of his Father with his angels; and then he shall reward every man according to his works. 28. Verily I say unto you, There be some standing here, which shall not taste of death, till they see the Son of man coming in his kingdom.*

> *Matthew 25:31-33*
> *When the Son of man shall come in his glory, and all the holy angels with him, then shall he sit upon the throne of his glory: 32. And before him shall be gathered all nations: and he shall separate them one from another, as a shepherd divideth his sheep from the goats: 33. And he shall set the sheep on his right hand, but the goats on the left.*

Moses overcame or laid out the path for humans to access "the Throne of God" but he did not overcome "fleshy death", that which kills humans perpetually. In the case of Jesus Christ, with access secured as a human to "the Throne of God", a path laid out for him and everyone else by Moses, he pushed the bar further and secured the power to accomplish overcoming "fleshy death" as a human, this death is also referred to as "the wrath of God" in certain scriptural context, it is also called "the weight of the consequence of the first Sin of Humanity".

That was the sin of "another son of man or Human" namely Adam & Eve which by separating Humanity from the LORD made them begin to die like other mortals, the ability to overcome it is now bequeathed to us by Jesus Christ, and is that which  fits into the grace perspective perfectly.

> *John 1:17*
> *For the law was given by Moses, but grace and truth came by Jesus Christ.*

We need to recognize that if Jesus Christ did not have access to "the Throne of God", which is the source of all the LORD's Power and Glory, he would have been unable to overcome "fleshy death" or that considered as "the wrath of God", which was destined upon all of us from the moment the human race fell or when we were separated from God's Presence at Eden.

Jesus Christ fulfilled the prophecy of overcoming "death", by being "a son of man" or a human first and also "a Son of God" or a divinely incarnated being as a result of his paternity originating from "the Spirit of God", and not of pure human seed according to Christian doctrine. If that was truly the case this configuration makes him a "mixed-breed human", and not a "pure-breed human" or "a son of man" by one of its definition. And by such status he became automatically disqualified from being "the Anointed One" or "expected Messiah", also called "a Son of man" in certain context, just as Ishmael was disqualified as the one to inherit the LORD's everlasting Covenant with Abraham.

The prophecy about the one who will be brought up to the Ancient of Days, specifies that "a Son of man", which suggest a pure human and not "a half-Human-half-Divine being", will be brought up to the Ancient of Days.

It will be wrong to assume that the one being brought up to God will be or was Jesus Christ because he was not a pure-human going by the virgin birth assumptions, and by now he is even no longer a human like us in two contexts as expressed below.

The first context in which Jesus Christ is no longer human arises from the fact that he is now a superhuman, and now possesses a supernatural body or "heavenly body", one which precludes him from being a mere human. He now has a body that overcame "the forces of death and the grave"; one that doesn't die or wither away like ours, his body has evolved way past that level or limits of a mere human body, his body is like ours was meant to be at Eden.

Additionally from obvious facts gleaned from the visions of the book of Revelations, he is already sitting on "the Throne of God", because he is noted to have ascended up to Heaven when he departed the Earth.

*Mark 16:15-19*
*And he said unto them, Go ye into all the world, and preach the gospel to every creature.  16.  He that believeth and is baptized shall be saved; but he that believeth not shall be damned.  17. And these signs shall follow them that believe; In my name shall they cast out devils; they shall speak with new tongues;  18.They shall take up serpents; and if they drink any deadly thing, it shall not hurt them; they shall lay hands on the sick, and they shall recover. 19.  So then after the Lord had spoken unto them, he was received up into heaven, and sat on the right hand of God.*

*Acts 1:7-9*
*And he said unto them, It is not for you to know the times or the seasons, which the Father hath put in his own power.  8.  But ye shall receive power, after that the Holy Ghost is come upon you: and ye shall be witnesses unto me both in Jerusalem, and in all Judaea, and in Samaria, and unto the uttermost part of the earth.  9.  And when he had spoken these things, while they beheld, he was taken up; and a cloud received him out of their sight.*

With all those stated in the verses above, don't we need to wonder why Jesus Christ would need to be brought up to "the Throne of God" by angels, especially when he already had access to it, or has already ascended into Heaven? By that I mean since he is noted to be already seated at the right hand of God according to what those scriptures reveal.

We really have to ask ourselves why Jesus Christ needs to be brought or assisted into "the Presence of the LORD", by angels when he has acquired a body that can avail him access in to "the Presence of the LORD". By which I mean he has a body that he could use to ascend into Heaven, the location of "the Throne of God" without any angelic assistance.

In order to fulfill the prophecies of Daniel about "a son of man" being taken to the LORD, a prophecy that most will agree could be considered as one not yet fulfilled. Any human who will fulfills this prophecy must be given angelic assistance to access Heaven.

This is because humans are still fallen beings by nature and have no access or ability to ascend into Heaven where "the Throne of God" is situated. The best one among humans or "sons of men" will in my view be the one given this assistance by the angels in order to bring "the Kingdom of Heaven" back upon the Earth.

The second context of Jesus Christ not being a human anymore, is that even if he was  considered a human or "a son of man" initially at birth, at present he no longer qualifies to be one because, to all those who believe in God like he did, the LORD gives them the power to become "a Son of God".

Believing in this context, does not mean affirming a faith in God as we have been taught by faulty religious doctrine. Rather it is obtaining "a union with God" by virtue of seeking him with all of ones heart until that union is established, and when that union becomes established one is then considered as believing in God or "a disciple of Christ" or "a son of God".

> *John 1:12*
> *But as many as received him, to them gave he power to become the sons of God, even to them that believe on his name:*

There is also a clearer perspective of being "a Son of God", one emanating from being led by "the Spirit of God". We all know such can only happen if we submit our will or heart to such a Spirit and such a submission process is what is tagged believing by scriptures.

> *Romans 8:14-16*
> *For as many as are led by the Spirit of God, they are the sons of God. 15. For ye have not received the spirit of bondage again to fear; but ye have received the Spirit of adoption, whereby we cry, Abba, Father. 16. The Spirit itself beareth witness with our spirit, that we are the children of God:*

Such status we know Jesus Christ already accomplished, and by accomplishing it he was no longer a "son of man" but now one of the "sons of God" in the Universe. Any attempt to say he is the one these future prophecies concerning a "Son of man" are pointing to is simply an attempt to demote the status of Jesus Christ from "a Son of God" back into "a son of man" status. Which is purely a blasphemous act committed in human attempts to make their promoted doctrine fit with what religion has put forward as a kosher theory of the Messiah being Jesus Christ.

The bible is littered with references that indicate that the phrase "a son of man" means one of human form, never does it suggest otherwise that "a son of man" could be a mixed-breed human. Even in Genesis 6, those tagged as "daughters of men" who were cross-bred with "the sons of God", had their offspring referred to as "Giants or Nephelims". Not as "sons of men" or "seeds of Adam". I am citing this perspective to re-emphasise the view that the "son of man" who will be taken up to "the Throne of God", by the angels must be a pure human and is not Jesus Christ, because he was never even a pure human from the onset by the virgin birth doctrine accounts of his persona and by other evolutions in his life.

*Daniel 7:13-14*
*I saw in the night visions, and, behold, one like the Son of man came with the clouds of heaven, and came to the Ancient of days, and they brought him near before him. 14. And there was given him dominion, and glory, and a kingdom, that all people, nations, and languages, should serve him: his dominion is an everlasting dominion, which shall not pass away, and his kingdom that which shall not be destroyed.*

If the one to inherit a kingdom that will never be destroyed or pass away is a human, it also follows that this human will be the one who God told to sit with him on the Throne. This human is also the one who will rule with a rod of iron, this human is also the one who overcomes as expressed and expected by Jesus Christ while he was putting forward all those — to him who overcome — declarations in Revelations. This human is also the one who is "a seed of David", this human is the one who is "a seed of Jacob", and finally I do believe, it is this human getting caught up unto God, as iterated below in the book of Revelation's visions, which is most likely a future event, one which bears close similarities to that event illustrated by Daniel's prophetic vision. It is crucial to note that there would have been no point in relaying a vision to John in the book of Revelations, about events that had already been fulfilled in the past as a prophecy for something that will happen in the future; such will simply confuse us utterly and is really of no use to us. I say that to emphasise that it is highly unlikely that Jesus Christ was the subject or person to fulfill this prophecy; rather it is a pure breed human that will fulfill these prophecies.

Most importantly, I don't see the LORD changing his position to suit our religious preferences, or flawed interpretation of prophecies simply because we have become dogmatic about them and our expectations of what God's plans are. That may explain why He laughs when humans come together to gang-up against his chosen anointed one as depicted in Psalm 2.

> *Revelation 12:3-5*
> *And there appeared another wonder in heaven; and behold a great red dragon, having seven heads and ten horns, and seven crowns upon his heads. 4. And his tail drew the third part of the stars of heaven, and did cast them to the earth: and the dragon stood before the woman which was ready to be delivered, for to devour her child as soon as it was born. 5. And she brought forth a man child, who was to rule all nations with a rod of iron: and her child was caught up unto God, and to his throne.*

Again various biblical scholars suggest that the one being born in the prophecy above was Jesus Christ. Crucially, we need to ask why would there be a prophecy for his birth, when the event prophesied already occurred in the past ages. Those visions recorded in the book of Revelations signify things that will happen, not things that have already happened, there has to be a distinction between both.

> *Revelation 1:1-2*
> *The Revelation of Jesus Christ, which God gave unto him, to shew unto his servants things which must shortly come to pass; and he sent and signified it by his angel unto his servant John: 2. Who bare record of the word of God, and of the testimony of Jesus Christ, and of all things that he saw.*

There are also some scholars, who interpret the woman giving birth as the nation of Israel. Well if the woman was Israel; shouldn't we wonder what happened to the other parts of the prophecy? How can those be explained away? We surely didn't miss the other parts of the prophecy, because it is not chronicled in any historical accounts of the nation of Israel or events during or after the birth of Jesus Christ.

There was no flood, and equally no dragon was seen casting down stars out of heaven, so it appears the prophecy was not matching to his birth or appearance. It is for another expected birth or appearance of one, also called "a Son of man" or "the Anointed One".

We tend to find ourselves entangled in such quandary about fulfillments or expectations, if we choose to interpret prophecies as both literal and figuratively simultaneously, a prophecy is not a parable and will never be.

My opinion about this prophecy is that the one being born here and his birth, may have been a spiritual event, and I hold that view because it played out in "the Heavens" or that considered as the spiritual realm first as detailed, before the earthly drama or manifestation followed. But if my opinion on that is inaccurate, then we should all be on the lookout for a male child who is to be born before a major flood after a battle in the heavens with a serpent or dragon, because only such a person will fulfill the requirements of being caught up unto God and his Throne as predicted in that prophecy's context.

In my view the woman in that prophecy represents "a race of Humanity" and that description dovetails with the "seed of woman" perspective in Geneses 3 which connotes same meaning. However, the actual identities of these people are revealed in the last verse of the chapter.

> *Revelation 12:17*
> *And the dragon was wroth with the woman, and went to make war with the remnant of her seed, which keep the commandments of God, and have the testimony of Jesus Christ.*

The "remnant seeds of the woman" can be collectively described as "those who have a testimony of Jesus Christ". We should realise that anyone who has "the testimony of Jesus Christ" must be one of those walking the Earth in days after this testimony (or testament) was executed or given to Earth dwellers.

I know that view may swiftly lead people into thinking that it is the Church been referenced here, well not quite so. If we consider that the whole human race was depicted as "the woman", from which one was born and brought up to God's Throne, then we can see a reason to accept my view that the devil is busy waging war against all other humans dwelling on Earth. It should be noted that this war begins right after he failed at stopping the man child's birth, because he knows his time is short.

This war perhaps fits perfectly with the troubling times that will precede the return of "the Spirit of the LORD", tagged as the tribulation period of some doctrines. This man child or "seed of the woman" is the one who bruises the head of the serpent (or devil) as foretold by the LORD God after "the Fall of man", this is wisdom.

That phrase "having the testimony of Jesus Christ", surely does not mean those who believe in Christianity and its flawed doctrines. Rather in my view it means all those who believe in the LORD God and has accepted into their heart or become one with "the Spirit of God", people who can now use such union to their benefit. In my view, I will de-select those who already truly believe in God from the whole of subset Humanity, for those left in this subset are those being persecuted and those who are referenced in that prophecy. Those who truly believe will be empowered to overcome the dragon and his co-demons, because he is no threat to such people, and he won't mess around with them.

The devil can only trouble those who are not truly born again, or those who do not truly believe, who are also those who do not have a union with "the Spirit of the LORD", also known as partaking in the benefits of the executed "testimony of Jesus Christ", a privilege which those who overcome can use against the devil.

Somehow in light of that persecution expected in those times, we have to wonder if it is the LORD God judging the Earth, or the devil tormenting it. Sadly my opinion on that question is that, both are occurring contemporaneously, because right after the LORD removes his hedge of protection, or the seal gets broken, it is trouble from both sides, because the final battle begins between good and evil forces over the entire Human race.

My opinion is that without "the testimony of Jesus Christ", the man child born and caught up to God's Throne would not have accomplished that feat either. His accomplishment was purely one assisted by that testimony or testament execute by Jesus Christ prior to his birth, just as Jesus Christ leveraged on the victories of Moses — executed before his own birth — to aid Humanity with overcoming "the forces of death" separating us from God's Throne.

That explains why the serpent is eager to wage war with his brethrens too, it is so that they get distracted and can't do what this man child has done too.

I believe it was this "man-child" or "son of man" who was assisted by the angels in casting the devil out of the Heavens. If we observe clearly what scriptures reveal, we will notice that the angels did not fight the battle with the devil until this man child was born. To me that sort of suggests that "this man child" is the key to winning the battle for them, and such a view may make more sense if we consider that his birth was what the devil did not want to happen and tried to prevent. In addition to that the man child is the one who leads the Heavenly host in battle.

> *Revelation 19:14-15*
> *And the armies which were in heaven followed him upon white horses, clothed in fine linen, white and clean. 15. And out of his mouth goeth a sharp sword, that with it he should smite the nations: and he shall rule them with a rod of iron: and he treadeth the winepress of the fierceness and wrath of Almighty God.*

The verses below tells us they overcame by "the blood of the Lamb", which again is symbolic of "the testimony of Jesus Christ" executed for Humanity by shedding of his blood on the cross "as a Lamb" to overcome "the forces of death and the grave" which plagued the human flesh.

Without that testimony (or testament) executed prior to the birth of this "one man child" who activates its potential, the devil will still be sitting in the Heavens (the earthly heaven though) and ruling over Humanity.

For no one among the humans can contend against his authority without taking out the devil's lieutenants first who fight with him first and afterwards the devil himself. We must note that the heavens in this context refers to the spiritual realm or dimension, it is not the place where "the Spirit of the LORD" dwells or is domiciled, there are various interpretations to the word heaven in scriptures and we all would agree that both the LORD and the devil are not in the same location though scriptures references both as heaven.

> *Revelation 12:9-11*
> *And the great dragon was cast out, that old serpent, called the Devil, and Satan, which deceiveth the whole world: he was cast out into the earth, and his angels were cast out with him. 10. And I heard a loud voice saying in heaven, Now is come salvation, and strength, and the kingdom of our God, and the power of his Christ: for the accuser of our brethren is cast down, which accused them before our God day and night. 11. And they overcame*

On the other hand, the prevalent preaching we get is that nothing is required of Humanity, and that we should all just seat back and keep waiting for Jesus Christ to return, because he has done everything for us. Such is a misinterpretation of the "it is finished" comment made by him on the cross, used by many to justify such suggestions. What was finished was the role he came to play on Earth, not the whole plan of the LORD God for Humanity.

Strangely, if we come to think of it, Islam has been stating by its teaching all along that Jesus Christ was a Prophet of God sent on a mission, that fact rings true in this perspective, though I know most Christians would become incandescent hearing such being put forward, simply because it upsets their doctrinal views.

The view that the woman giving birth depicts the collective set of earth dwellers is also clearly validated, when we consider that the other woman riding the beast was also depicting other seeds of the devil ruling the earth, just before the LORD's Spirit returns and executes judgment upon such people. From what we all know, only humans rule on the earth, though they may be ruling on behalf of evil entities as puppets just like Pharaoh was ruling on behalf of another god (or entity) over Egypt in those days.

> *Revelation 17:15-18*
> *And he saith unto me, The waters which thou sawest, where the whore sitteth, are peoples, and multitudes, and nations, and tongues. 16. And the ten horns which thou sawest upon the beast, these shall hate the whore, and shall make her desolate and naked, and shall eat her flesh, and burn her with fire. 17. For God hath put in their hearts to fulfil his will, and to agree, and give their kingdom unto the beast, until the words of God shall be fulfilled. 18. And the woman which thou sawest is that great city, which reigneth over the kings of the earth.*

For serious consideration, is the view that if Jesus Christ who is not a pure-human as presented and put forward by Christian doctrine, can be classified as "a son of man"; or "a seed of Adam"; or "the man child"; and for such reasons he is considered "the Messiah" or "the Anointed One", then any one of the off-spring of the "Giants or Nephelims" who were also not pure humans, could equally claim a likewise status for the same such reasons, that is a recipe for doctrinal kiosk.

The Messiah or "the Anointed One's" identity seems to have been misrepresented in certain biblical context by a similar trend that occurs in modern day governance, where the policy of a government is given an appellation made up of the name of the one in government who decreed it into law or executed it. The Iraqi war is also called "the Bush war on Iraq", even though it was a war waged on the Iraq government of Saddam Hussein, by the American government, not by any of the Bush family individually.

Likewise, "the Healthcare bill" is usually referred to as "Obama care", simply because it came into legislative effect under the presidency of Barrack Obama. It is not Obama's legislation but one made and sanctioned by the whole American democratic government.

Concerning prophecies of "the Anointed One", there are lots of references about David sitting on the Throne every time "the Throne of God" is mentioned, and this is because he sat on "the Throne of God" at its first establishment at the city of Jerusalem. That is why references such as "the Throne of David" show up in other prophecies or expectations. Jesus Christ is expected to return to rule over the world sitting on "the Throne of God" too by Christian doctrinal expectations.

The fact remains, that the one ruling over the world or nations is the same one who gets to sit on "the Throne situated at Jerusalem", also called "the Throne of David" in some context. That means we really have to ask if it is David according to prophecy. Or is it going to be Jesus Christ sitting on it as expected by the Christians?

The fact is there is only going to be one Throne ruling over the world, upon which someone bearing "son of man attributes" is expected to sit. This throne is a united one made of the two parts, the heavenly and earthly parts. In light of that whoever  is seating on it must posses "David-like attributes" for the Earthly portion and also posses "Jesus-like attributes" for the Heavenly portion to fulfill the laid out criteria for seating on it. Hence another attribute is desired for occupying it called the "son of God attribute" similar to that manifested by Jesus Christ. And in addition to those requirements, any individual who the cap will fit must fulfill other criteria laid out for "the Anointed One".

That in my view is why Jesus Christ was noted to talk about one coming who will be "a Son of man", coming in his glory. If it was himself, I think he will have stated when I return in my Glory. That is a nuance that cannot and should not be overlooked.

Again we have to observe that his statement, speaks of one returning who is leading the holy angels, a parallel depiction bearing resemblance with that of the one on the white horse in the book of Revelations who was leading the armies of Heaven. It shouldn't be too hard for us to agree that "the holy angels" and "armies of Heaven" depict essentially the same thing.

> *Matthew 25:31-33*
> *When the Son of man shall come in his glory, and all the holy angels with him, then shall he sit upon the throne of his glory: 32. And before him shall be gathered all nations: and he shall separate them one from another, as a shepherd divideth his sheep from the goats: 33. And he shall set the sheep on his right hand, but the goats on the left.*

Again it is crucial to note that when Jesus Christ responded to the question put to him by the chief priest he stated in his response, you will see the "Son of man" sitting at "the right hand of power". That phrase depicts "the Right hand of God" or suggests "one being empowered by the LORD God". Again, we must note he did not say you will see me coming in my glory, but rather made reference to a "Son of man", such nuances should not be overlooked even though a lot of mis-translations of scriptural text may have effaced their significance.

*Mark 14:60-63*
*And the high priest stood up in the midst, and asked Jesus, saying, Answerest thou nothing? what is it which these witness against thee? 61. But he held his peace, and answered nothing. Again the high priest asked him, and said unto him, Art thou the Christ, the Son of the Blessed? 62. And Jesus said, I am: and ye shall see the Son of man sitting on the right hand of power, and coming in the clouds of heaven. 63. Then the high priest rent his clothes, and saith, What need we any further witnesses?*

We also need to pay attention to the prophecy stated in Psalm 80, about the one who is to rule and conquer, who by description is a man strengthened by the LORD for this purpose, to understand what Jesus Christ meant by his comments.

*Psalms 80:17*
*Let thy hand be upon the man of thy right hand, upon the son of man whom thou madest strong for thyself.*

Though Jesus Christ referenced himself as "a Son of man", one with power and authority in certain context and narratives, a lot of facts show us that he was simply referring to himself as "a Son of man" just as referred to himself as "a Messiah" and also as "the Christ" in other context, because all such titles are fitting for anyone bearing "the Spirit of the LORD" or was anointed by God.

Most especially is that we must note that it could be, that while all those utterances were being made, that it was "the Spirit of God" speaking and not Jesus Christ, such a realisation will open up new perspectives for interpreting such comments.

The clearest distinction between the two "Son of man" identities, "Jesus Christ" and "the Expected One", can be spotted when Jesus Christ was asked by the Jews to explain why he should die or go away. They put this question to him because "the Christ or Messiah" who they were expecting also known as "a Son of man" was supposed to abide or reign forever, meaning eternally according to prophecies about him and his kingdom upon the Earth.

Such nuances must never be overlooked because they reveal hidden truths, and we must never forget that Jesus Christ did not assert to these people that I am "the Son of man" you are expecting, though flawed doctrines now suggest and promote this.

*John 12:31-35*
*Now is the judgment of this world: now shall the prince of this world be cast out. 32. And I, if I be lifted up from the earth, will draw all men unto me.*

*33. This he said, signifying what death he should die. 34. The people
answered him, We have heard out of the law that Christ abideth for ever: and
how sayest thou, The Son of man must be lifted up? who is this Son of man?
35. Then Jesus said unto them, Yet a little while is the light with you. Walk
while ye have the light, lest darkness come upon you: for he that walketh in
darkness knoweth not whither he goeth.*

## The Anointed One is the one with "the Word of God" in his mouth

"The Spirit of God" is the LORD God or is the LORD's Authority to speak for
Him and it happens as spoken. That was what existed at the beginning, and it
was what brought about everything we perceive as Creation by virtue of the
famously spoken "Let there be" commands recorded in the book of Genesis.

"The Spirit of God" is also identified or referenced as "the Word of God" in
several passages in the bible, though due to wrong translation it is
misinterpreted religiously as meaning an audible message from God.

"The Word of God" is also called "the Word of the LORD" in some parts of
the bible, and is simply another name or means to represent "the Spirit of
God". By equalisation, its presence with any individual indicates that "the
Presence of God" is with that person. And whoever God's Presence is with,
bears the LORD God's Authority and Power, and such a person is "an
Anointed Servant of God" because the anointing must surely precede "the
Presence of God" with any person.

All anointing from God doesn't come in a one-size-fit-all attribute. The level
of dedication of the anointed one to the LORD, determines the level of
manifesting their anointing as miracles, signs or wonders, the anointing that
will be upon "the expected Anointed One", is greater than has ever been seen
or experienced in the history of the Earth or Humanity.

Because it bears the authority to vanquish the devil and his acolytes
together, such is a feat no other servant of the LORD has ever accomplished.

Jesus Christ overcame death and not the devil (or serpent), which is why
even after his resurrection Humanity was still subject or slaves to evil
temptations all coming from the devil's kingdom existing on Earth.

The "Word of the LORD" can be gleaned as an entity or authority present
with or known to be with the characters as expressed in the verses below,
without it these characters — or men of God — will not bear the LORD's
Authority or Power to act on his behalf.

*1 Samuel 3:7-9*
*Now Samuel did not yet know the LORD, neither was the word of the LORD
yet revealed unto him. 8. And the LORD called Samuel again the third
time. And he arose and went to Eli, and said, Here am I; for thou didst call
me. And Eli perceived that the LORD had called the child. 9. Therefore Eli
said unto Samuel, Go, lie down: and it shall be, if he call thee, that thou shalt
say, Speak, LORD; for thy servant heareth. So Samuel went and lay down in
his place.*

*1 Kings 17:22-24*
*And the LORD heard the voice of Elijah; and the soul of the child came into him again, and he revived. 23. And Elijah took the child, and brought him down out of the chamber into the house, and delivered him unto his mother: and Elijah said, See, thy son liveth. 24. And the woman said to Elijah, Now by this I know that thou art a man of God, and that the word of the LORD in thy mouth is truth.*

*2 Kings 3:10-12*
*And the king of Israel said, Alas! that the LORD hath called these three kings together, to deliver them into the hand of Moab! 11. But Jehoshaphat said, Is there not here a prophet of the LORD, that we may enquire of the LORD by him? And one of the king of Israel's servants answered and said, Here is Elisha the son of Shaphat, which poured water on the hands of Elijah. 12. And Jehoshaphat said, The word of the LORD is with him. So the king of Israel and Jehoshaphat and the king of Edom went down to him.*

*Jeremiah 1:9-10*
*Then the LORD put forth his hand, and touched my mouth. And the LORD said unto me, Behold, I have put my words in thy mouth. 10. See, I have this day set thee over the nations and over the kingdoms, to root out, and to pull down, and to destroy, and to throw down, to build, and to plant.*

All those who are "Anointed by God" are also "Prophets of God", but not all those who are "Prophets of God" are "Anointed by God". To be a prophet for God that which needs to happen is for "the Spirit of God", also called "the Word of the LORD", to come upon an individual and use them for the purpose of speaking on behalf of God.

The classic instance of a donkey that spoke to Balaam is a good example for iterating the ability of "the Spirit of God" coming upon a person or entity, in order to use them to accomplish an utterance or speech objective for the LORD. In the case of the donkey, it also became a prophet by that definition because it was caused to speak by God for His purpose at that moment, perhaps a better description for those individuals who fall under such category will be "accidental prophets".

*Numbers 22:24-31*
*But the angel of the LORD stood in a path of the vineyards, a wall being on this side, and a wall on that side. 25. And when the ass saw the angel of the LORD, she thrust herself unto the wall, and crushed Balaam's foot against the wall: and he smote her again. 26. And the angel of the LORD went further, and stood in a narrow place, where was no way to turn either to the right hand or to the left. 27. And when the ass saw the angel of the LORD, she fell down under Balaam: and Balaam's anger was kindled, and he smote the ass with a staff. 28. And the LORD opened the mouth of the ass, and she said unto Balaam, What have I done unto thee, that thou hast smitten me*

*these three times? 29. And Balaam said unto the ass, Because thou hast mocked me: I would there were a sword in mine hand, for now would I kill thee. 30. And the ass said unto Balaam, Am not I thine ass, upon which thou hast ridden ever since I was thine unto this day? was I ever wont to do so unto thee? And he said, Nay. 31. Then the LORD opened the eyes of Balaam, and he saw the angel of the LORD standing in the way, and his sword drawn in his hand: and he bowed down his head, and fell flat on his face.*

All those who judged Israel on their way towards the Promised Land, were mostly "Acting-Prophets", acting in the sense that they all spoke and acted on the LORD's behalf in certain instances, but it appears none was fully-anointed by the LORD. It must be noted that judging Israel is almost the same things as ruling or being a king over Israel.

Nevertheless the Judges too accomplished great victories by virtue of "the Word of God", also known as "the Spirit of the LORD" momentarily coming upon them to strengthen them. And also by virtue of "the Word of the LORD" coming forth from their mouth in such instances, a phrase used to depict when people speak under the influence of "the Spirit of God". In such cases, whenever they spoke under the influence of "the Spirit of the LORD", it was as if the LORD God Himself was speaking.

Surely all those things they say under such an influence always came to pass, and at every such instance, they became "temporary-Anointed" or "accidental-Prophets". Sometimes they could also at best be described as "Mighty men" because they did things which no mere mortal could do by action or accomplish with mere words.

## Gideon

*Judges 6:34*
*But the Spirit of the LORD came upon Gideon, and he blew a trumpet; and Abiezer was gathered after him.*

## Samson

*Judges 14:5-6*
*Then went Samson down, and his father and his mother, to Timnath, and came to the vineyards of Timnath: and, behold, a young lion roared against him. 6. And the Spirit of the LORD came mightily upon him, and he rent him as he would have rent a kid, and he had nothing in his hand: but he told not his father or his mother what he had done.*

## Saul

*1 Samuel 11:6*
*And the Spirit of God came upon Saul when he heard those tidings, and his anger was kindled greatly.*

If "the Spirit of God", or "the Word of the LORD", also described as "the Spirit of the LORD", comes upon an individual and rests with such a person, then such a person becomes during such periods "an Anointed one of the LORD".

There are several instances recorded in scriptures when "the Spirit of the LORD", momentarily takes control of a person on which it did not rest or have any association with previously. This happens because there is a need for that person to act for, or execute a task for God at such a moment. Any available person is selected to execute such tasks when such a need arises. Just like a police officer in pursuit of a bandit could commandeer any car or bicycle closest to him to accomplish his pursuit objective. Individuals who are momentarily used by the LORD are best described as "accidental-prophets or temporary-anointed", the donkey and the old prophet in Israel fit into this subset perfectly.

In the instance of the old prophet, a man of God was sent to proclaim under the influence of "the Word of the LORD" against the altar in Bethel. Even though this man was sent on a mission, one which he executed as "the Word of the LORD" or "the Spirit of the LORD" desired of him, he lost his life on the mission, because he failed to obey the instruction given to him by the LORD's Spirit attached to or upon him. The instruction was that he should return to his home base immediately after delivering the prophetic utterance which he didn't. Despite his disobedience everything this man said came to pass as he had pronounced because it was the LORD's Spirit speaking and not the man when the utterances were made.

Reading through the passage you will notice that the fact that he spoke "in the Word of the LORD" was being emphasised. That simply means he was speaking as man for the LORD God under the influence of "the Spirit of God" which is also called "the Word of the LORD".

*1 Kings 13:1-5*
*And, behold, there came a man of God out of Judah by the word of the LORD unto Bethel: and Jeroboam stood by the altar to burn incense. 2. And he cried against the altar in the word of the LORD, and said, O altar, altar, thus saith the LORD; Behold, a child shall be born unto the house of David, Josiah by name; and upon thee shall he offer the priests of the high places that burn incense upon thee, and men's bones shall be burnt upon thee. 3. And he gave a sign the same day, saying, This is the sign which the LORD hath spoken; Behold, the altar shall be rent, and the ashes that are upon it shall be poured out. 4. And it came to pass, when king Jeroboam heard the saying of the man of God, which had cried against the altar in Bethel, that he put forth his hand from the altar, saying, Lay hold on him. And his hand, which he put forth against him, dried up, so that he could not pull it in again to him.*
*5.The altar also was rent, and the ashes poured out from the altar, according to the sign which the man of God had given by the word of the LORD.*

This prophet after prophesying against the altar was deceived by another old prophet to stop over in Bethel for a meal, and by falling for the deceiver's con-trick he lost his life by a prophetic utterance that came forth from the mouth of the one who deceived him. This man — the deceiver — instantly became an "accidental or temporary Prophet", who spoke or prophesied the judgment from "the Spirit of God's mouth", unto the one who disobeyed the explicit instructions given to him by the LORD's Spirit earlier. Because the deceiver was the best tool available to accomplish the LORD's mission, he was used for the purpose by the LORD even though he was a contributor to the ugly situation. That is quite strange, but again such symbolizes that if we allow the devil or evil entities to deceive us, we will still pay the price. Just like when humans fell, they paid the price for their gullibility to the serpent. We must note that our free-will is not given to disobey the LORD God.

> *1 Kings 13:18-26*
> *He said unto him, I am a prophet also as thou art; and an angel spake unto me by the word of the LORD, saying, Bring him back with thee into thine house, that he may eat bread and drink water. But he lied unto him. 19. So he went back with him, and did eat bread in his house, and drank water. 20. And it came to pass, as they sat at the table, that the word of the LORD came unto the prophet that brought him back: 21. And he cried unto the man of God that came from Judah, saying, Thus saith the LORD, Forasmuch as thou hast disobeyed the mouth of the LORD, and hast not kept the commandment which the LORD thy God commanded thee, 22. But camest back, and hast eaten bread and drunk water in the place, of the which the LORD did say to thee, Eat no bread, and drink no water; thy carcase shall not come unto the sepulchre of thy fathers. 23. And it came to pass, after he had eaten bread, and after he had drunk, that he saddled for him the ass, to wit, for the prophet whom he had brought back. 24. And when he was gone, a lion met him by the way, and slew him: and his carcase was cast in the way, and the ass stood by it, the lion also stood by the carcase. 25. And, behold, men passed by, and saw the carcase cast in the way, and the lion standing by the carcase: and they came and told it in the city where the old prophet dwelt. 26. And when the prophet that brought him back from the way heard thereof, he said, It is the man of God, who was disobedient unto the word of the LORD: therefore the LORD hath delivered him unto the lion, which hath torn him, and slain him, according to the word of the LORD, which he spake unto him.*

Another instance that verifies speaking as the LORD occurs when a man speaking in "the Word of the LORD" to his neighbour requested to be smitten by the neighbour. When his neighbour refused to grant his request, he told the neighbour that because you disobeyed "the Voice of the LORD" you will be killed by a Lion. Strangely, because it was the LORD's Spirit speaking to him, what was said to this neighbour came to pass immediately the man left him, he got killed by a Lion. It happened so because it was "the Spirit of the LORD" talking to the neighbour through the man's mouth when he requested to be smote, not the person who owned the body making the request to be smitten. I find this instance both interesting and intriguing, often times I wonder if the man had been smitten by his neighbour as requested of him, what would happen to the wound sustained from the smiting? Would it still be visible after "the Spirit of the LORD" lifted off the one smote? How will he explain the wound?

I know healing a wound sustained from such smiting is simply a piece of cake to the LORD, so my assumption is that the man would have fully recovered or been instantly healed from the smiting once the purpose for which the wound was needed became exhausted.

The one I pity the most would have been the person who smote his neighbour as  requested of him, because that individual will be shocked the next time he saw the one he smote, who should naturally bear a wound from the smiting not having  any wounds or scars, because it had been healed miraculously by the LORD.

I am quite certain he will be somewhat confused and he would swear to everyone that cared to listen to his story that he stabbed or smote this man today, but the one he smote sustained a wound initially which has now disappeared. Quite hard to believe by anyone not present when those events occurred, such are the ways of the LORD, beyond human comprehension at times

> *1 Kings 20:35-37*
> *And a certain man of the sons of the prophets said unto his neighbour in the word of the LORD, Smite me, I pray thee. And the man refused to smite him. 36.  Then said he unto him, Because thou hast not obeyed the voice of the LORD, behold, as soon as thou art departed from me, a lion shall slay thee. And as soon as he was departed from him, a lion found him, and slew him. 37.  Then he found another man, and said, Smite me, I pray thee. And the man smote him, so that in smiting he wounded him.*

Anyone who speaks under the influence of "the Spirit of God" is best considered as having the "the Word of God" or "Word of the LORD" in his mouth, at such a moment. Speaking under the influence of "the Spirit of God" is accomplished by either becoming a host to "the Spirit of the LORD" or by the body being taken over by "the Spirit of God", momentarily to execute a desired task. Every thing said by such people always comes to pass as uttered, though I have discerned a pattern that for some individuals, that the manifestations of their words or pronouncements occur faster than it does in others.

This in my view could be relative to how tight the connection between "God and Man" was made when "the Spirit of God" came upon them, which may also be a function of the state of their hearts in holiness context.

The fact remains that such people just like God, cannot lie whenever they are under "the Spirit of the LORD's" influence; whatever they say comes to be as spoken by them. All prophecies of David littered in the Psalms are all coming to pass one after the other and surely the one about "the Anointed One" too, will come to pass.

This is because he spoke those words as a prophet, though it appears that in King David's case, all those words and their manifestation time lines are staggered intentionally to suit the LORD's Plans and Purposes.

Such a view should hint to anyone who is wise that we are somewhat all sleep-walking into an already decided future for Humanity, though our only consolation is that we can still deploy our freewill to work with the One who decides these things and has planned everything ahead, as smart ones.

*2 Samuel 23:1-2*
*Now these be the last words of David. David the son of Jesse said, and the man who was raised up on high, the anointed of the God of Jacob, and the sweet psalmist of Israel, said,  2.  The Spirit of the LORD spake by me, and his word was in my tongue.*

*1 Samuel 3:19-21*
*And Samuel grew, and the LORD was with him, and did let none of his words fall to the ground.  20.  And all Israel from Dan even to Beersheba knew that Samuel was established to be a prophet of the LORD.  21.  And the LORD appeared again in Shiloh: for the LORD revealed himself to Samuel in Shiloh by the word of the LORD.*

## The "Anointed One" is he who is to be called "Faithful and True"

This "Anointed One" is also expected to possess this attribute of "the Spirit of the LORD". Speaking through him, meaning everything he says will come to pass, this is because "the Word of God" will be the tool with which he accomplishes all the mission the LORD wants accomplished on the Earth.

*Isaiah 30:30-31*
*And the LORD shall cause his glorious voice to be heard, and shall shew the lighting down of his arm, with the indignation of his anger, and with the flame of a devouring fire, with scattering, and tempest, and hailstones.  31. For through the voice of the LORD shall the Assyrian be beaten down, which smote with a rod.*

This tool of speech or utterance "the Voice of the LORD" is also known or called "the Sharp sword"; or "the Rod of his mouth"; or "a Rod of iron"; or "the Spoken word".

"The Spoken Word" can be described as any sentence or phrase uttered by "the Spirit of the LORD", through the mouth of a human, and in most case such humans are "Prophets of God" or "His Anointed Servants" or "temporary, acting or accidental speech-vessels" as the case may apply.

"The Spoken Word" could be a good word to bless, heal or comfort. It could be words to judge or destroy the evil ones also. The Spoken word is described as such to signify and highlight that not all the person's words are utterances of "the Spirit of the LORD".

A typical symbolism of the spoken word occurs in the New Testament, where in some versions of the bibles, the utterances of Jesus Christ are highlighted in red ink. That is actually not the real representation of it, because it wasn't everything that came out of the mouth of Jesus Christ, that was an utterance of "the Spirit of God"; or a speech of "a Son of God"; or  that of "a Prophet of God"; because he played all those roles simultaneously, some of his utterances were simply those of "the son of man" or "the human part" of his personality as he interacted with other humans on Earth.

*Hosea 6:5*
*Therefore have I hewed them by the prophets; I have slain them by the words of my mouth: and thy judgments are as the light that goeth forth.*

*Hosea 12:9-10*
*And I that am the LORD thy God from the land of Egypt will yet make thee to dwell in tabernacles, as in the days of the solemn feast.10. I have also spoken by the prophets, and I have multiplied visions, and used similitudes, by the ministry of the prophets.*

This tool called "a Sharp Sword" in his mouth, is a figurative description of "the Spoken Word of God", when used for judgment against evil. Such was also possessed by Jesus Christ, and we can spot from accounts about his life, that he never cursed, slayed or killed anyone by "the Spoken Word", because no negative utterances came from his mouth, though in a noticeable demonstration of possessing such abilities he made a fig tree die, and dry up overnight.

This demonstration was to highlight that what he bore was also an authority to both bless and curse; the same criteria applies to "the Anointed One", he who hath an ear let him hear.

We have to realise that it surely wasn't that Jesus Christ could not curse or speak judgment to those persecuting him, because he had "the Sharp Sword ability" to deliver the necessary if desired. Also known as, "the Spoken Word" in his mouth, his mission from God was to be "a Lamb taken to the slaughter", and not one to fight those who desired to kill him and hated the LORD who he represented. That is why he was noted saying, "not my will but thine be done Father". He was also noted to be asking the LORD to forgive those persecuting him, because Jesus Christ knew they were messing with "a Great One", and quite similar to that were entreaties and pleas from Stephen to the LORD for those who stoned him to death, these guys knew something those persecuting them didn't about the one they were messing with.

The verses below show us that the "Word of God" is also referred to as a "Rod of Iron"; or "a Sharp Sword"; or "Rod of Iron in his mouth".

All these various names are used in different contexts and perhaps interpreted differently by the various composers or writers of the scriptures, but they all refer to essentially the same thing or attribute borne by "the Anointed One" of the LORD God.

*Revelation 19:11-16*
*And I saw heaven opened, and behold a white horse; and he that sat upon him was called Faithful and True, and in righteousness he doth judge and make war. 12. His eyes were as a flame of fire, and on his head were many crowns; and he had a name written, that no man knew, but he himself. 13. And he was clothed with a vesture dipped in blood: and his name is called The Word of God. 14. And the armies which were in heaven followed him upon white horses, clothed in fine linen, white and clean. 15. And out of his mouth goeth a sharp sword, that with it he should smite the nations: and he shall rule them with a rod of iron: and he treadeth the winepress of the fierceness and wrath of Almighty God. 16. And he hath on his vesture and on his thigh a name written, KING OF KINGS, AND LORD OF LORDS.*

*Isaiah 49:1-2*
*Listen, O isles, unto me; and hearken, ye people, from far; The LORD hath called me from the womb; from the bowels of my mother hath he made mention of my name. 2. And he hath made my mouth like a sharp sword; in the shadow of his hand hath he hid me, and made me a polished shaft; in his quiver hath he hid me;*

*Psalms 2:7-9*
*I will declare the decree: the LORD hath said unto me, Thou art my Son; this day have I begotten thee. 8. Ask of me, and I shall give thee the heathen for thine inheritance, and the uttermost parts of the earth for thy possession. 9. Thou shalt break them with a rod of iron; thou shalt dash them in pieces like a potter's vessel.*

*Isaiah 11:1-4*
*And there shall come forth a rod out of the stem of Jesse, and a Branch shall grow out of his roots: 2. And the spirit of the LORD shall rest upon him, the spirit of wisdom and understanding, the spirit of counsel and might, the spirit of knowledge and of the fear of the LORD; 3. And shall make him of quick understanding in the fear of the LORD: and he shall not judge after the sight of his eyes, neither reprove after the hearing of his ears: 4. But with righteousness shall he judge the poor, and reprove with equity for the meek of the earth: and he shall smite the earth with the rod of his mouth, and with the breath of his lips shall he slay the wicked.*

*Revelation 2:26-27*
*And he that overcometh, and keepeth my works unto the end, to him will I give power over the nations: 27. And he shall rule them with a rod of iron; as the vessels of a potter shall they be broken to shivers: even as I received of my Father.*

There is a need to realise that there exists also a sub-set of humans, called "false prophets", who claim to speak for the LORD and prophesy or speak things supposedly under the influence of the LORD's Spirit to the undiscerning. The only way to confirm they are not what or who they claim to be, is by comparing their words with the results or what comes to be, after they have spoken for the LORD.

Such people are described as not having "the Word of the LORD" in them; such are those referenced to in the various verses below.

> *Jeremiah 5:11-13*
> *For the house of Israel and the house of Judah have dealt very treacherously against me, saith the LORD. 12. They have belied the LORD, and said, It is not he; neither shall evil come upon us; neither shall we see sword nor famine: 13. And the prophets shall become wind, and the word is not in them: thus shall it be done unto them.*

> *Jeremiah 27:18*
> *But if they be prophets, and if the word of the LORD be with them, let them now make intercession to the LORD of hosts, that the vessels which are left in the house of the LORD, and in the house of the king of Judah, and at Jerusalem, go not to Babylon.*

Now it should be clear that the fact that false prophets are not with "the Word of the LORD"; or "the Word of God"; in them or in their mouths, does not mean they are not equipped with another tool of prophecy or curious spiritual ability to make things happen as they so desire. In actual fact, what makes them false is that they stand in counsel of − or union with − "other spirits or entities" that exist those called other gods.

Rather than in counsel of "the Spirit of the LORD" and be informed, some spirits are powerful, and can only be contended against by humans in a duet with "the Spirit of the Most High God or LORD God" because they are empowered by the devil, so don't go messing around with evil people if you haven't been anointed by God, this is wisdom.

False prophets also possess the capability to see or know things that are yet to occur, because the other spirits sometimes called familiar-spirits which they stand in counsel with or are joined to; reveal such things to them in dreams or by vision. And the onward relaying of such dreams to other humans before the events occurs avail them the opportunity to deceive people that they too are prophets of God, they may be prophets of some gods but not that of the LORD God, the commander-in-chief of all the Host in the Heavens.

All the Baal prophets killed by Elijah on Mount Carmel, and those killed by Jehu in Israel were false prophets. It is worthy to note that all these individuals even though they were called prophets in their days, and demonstrated such attributes previously could not see the sword of death coming to their own necks before they got slaughtered.

Neither could they predict beforehand the events leading to their execution, which is a glaring depiction that they were blind. Though to common men, they were presumed to possess foreseeing abilities. Just like the girl in the book of Acts who was a fortune-teller, she could not tell by divination that the source of the fortune of those who commercialised her abilities was coming to an end, prior to the day the evil spirit was cast out of her by Paul, for sound reasoning will cause us to accept that if she knew or if they knew this beforehand — her exploiters — will have avoided her stalking Paul.

> *Acts 16:16-20*
> *And it came to pass, as we went to prayer, a certain damsel possessed with a spirit of divination met us, which brought her masters much gain by soothsaying: 17. The same followed Paul and us, and cried, saying, These men are the servants of the most high God, which shew unto us the way of salvation. 18. And this did she many days. But Paul, being grieved, turned and said to the spirit, I command thee in the name of Jesus Christ to come out of her. And he came out the same hour. 19. And when her masters saw that the hope of their gains was gone, they caught Paul and Silas, and drew them into the marketplace unto the rulers, 20. And brought them to the magistrates, saying, These men, being Jews, do exceedingly trouble our city,*

False prophets could also be described as those who could read six months newspapers, even before they are printed in the printing press on Earth. But they cannot change anything that is meant to happen in the future, although they could warn people about what they have seen in the papers, they were referenced as those who peek, and those who mutter and have no light in them in verses below.

> *Isaiah 8:17-20*
> *And I will wait upon the LORD, that hideth his face from the house of Jacob, and I will look for him. 18. Behold, I and the children whom the LORD hath given me are for signs and for wonders in Israel from the LORD of hosts, which dwelleth in mount Zion. 19. And when they shall say unto you, Seek unto them that have familiar spirits, and unto wizards that peep, and that mutter: should not a people seek unto their God? for the living to the dead? 20. To the law and to the testimony: if they speak not according to this word, it is because there is no light in them.*

Real prophets can also see six months newspaper ahead. But they have the ability to change anything which will occur in the future because they have access to the power that can effect, execute and accomplish such changes, before it manifest in our realm.

And that power is "the Word of the LORD" also called "the Spirit of the LORD", and also sometimes referred to as "the Light" if it is in them.

That Light is also "the Word of God". That which will come forth from the mouth of "the Anointed One"; It will come just as light came and overcame darkness at the beginning, this person will overcome ignorance about the LORD and all evil and darkness in our world by its power.

*John 1:3-5*
*All things were made by him; and without him was not any thing made that was made. 4. In him was life; and the life was the light of men. 5. And the light shineth in darkness; and the darkness comprehended it not.*

*Jeremiah 27:17-18*
*Hearken not unto them; serve the king of Babylon, and live: wherefore should this city be laid waste? 18. But if they be prophets, and if the word of the LORD be with them, let them now make intercession to the LORD of hosts, that the vessels which are left in the house of the LORD, and in the house of the king of Judah, and at Jerusalem, go not to Babylon.*

## The Anointed builds the Temple, sits in the Temple and bears "the Glory of the LORD"

Every time the word "Temple" comes up in the bible, the observed default is one of perceiving it as Solomon's Temple, or the rebuilt edifice by those returning from exile to Jerusalem. However, astute biblical scholars are aware that there can be more than one meaning to the word "Temple", when it shows up in the scriptures.

A sound clarification about the word "Temple" having more than one meaning was made by Jesus Christ when he explained that the word "Temple" also meant "the Human body", as a place where "the Spirit of the LORD" could dwell within.

*John 2:18-21*
*Then answered the Jews and said unto him, What sign shewest thou unto us, seeing that thou doest these things? 19. Jesus answered and said unto them, Destroy this temple, and in three days I will raise it up. 20. Then said the Jews, Forty and six years was this temple in building, and wilt thou rear it up in three days? 21. But he spake of the temple of his body.*

"The Anointed One" is the human who successfully builds in his heart a temple for "the Spirit of the LORD" to dwell in, and when this "Temple" becomes fully built, the LORD by placing His Spirit in it will come into this temple and begins to dwell in it, just as he placed His Spirit in the Ark and upon Jesus Christ.

After that is done, He starts interacting with humans on Earth from within this "Temple", just like it was at the beginning of Creation, before the deceptions of the Serpent, that which separated Humanity from the LORD's Presence, and just like it was experienced during the days when Jesus Christ walked upon the Earth, when it was noted that "God was with us" and signs to such effect manifested by him.

The person who rebuilds this "Temple for God" will be "the expected Messiah" or "the Christ" of that age or generation. It is he who will bear "the LORD's Glory and be His Priest" on Earth. Bearing such glory is in a way shining "the Light of God", outwards from within the Temple built by him, making him a transmitter or magnifier of the LORD's Glory. We must remember God is Light and in Him is no darkness, such manifestations of Him is similar to what Moses and Jesus Christ did exhibit in their days.

It appears some still expect the rebuilding of a physical temple on the mount, bearing similarities to the one built by Solomon in Israel as pre-cursors to the LORD's return, that is simply because they do not understand the scriptures or such prophecies concerning "the Temple of God".

The person who builds this temple is also the one who fulfils the promise of the LORD to King David, for that to occur, the person must possess "David-like attributes" which makes him or her "a seed of David".

That is what it will take for anyone to desire building "a Temple for God" in their heart. It would take just as much love and thoughtfulness as King David had for the LORD, or better still, even greater love than that which King David had for the LORD, to push such a person into the desire to build "a house for God to dwell in", at this time on Earth where humans have forsaken God.

This house will be one within his human heart and not a physical structure on a physical terrain as erroneously expected.

Since we live in an age where human hearts are consumed and distracted by various other cravings, lust, obsession or distractions, whoever labours to achieve that feat is one that overcomes all the aforementioned obstacles, in order to become a true "son of King David", and who will rule in duet with the LORD God.

> *Zechariah 6:12-13*
> *And speak unto him, saying, Thus speaketh the LORD of hosts, saying, Behold the man whose name is The BRANCH; and he shall grow up out of his place, and he shall build the temple of the LORD: 13. Even he shall build the temple of the LORD; and he shall bear the glory, and shall sit and rule upon his throne; and he shall be a priest upon his throne: and the counsel of peace shall be between them both.*

> *Malachi 3:1-2*
> *Behold, I will send my messenger, and he shall prepare the way before me: and the Lord, whom ye seek, shall suddenly come to his temple, even the messenger of the covenant, whom ye delight in: behold, he shall come, saith the LORD of hosts. 2. But who may abide the day of his coming? and who shall stand when he appeareth? for he is like a refiner's fire, and like fullers' soap:*

> *Zechariah 3 :8*
> *Hear now, O Joshua the high priest, thou, and thy fellows that sit before thee: for they are men wondered at: for, behold, I will bring forth my servant the BRANCH.*

*Jeremiah 33:14-15*
*Behold, the days come, saith the LORD, that I will perform that good thing which I have promised unto the house of Israel and to the house of Judah. 15. In those days, and at that time, will I cause the Branch of righteousness to grow up unto David; and he shall execute judgment and righteousness in the land.*

*Jeremiah 23:5-6*
*Behold, the days come, saith the LORD, that I will raise unto David a righteous Branch, and a King shall reign and prosper, and shall execute judgment and justice in the earth. 6. In his days Judah shall be saved, and Israel shall dwell safely: and this is his name whereby he shall be called, THE LORD OUR RIGHTEOUSNESS.*

The person who "the Spirit of the LORD" will come into his temple — his body in this case — must be a human pure in heart. And to be pure in heart requires utmost discipline, which those bearing a fickle response towards the desires of the LORD can never accomplish.

The commandment to love the LORD with all our heart, mind, soul and strength simply means we should crave a union with Him with everything we have or are, for without such we cannot accomplish that objective.

There is a need to wonder why the criterion for one with a pure heart matters if the LORD is keen on returning to dwell with Humanity. To answer that I will simply respond, wouldn't it be stupid of any government spending billions of currency developing a weapons system only to open up access, or leak the secrets concerning using or deploying it to their enemies or an unsupportive factional state or a country not on their side.

Well, anyone not pure in heart is a human not on the LORD's side fully, and such a person could be used as a pawn or double-agent by the devil to gain access to "the Throne of God" where all Humanity's secrets and powers are domiciled and from which they could be activated.

Not being pure in heart means the respective human possesses some evil spirit or consciousness within their heart. If that consciousness by its deceitful status of being holy is allowed access to "the Throne of God", what can we expect such an evil consciousness to do with the privileges of the powers domiciled at "the Throne of God", after it sneaks into such a zone undetected. That is best left imagined to those who understand the stakes of the on-going battle between good and evil, an extremely high stakes duel it is.

The access restriction view is also validated and symbolised by the fact that in old days, before going into "the Holy of Holies", the priest had bells sewn on their garments which rang while he moved within the inner court of the temple where God's presence was presumed to be.

This was in order for those outside to tell that their priest had not been struck dead by the LORD for guilt or sin. The priest only gets struck dead if he possessed things that are a threat to "the Throne of God" or "His Presence".

In those days, this Throne was symbolized as "the Holy of Holies" or "the Presence of the LORD", any human that shows up there must be perfect, and it was better killing any human who was imperfect than risking a chance of compromising "the Holy of Holies" or giving an evil entity privilege into it .

> *Exodus 28:33-36*
> *And beneath upon the hem of it thou shalt make pomegranates of blue, and of purple, and of scarlet, round about the hem thereof; and bells of gold between them round about: 34. A golden bell and a pomegranate, a golden bell and a pomegranate, upon the hem of the robe round about. 35. And it shall be upon Aaron to minister: and his sound shall be heard when he goeth in unto the holy place before the LORD, and when he cometh out, that he die not. 36. And thou shalt make a plate of pure gold, and grave upon it, like the engravings of a signet, HOLINESS TO THE LORD.*

Another perspective by which we can understand this view is by considering the precautionary measures adopted into the field of mechanical automation or artificial intelligence, usually to protect humans from machines which may malfunction and hurt them. This protection is achieved by restricting the autonomous abilities of such machines to certain levels which can only be over-ridden when a human is currently in control of such machine.

A similar measure to keep Humanity safe from annihilation is what the LORD has implemented with human abilities considered supernatural and available at His Throne a place which is also His Temple by equalisation.

These abilities can only be activated in humans when "the Spirit of the LORD" dwells within their heart or comes upon them, once the Spirit dwells in a human's heart, it transforms the status of that respective human into "a Temple of the LORD", which bears other names such as "the City of the LORD"; or "the Zion of the Holy One in Israel"; and activates the powers associated with such thereafter.

> *Isaiah 60:14*
> *The sons also of them that afflicted thee shall come bending unto thee; and all they that despised thee shall bow themselves down at the soles of thy feet; and they shall call thee, The city of the LORD, The Zion of the Holy One of Israel.*

Perhaps the most illuminating prophecy about a true meaning of "the Temple of God", is one voiced by "the Spirit of God", when it spoke through Prophet Amos. The message passed across was that, one day "the tabernacle of King David" will be rebuilt to restore things back to the way they were in days of old.

Anyone who knows their bible very well will know that King David never built a physical temple or a tabernacle. All he had was an Ark located in a tent, though he expressed a desire to build a temple to house that Ark. Such knowledge should prompt us to wonder, what was being associated to King David, also called a tabernacle built in the past which the LORD still bears a desire or longing for it to be rebuilt? It surely isn't an Ark parked in a tent, because Moses built the Ark in reference. What it is, is simply a heart with strong love for the LORD, and that was the only thing King David had as a legacy which is now associated with him.

It was also for reasons of such love that King David worshipped the LORD daily in a tabernacle, but we must realise that even before David became King, he was known to have a heart after God's Heart. This is also that which the LORD desires from another Human who will become "the Anointed One" or the much expected "son of David".

*Amos 9:11*
*In that day will I raise up the tabernacle of David that is fallen, and close up the breaches thereof; and I will raise up his ruins, and I will build it as in the days of old:*

We should pay close attention to the fact that if the LORD was intent on referencing the temple built by Solomon, it will have been named or highlighted as what was to be rebuilt. The LORD God is not senile, He can tell the difference between David and Solomon clearly, and so should we whenever spot references to a tabernacle built by David. Such a tabernacle — or temple — is what He desires to be rebuilt in a human heart.

### The Anointed is the one who rules the Earth "In a Duet with God"

The "Anointed One"; or "the expected Messiah"; is a human who will rule with God over the Earth, or better still the one who will rule the Earth on behalf of the LORD God. This is because he has successfully approached "the Throne of God" as a human, or that is better expressed as he has been taken up to this Throne by "angels of the LORD".

Such occurs only after fulfilling of the criteria for such assistance by them. From this position, such a person has access to "the Powers and Authority of God", and thereby becomes the one interfacing "or standing in the gap" between the LORD and Humanity, something God has sought for over the ages.

For this person to come to God, or be allowed access into Heaven or "the Presence of the LORD"; or into "the Throne of God"; he must have submitted his will to the LORD and pleased the LORD to His utmost desire. Just like Jesus Christ did, while playing "a High priest & Scape goat role" for Humanity, and quite similar to that played by Aaron in the days of Moses.

Such a person is expected to rule over the whole Earth one day, because he will have the supportive backing and authority, or power from the LORD to accomplish this task.

He will purge the Earth of all evil and break the evil bondage over its inhabitants causing PEACE and LOVE to reign on the Earth. This person will appear to be the one doing all the things he does as a human. But that is an illusion because the one doing the things being done, is actually the LORD

Himself. That is because HE has control over the will of this human as HE had over that of Jesus Christ. These or such humans like him have submitted their will back to the LORD and said "thine will be done, Father in our hearts and lives Oh LORD God". Such a submission is required from everyone in order to return fully to the LORD and fully reverse our states of existence, it is that called "Repentance".

*Micah 5:4-5*
*And he shall stand and feed in the strength of the LORD, in the majesty of the name of the LORD his God; and they shall abide: for now shall he be great unto the ends of the earth. 5. And this man shall be the peace, when the Assyrian shall come into our land: and when he shall tread in our palaces, then shall we raise against him seven shepherds, and eight principal men.*

*Isaiah 49:1-6*
*Listen, O isles, unto me; and hearken, ye people, from far; The LORD hath called me from the womb; from the bowels of my mother hath he made mention of my name. 2. And he hath made my mouth like a sharp sword; in the shadow of his hand hath he hid me, and made me a polished shaft; in his quiver hath he hid me; 3. And said unto me, Thou art my servant, O Israel, in whom I will be glorified. 4. Then I said, I have laboured in vain, I have spent my strength for nought, and in vain: yet surely my judgment is with the LORD, and my work with my God. 5. And now, saith the LORD that formed me from the womb to be his servant, to bring Jacob again to him, Though Israel be not gathered, yet shall I be glorious in the eyes of the LORD, and my God shall be my strength. 6. And he said, It is a light thing that thou shouldest be my servant to raise up the tribes of Jacob, and to restore the preserved of Israel: I will also give thee for a light to the Gentiles, that thou mayest be my salvation unto the end of the earth.*

*Micah 6:9*
*The LORD'S voice crieth unto the city, and the man of wisdom shall see thy name: hear ye the rod, and who hath appointed it.*

*Psalms 80:17-19*
*Let thy hand be upon the man of thy right hand, upon the son of man whom thou madest strong for thyself. 18. So will not we go back from thee: quicken us, and we will call upon thy name. 19. Turn us again, O LORD God of hosts, cause thy face to shine; and we shall be saved.*

The Anointed is the one who satisfies all criteria for the role.

"The Anointed One" is a human who is chosen for the position by the LORD. However, being chosen is not the only requirement. In my view, it is the first of a series of criteria that have to be satisfied, because all humans are chosen to become "anointed sons and daughters of God", because we are all created to bear "the uncorrupted Image of God".

Another criterion for being "the Anointed One", will be a decision and dedication to build "a Temple for God", also known or better perceived as to approach the LORD with his or her heart. This is an utmost requirement because whoever is to play this role, must dwell within "the Presence of the LORD God", in a place also known as "the Throne of God"; or "the Temple of God"; or "The LORD's Holy Temple"; or "Zion".

It is crucial for this person to be in God's Presence, which is also symbolized by being brought up to "the Throne of the Most High", by the angels in some prophecies. This is because such a person will be the LORD's personal assistant on all Earthly affairs. To be a personal assistant to the LORD, you have to be physically present with Him and additionally He must have full access to you at all times. It can only be so after a human submits totally to the LORD God, hence this person will also be like "a Priest to the LORD", or the one upon who the LORD's Spirit rest and controls as He so pleases.

*Psalms 65:1-4*
*To the chief Musician, A Psalm and Song of David. Praise waiteth for thee, O God, in Sion: and unto thee shall the vow be performed. 2. O thou that hearest prayer, unto thee shall all flesh come. 3. Iniquities prevail against me: as for our transgressions, thou shalt purge them away. 4. Blessed is the man whom thou choosest, and causest to approach unto thee, that he may dwell in thy courts: we shall be satisfied with the goodness of thy house, even of thy holy temple.*

*Isaiah 28:5-6*
*In that day shall the LORD of hosts be for a crown of glory, and for a diadem of beauty, unto the residue of his people 6.And for a spirit of judgment to him that sitteth in judgment, and for strength to them that turn the battle to the gate.*

*Isaiah 42:1-9*
*Behold my servant, whom I uphold; mine elect, in whom my soul delighteth; I have put my spirit upon him: he shall bring forth judgment to the Gentiles. 2. He shall not cry, nor lift up, nor cause his voice to be heard in the street. 3. A bruised reed shall he not break, and the smoking flax shall he not quench: he shall bring forth judgment unto truth. 4.He shall not fail nor be discouraged, till he have set judgment in the earth: and the isles shall wait for his law. 5. Thus saith God the LORD, he that created the heavens, and stretched them out; he that spread forth the earth, and that which cometh out of it; he that giveth breath unto the people upon it, and spirit to them that walk therein: 6. I the LORD have called thee in righteousness, and will hold thine hand, and will keep thee, and give thee for a covenant of the people, for a light of the Gentiles; 7. To open the blind eyes, to bring out the prisoners from the prison, and them that sit in darkness out of the prison house. 8. I am the LORD: that is my name: and my glory will I not give to another, neither my praise to graven images. 9. Behold, the former things are come to pass, and new things do I declare: before they spring forth I tell you of them.*

*Psalms 68:28-30*
*Thy God hath commanded thy strength: strengthen, O God, that which thou hast wrought for us. 29. Because of thy temple at Jerusalem shall kings bring presents unto thee. 30. Rebuke the company of spearmen, the multitude of the bulls, with the calves of the people, till every one submit himself with pieces of silver: scatter thou the people that delight in war.*

*Psalms 66:3-7*
*Say unto God, How terrible art thou in thy works! through the greatness of thy power shall thine enemies submit themselves unto thee. 4. All the earth shall worship thee, and shall sing unto thee; they shall sing to thy name. Selah. 5. Come and see the works of God: he is terrible in his doing toward the children of men. 6. He turned the sea into dry land: they went through the flood on foot: there did we rejoice in him. 7. He ruleth by his power for ever; his eyes behold the nations: let not the rebellious exalt themselves. Selah.*

Like a sperm cell which successfully fertilizes the egg in a female ovum is considered the best out of all the millions of sperm cells released during that copulation period. And this is simply because it was the fastest and also the strongest cell that penetrated the female egg wall which other sperm cells couldn't reach, penetrate or overcome.

By similar considerations, "the Anointed One", who enters "the Holy of Holies", and gets to sits upon "the Throne of the LORD"' with God and thereby becoming the "one of the LORD's Right hand", because he is the first pure human to do all that is desired of Humanity by the LORD God.

While other humans before him may have ticked some of the boxes before him, they did not tick all boxes. "The Anointed One" will tick all the boxes of these requirements. Such a person is the first of many to come after him hence his title "the First-Born".

Such a person is "the ne plus ultra of Humanity" of that age; he is also "the First-Born of God". A title which should not be misconstrued with another similar title to it "the First-Born of Death" title which exclusively belongs to Jesus Christ eternally. And that is because he fulfilled all the requirements for that title too, and by doing that he provided solutions that will aid "the First-Born of God" to achieve that status of "the one who sits on the LORD's Right hand", these requirements are those termed "the testimony of Jesus Christ".

*Psalms 80:17-19*
*Let thy hand be upon the man of thy right hand, upon the son of man whom thou madest strong for thyself.*

*James 1:18*
*Of his own will begat he us with the word of truth, that we should be a kind of firstfruits of his creatures.*

There are still several things we do not know about the LORD or His Purposes for Humanity presently. I boldly take this view because after deep ponderings, it becomes obvious that if truly we have figured it all out, and know it all, then Humanity should not exist in the position of misery that it currently finds itself in our days.

There is lesser manifestation of the LORD's Power in our midst than in biblical days. This is despite our generation's opinion about being saved by or into grace, or our consideration as being most favoured. What we are experiencing can surely not be the best our faith or the grace of God can offer, neither is it the best the LORD God has planned for His people.

We are suppose to get better, evidence of progress should abound in our midst, the bible we read should by now be like a kindergarten study book for toddlers, if we had advanced our faith as expected of Humanity.

The Jews who persecuted Jesus Christ for perverting their religious culture with his own doctrinal interpretations, did also believe they knew everything about the LORD, His Works and what their faith in Him entails, even though they could not manifest His Power or Glory in any way.

When one came from the LORD, who by bearing the LORD's Spirit could manifest His Power and Glory in their midst, for trying to show them the right ways, and rectify their misinterpretations and for doing what they couldn't do, they chose to persecute him. This was because they would rather remain steadfast in ignorance with their presumed pitch perfect religious ways and lifestyle, than change ways to that of "the Truth". Hence by their obstinacy and folly they considered themselves as perfect defenders of a faulty faith and doctrine, we now know they were not as they thought, this has been revealed to us through the benefit of hindsight.

We all must really consider if it is the same with our generation as it was with that generation which persecuted Jesus Christ? Are we not set to reject anything contrary to that we also have been taught or brought to believe as true? Are we prepared to adjust our understanding and forsake dogmas?

We need to ask ourselves why we are still experiencing an absence of the LORD's Glory among us, despite all our claims that Jesus Christ has solved all our problems, and all our sins forgiven by the faulty Grace suppositions? We need to wonder why we can not heal the sick in our midst, despite authority being given to us to do such by Jesus Christ.

We need to know why we can not do greater works than he did, despite the fact that Jesus Christ promised this to those who believe in the Father "the LORD GOD". If we can't do the things promised to those who believe in the Father, it simply means we do not believe in the Father, and such calls for us to re-check what it means to believe in the Father if we originally assumed we do.

The "Anointed One" or "expected Messiah" will be the one who will enlighten all those who need enlightenment, reveal hidden knowledge or mysteries, about our faith in the LORD; such will bring answers to those troubling questions. Few who are not full of conceit or bear and hold dogmatic arrogance will take enlightenment from him at his appearance. But those who presume they know everything already with nothing to show or prove their knowledge will despise him because their religion has laid that path out for them to follow, herein lies wisdom.

*Isaiah 52:13-15*
*Behold, my servant shall deal prudently, he shall be exalted and extolled, and be very high. 14. As many were astonied at thee; his visage was so marred more than any man, and his form more than the sons of men: 15. So shall he sprinkle many nations; the kings shall shut their mouths at him: for that which had not been told them shall they see; and that which they had not heard shall they consider.*

*Isaiah 29:18-24*
*And in that day shall the deaf hear the words of the book, and the eyes of the blind shall see out of obscurity, and out of darkness. 19. The meek also shall increase their joy in the LORD, and the poor among men shall rejoice in the Holy One of Israel. 20. For the terrible one is brought to nought, and the scorner is consumed, and all that watch for iniquity are cut off: 21. That make a man an offender for a word, and lay a snare for him that reproveth in the gate, and turn aside the just for a thing of nought. 22. Therefore thus saith the LORD, who redeemed Abraham, concerning the house of Jacob, Jacob shall not now be ashamed, neither shall his face now wax pale. 23. But when he seeth his children, the work of mine hands, in the midst of him, they shall sanctify my name, and sanctify the Holy One of Jacob, and shall fear the God of Israel. 24. They also that erred in spirit shall come to understanding, and they that murmured shall learn doctrine.*

We must never forget that the lady at the well said to Jesus Christ, "we await the Messiah, and he will tell us things we do not know and teach us more about God". Jesus Christ also confirmed the absence of some knowledge concerning things about the LORD God to those of his days, hence his efforts to enlighten then.

Such perspective illustrate there are unknowns which need to be revealed to us, and such cometh forth from the mouth of "the Anointed one of the LORD".

## The Anointed One is "a Light for the Gentiles"

The Jews are expecting a Messiah; likewise several other faiths have similar expectations. There is a very interesting scripture that makes reference to the one being empowered by the LORD. Who was being made "a Light for the Gentiles", this individual is also one that fulfills an outstanding Covenant of God with his people, and he is the one who brings judgment to the earth and has the LORD's Spirit put upon him. All these are outstanding roles for "the Messiah or expected Anointed One", and such co-entanglement suggests that whoever it is, will have a Gentile relationship or lineage and minister to a

Gentile flock too.

For this person to become a light, "the Glory of the LORD", is expected to be seen on him, after which the Gentiles and kings will gather to celebrate such a Glory, this Glory is simply "the Light of God" shining upon the subject of these prophecies, just as the star of Jesus' birth attracted the wise men.

*Isaiah 42:1-6*
*Behold my servant, whom I uphold; mine elect, in whom my soul delighteth; I have put my spirit upon him: he shall bring forth judgment to the Gentiles. 2. He shall not cry, nor lift up, nor cause his voice to be heard in the street. 3. A bruised reed shall he not break, and the smoking flax shall he not quench: he shall bring forth judgment unto truth. 4. He shall not fail nor be discouraged, till he have set judgment in the earth: and the isles shall wait for his law. 5. Thus saith God the LORD, he that created the heavens, and stretched them out; he that spread forth the earth, and that which cometh out of it; he that giveth breath unto the people upon it, and spirit to them that walk therein: 6. I the LORD have called thee in righteousness, and will hold thine hand, and will keep thee, and give thee for a covenant of the people, for a light of the Gentiles;*

*Isaiah 60:1-6*
*Arise, shine; for thy light is come, and the glory of the LORD is risen upon thee. 2. For, behold, the darkness shall cover the earth, and gross darkness the people: but the LORD shall arise upon thee, and his glory shall be seen upon thee. 3. And the Gentiles shall come to thy light, and kings to the brightness of thy rising. 4. Lift up thine eyes round about, and see: all they gather themselves together, they come to thee: thy sons shall come from far, and thy daughters shall be nursed at thy side. 5. Then thou shalt see, and flow together, and thine heart shall fear, and be enlarged; because the abundance of the sea shall be converted unto thee, the forces of the Gentiles shall come unto thee. 6. The multitude of camels shall cover thee, the dromedaries of Midian and Ephah; all they from Sheba shall come: they shall bring gold and incense; and they shall shew forth the praises of the LORD.*

The words by Jesus Christ, that "the Kingdom of God" was taken away from the Jews, and given to another nation — which could also be interpreted to mean another tribe or race — one that will bring forth the Kingdom's fruits. Such pronouncements could also bear significance, if we consider that "the Light of God" is the resultant effect of the presence of "the Spirit of God" upon or with a person, just as "the roar of a Lion" heard within a neighbourhood signifies the presence of a Lion nearby.

Then considering that such a light according to prophecy is expected to arise upon a person from a Gentile nation, simply means this person will come from another nation, tribe or race apart from the Jewish nation hence not a Jew.

If he was going to be a Jew, then we may need to understand what those comments by Jesus Christ (which potentially are utterances of the LORD God via His Spirit) really meant.

*Matthew 21:43*
*Therefore say I unto you, The kingdom of God shall be taken from you, and given to a nation bringing forth the fruits thereof.*

In another perspective we must pay attention to the fact that certain Eastern religions or faith speak about how humans must search for the light within them. In my opinion what these faiths are talking about is the effects of lights manifesting in a human after such a human has accomplished the task of connecting with the LORD God who is and dwells in pure Light.

## The Anointed One is "the Bridegroom"

There exist several biblical references to "the Bride" and its alternate personality called "the Bridegroom" in scriptures. Such are symbolisms to express the various parts of "a Marriage", which in itself symbolizes a union that is to be consummated after a separation that occurred in Humanity's past.

The separation I refer to is the sending away of "Adam and Eve" from "the Presence of God" after falling for the deception by the serpent and breaking the union (or marriage) that existed between "Man and God."

*Isaiah 54:5*
*For thy Maker is thine husband; the LORD of hosts is his name; and thy Redeemer the Holy One of Israel; The God of the whole earth shall he be called.*

"The Bride" of the marriage is "the Spirit of the LORD", this perspective is best amplified or accentuated when we examine the comments of John the Baptist when he was being hounded by those who thought he was the expected saviour or "the Anointed One", also translated as "Messiah" or "the Christ", who is the person expected to bear "the Spirit of God" in those days by the Jews doctrine and prophecy.

The act of bearing this bride is preceded by a marriage, such was that which King David intended by his desires to build the LORD a house to dwell in.

*John 3:27-29*
*John answered and said, A man can receive nothing, except it be given him from heaven. 28. Ye yourselves bear me witness, that I said, I am not the Christ, but that I am sent before him. 29. He that hath the bride is the bridegroom: but the friend of the bridegroom, which standeth and heareth him, rejoiceth greatly because of the bridegroom's voice: this my joy therefore is fulfilled.*

"The Bride" as expressed in this context is what bequeaths the status of "the Bridegroom" to whom ever has her hand in marriage. This marriage is one that happens in the heart of a human, and is not a typical marriage between a man and a woman; such a marriage is desired for all humans and is the underlying purpose of every call for "Repentance".

Before glossing over it, we have to realise that though we get married or joined to "the Spirit of the LORD" on one side, the one from who the Spirit came also gets connected to us on the other side by releasing His Spirit into our midst. So just as both parties in a marriage make individual vows of commitment to their partner, in quite a similar way two marriages are occurring simultaneously as a Human accepts "the Spirit of the LORD", and that is why two possible perspectives of bride and bridegroom exists at the same time, each of which simply expresses our union with the LORD from both sides His and ours.

The first of such marriage was fully consummated in the life of the man we call Jesus Christ, when the "Spirit of the LORD" or "the Bride" descended upon him during the baptism at the river Jordan by his cousin John the Baptist. Although I prefer to perceive it as a transfer of the LORD's Spirit from John the Baptist unto Jesus Christ. John was filled with this Spirit from conception, while Jesus Christ was the filled with or the one bearing the ability to manifest its powers and potentials on Earth, both individuals were carrying different components to accomplish the same mission, the manifestation of the LORD's Power and Glory in our realm.

It is like giving one man knowledge about how to build a rifle, and giving a second man knowledge about how to make bullets needed to fire the rifle after it had been built. Such was the dispatch from Heaven to Humanity. And when the time became right and both parties were ready for the task before them, the transfer occurred and the Spirit within John came into "a Temple" which Jesus Christ had built for it in his heart.

Such was the reason why Jesus referred to his body as a temple in other conversations, because he hosted "the Spirit of the LORD" inside it, such was also the reason why John the Baptist made comments to the effect that the one bearing the Bride was the Bridegroom not him. From another perspective, it is also possible that it was the LORD's Spirit calling or pronouncing Jesus Christ's body a Temple, simply because He was dwelling in it at that moment those words were spoken.

Jesus Christ was not the only one upon whom "the Spirit of the LORD" had descended. There were many before him, but one unique thing about him was that his heart was fully ready to receive this guest called "the Spirit of God", and that perspective is high-lighted by the parable of the five wise and foolish virgins.

Unlike other humans before him, whose hearts were partially ready or not available to become perfect hosts to "the Spirit of God". Simply because the other cares of their hearts, or for things in the world, or things gratifying the flesh, and the erroneous teachings of the various religions they practiced, precluded them from preparing a pleasing place for "the Spirit of God" to come dwell within their body as had been prepared by Jesus Christ when he walked the Earth. Jesus Christ's doctrine was sound; he was able to discern all erroneous teachings embedded within the Jews' doctrines.

The only reason why Jesus Christ was "the Lamb" who took away "the sins of this world" is because his heart was fully set to comply with all the desires of "the Spirit of the LORD".

This was desired to accomplish that objective, and such a view becomes strikingly noticeable in several instances when Jesus Christ made comments saying, "it is not by saying God is our Father that gives us access into Heaven". Heaven in this case means "the Presence of His Spirit or the Throne of God", but rather by doing and pleasing the will of the Father. The verses below highlight this perspective of yielding to the will of "the Spirit of LORD" also some times called or referenced as "the Father" in these contexts.

*Matthew 12:46-50*
*While he yet talked to the people, behold, his mother and his brethren stood without, desiring to speak with him. 47. Then one said unto him, Behold, thy mother and thy brethren stand without, desiring to speak with thee. 48. But he answered and said unto him that told him, Who is my mother? and who are my brethren? 49. And he stretched forth his hand toward his disciples, and said, Behold my mother and my brethren! 50. For whosoever shall do the will of my Father which is in heaven, the same is my brother, and sister, and mother.*

*John 4:31-34*
*In the mean while his disciples prayed him, saying, Master, eat. 32. But he said unto them, I have meat to eat that ye know not of. 33. Therefore said the disciples one to another, Hath any man brought him ought to eat? 34. Jesus saith unto them, My meat is to do the will of him that sent me, and to finish his work.*

*John 5:30*
*I can of mine own self do nothing: as I hear, I judge: and my judgment is just; because I seek not mine own will, but the will of the Father which hath sent me.*

*John 6:38-40*
*For I came down from heaven, not to do mine own will, but the will of him that sent me. 39. And this is the Father's will which hath sent me, that of all which he hath given me I should lose nothing, but should raise it up again at the last day. 40. And this is the will of him that sent me, that every one which seeth the Son, and believeth on him, may have everlasting life: and I will raise him up at the last day.*

*Matthew 26:39*
*And he went a little further, and fell on his face, and prayed, saying, O my Father, if it be possible, let this cup pass from me: nevertheless not as I will, but as thou wilt.*

*Mark 14:36*
*And he said, Abba, Father, all things are possible unto thee; take away this cup from me: nevertheless not what I will, but what thou wilt.*

*Luke 22:41-42*
*And he was withdrawn from them about a stone's cast, and kneeled down, and prayed, 42. Saying, Father, if thou be willing, remove this cup from me: nevertheless not my will, but thine, be done.*

*Matthew 26:53-54*
*Thinkest thou that I cannot now pray to my Father, and he shall presently give me more than twelve legions of angels? 54. But how then shall the scriptures be fulfilled, that thus it must be?*

All these excerpts from the bible are to illustrate that if at any point in time Jesus Christ over-ruled the will of "the Spirit of the LORD" dwelling within his heart, he would have violated the essential requirement for being "the Lamb", which was to be taken to the slaughter.

This accomplishment was what no human before him had done, including all those who "the Spirit of LORD" had descended upon before him. They all in their own ways disobeyed the will of the LORD, causing him to retire or reject them for opting to please their own ways rather than that desired by the LORD's Spirit. Such a move by the LORD is similar to human bosses fire erring employees for violation of managerial instructions or guidelines.

*Isaiah 53:6-8*
*All we like sheep have gone astray; we have turned every one to his own way; and the LORD hath laid on him the iniquity of us all. 7. He was oppressed, and he was afflicted, yet he opened not his mouth: he is brought as a lamb to the slaughter, and as a sheep before her shearers is dumb, so he openeth not his mouth. 8. He was taken from prison and from judgment: and who shall declare his generation? for he was cut off out of the land of the living: for the transgression of my people was he stricken.*

*Jeremiah 11:19*
*But I was like a lamb or an ox that is brought to the slaughter; and I knew not that they had devised devices against me, saying, Let us destroy the tree with the fruit thereof, and let us cut him off from the land of the living, that his name may be no more remembered.*

"The Lamb" is the one who breaks the seal. This seal is what separates humans from "the Presence of the LORD". It is also considered as "fleshy death" a form of death trait or impurity in Humanity which must not be brought into the LORD's Presence because He is Holy.

"The Lamb" is the one who takes away those sins of the world or that of all humans, which is what, denies us access into "the LORD's Presence".

"The Lamb" is the one taken to the slaughter which is what Jesus Christ did for Humanity by facing the cross.

"And finally, "The Lamb" is the one who marries "the Bride". In this context she is "the Spirit of the LORD". For the marriage to occur amongst us, the heart of the next Lamb "who must be a pure human", must be ready and willing for this union. As figuratively expressed in requirements of the daily sacrifice under Moses' law, "a lamb must be without any blemishes", in this case the Lamb is the one who will host the Lord's Spirit within the temple of his body, and such a temple must be without any blemishes, meaning no evil within it. When all the criteria for this marriage to occur are fulfilled by any in the human race, or any from "the sea of Humanity", then "the Spirit of the LORD" descends to dwell with humans on Earth as it did when it came upon Jesus Christ. Just as it was in the beginning of Creation here, when "the Spirit of God" was on Earth with Humans, that location where this descent happens becomes "the Holy Mountain" of the LORD. That city where the human in question dwells or is located becomes "the Holy City". Also because wherever the LORD's presence dwells is also considered as "the Holy Jerusalem", once God's presence descends down to Earth to dwell with Humanity, the Earth becomes "the Holy Jerusalem" too by transfer of appellation. Like it applies for any aircraft the President of the United States of America is in, such becomes Air force One.

> *Revelation 21:9-10*
> *And there came unto me one of the seven angels which had the seven vials full of the seven last plagues, and talked with me, saying, Come hither, I will shew thee the bride, the Lamb's wife. 10. And he carried me away in the spirit to a great and high mountain, and shewed me that great city, the holy Jerusalem, descending out of heaven from God,*

## The Anointed One is the one referenced as "the Mountain of the LORD"

The Anointed One is sometimes also referenced as "the Mountain of the LORD's House". Such a phrase has identification with spiritual entities, because all such entities are referred to as "mountains or hills" in certain contexts of the scriptures. This is a lofty association ascribed to them because they are all considered to be one or several levels above humans by our perceptions of celestial layouts.

This person considered as "the Mountain of the LORD" will dwell in a place or the house known as that of "the God of Jacob". He is expected to teach people the ways of the LORD. Here we must again note that if the people knew everything concerning the ways of the LORD already, as assumed in our generation that should mean such a person has nothing to teach them in the last days as prophesied. He is expected to judge among nations; he is expected to bring an end to all forms of wars amongst humans; he is one who enforces peace and unites Humanity.

We all know that religion is a thorny subject that creates sharp divisions between humans all over the earth. Well this person is expected to somehow create a unifying situation where everyone holds on to their religious views about God whilst also at peace with others holding opposing views, a masterstroke it will be if such gets accomplished.

> *Micah 4:1-5*
> *But in the last days it shall come to pass, that the mountain of the house of the LORD shall be established in the top of the mountains, and it shall be exalted above the hills; and people shall flow unto it. 2. And many nations shall come, and say, Come, and let us go up to the mountain of the LORD, and to the house of the God of Jacob; and he will teach us of his ways, and we will walk in his paths: for the law shall go forth of Zion, and the word of the LORD from Jerusalem. 3. And he shall judge among many people, and rebuke strong nations afar off; and they shall beat their swords into plowshares, and their spears into pruninghooks: nation shall not lift up a sword against nation, neither shall they learn war any more. 4. But they shall sit every man under his vine and under his fig tree; and none shall make them afraid: for the mouth of the LORD of hosts hath spoken it. 5. For all people will walk every one in the name of his god, and we will walk in the name of the LORD our God for ever and ever.*

> *Isaiah 2:2-4*
> *And it shall come to pass in the last days, that the mountain of the LORD'S house shall be established in the top of the mountains, and shall be exalted above the hills; and all nations shall flow unto it. 3. And many people shall go and say, Come ye, and let us go up to the mountain of the LORD, to the house of the God of Jacob; and he will teach us of his ways, and we will walk in his paths: for out of Zion shall go forth the law, and the word of the LORD from Jerusalem. 4. And he shall judge among the nations, and shall rebuke many people: and they shall beat their swords into plowshares, and their spears into pruninghooks: nation shall not lift up sword against nation, neither shall they learn war any more.*

By equalising and applying the housekeeper perspective, we can observe that this person is expected in many ways to enforce a peace order that spans every realm, bringing about a never experienced peace for humans dwelling on the Earth.

This happens because Humans are "Images of God" and He has declared peace for His children because the LORD's Spirit has descended to dwell with them and keep them safe from everything that troubles them. It should also be noted that the authority that issues such an order that even "the beasts of the field" and "fowls of the heaven" will obey, can only be that of the LORD of all the Hosts of Heaven, for only him has control over everything existing.

*Hosea 2:18-23*
*And in that day will I make a covenant for them with the beasts of the field,
and with the fowls of heaven, and with the creeping things of the ground: and
I will break the bow and the sword and the battle out of the earth, and will
make them to lie down safely.  19.  And I will betroth thee unto me for ever;
yea, I will betroth thee unto me in righteousness, and in judgment, and in
lovingkindness, and in mercies.  20.  I will even betroth thee unto me in
faithfulness: and thou shalt know the LORD.*

# JESUS CHRIST, A MESSIAH OR NOT?

The case about Jesus Christ being "the Messiah" comes both strongly and weakly, this is because we can say he has fulfilled almost all of the criteria for "the expected Messiah" prophesied about. However, almost is certainly not all, and that nuance cannot be glossed over, especially once we can discern the existence of more than one "Son of Man" perspective in scriptures.

"The Messiah" was expected to bring "the Presence of God" back to the Earth, judge and rule the world with it, and also wipe out or put an end to all evil. Jesus Christ brought "the Presence of God" to the Earth and overcame "death and the grave" with it, and afterwards he ascended back into heaven without judging anyone or wiping off evil.

Such was according to the instructions of the Father who sent him. Judging is in a way repaying evil-doers for their evil deeds, as well as ruling over everything with an incontestable authority. Such we must note that Jesus Christ resisted strictly because it was not within his remit or assignment.

*Luke 9:54-56*
*And when his disciples James and John saw this, they said, Lord, wilt thou that we command fire to come down from heaven, and consume them, even as Elias did? 55. But he turned, and rebuked them, and said, Ye know not what manner of spirit ye are of. 56. For the Son of man is not come to destroy men's lives, but to save them. And they went to another village.*

*John 8:15-18*
*Ye judge after the flesh; I judge no man. 16. And yet if I judge, my judgment is true: for I am not alone, but I and the Father that sent me. 17. It is also written in your law, that the testimony of two men is true. 18. I am one that bear witness of myself, and the Father that sent me beareth witness of me.*

After his ascension, things deteriorated and have even become worse than they were before he left. The presence of God has vanished, and for that reason, there is a compelling need to question, if Jesus Christ was truly "the expected Messiah". We should wonder if God has forgiven Humanity's sins, why does He still allow evil to torment them and dwell within their midst?

If Jesus Christ was "the expected Messiah", why is God not dwelling with us on the Earth as foretold in prophecy? And why is the expected peace absent in our world?

We also must note that Jesus Christ prayed to the LORD to keep his disciples from evil in the world before his crucifixion. That hints that he was aware that evil was still going to exist or be present on the Earth after his crucifixion and him leaving this world. By such pleas to the Father, we can say he wasn't the one to take out evil from the world even though he said he was "a Messiah" in other conversations. That shows more than one Messiah exists.

> *John 17:12-17*
> *While I was with them in the world, I kept them in thy name: those that thou gavest me I have kept, and none of them is lost, but the son of perdition; that the scripture might be fulfilled. 13. And now come I to thee; and these things I speak in the world, that they might have my joy fulfilled in themselves. 14. I have given them thy word; and the world hath hated them, because they are not of the world, even as I am not of the world. 15. I pray not that thou shouldest take them out of the world, but that thou shouldest keep them from the evil. 16. They are not of the world, even as I am not of the world. 17. Sanctify them through thy truth: thy word is truth.*

Several excuses have been proffered by apologists to justify the case for Jesus Christ being "the expected Messiah". But one which may be most ridiculous is that his fulfillment of the Messianic prophecies is to be executed in two stages.

The first stage which they claim is already complete while the second stage which is expected to happen in the future. This explanation does have reasons to be doubted because we need to note that there is nothing in any of the LORD's prophecies concerning "the expect Messiah" or "Anointed One", that suggests a two stage fulfillment. Such explanations are human concoctions mooted to mesh with a melange of existing religious doctrines that put forward claims of Jesus Christ as "the expected Messiah".

When closely examined, all prophecies about "the expected Messiah" or "Anointed One" can be separated into two, one depicting a suffering servant who will be hated, for pleasing the Father and fulfilling the prophecy.

> *John 15:23-25*
> *He that hateth me hateth my Father also. 24. If I had not done among them the works which none other man did, they had not had sin: but now have they both seen and hated both me and my Father. 25. But this cometh to pass, that the word might be fulfilled that is written in their law, They hated me without a cause.*

While the other depicts a conquering king, however nothing depicts or suggests that the suffering servant is also to be the conquering king at a later date in these prophecies, save "the Son of Man" identity or similarity in reference, which is also title for anyone that is anointed with "the Spirit of the LORD". Presuming or assuming that every prophecy about "the Anointed One", or "the expected Messiah", refers to just one individual leads to such misunderstanding. And if such views are accepted without questioning it, it is easy to realise how wrong doctrines has solidly asserted that "the one who is to come last", is "the one who comes before him". Hence the truth becomes jumbled up leaving everyone confused.

In my opinion, the best way to explain all Jesus Christ has done for Humanity is this, Jesus Christ is "a begotten Son of God", as Christianity wants us to see him or in a perhaps alternate view was "one of the Sons of God" existing in eternity. He got dispatched down to the Earth, simply for the sole purpose of assisting humans in fulfilling this great task ahead of Humanity, a task which was raising up one fit for anointing by the LORD.

As part of his duties, he was sent to teach us what is right in terms of pleasing the LORD's Spirit, and most especially creating a path for humans to follow. Such a path will take them to the destination called "the Throne of God". This path if they followed in a straight and narrow manner, will guide and help them towards fulfilling the outstanding requirements Humanity needs to satisfy, before a transformation of the Earth back into "a Kingdom of Heaven" can occur. Such is also a transforming of the Earth back into a place where "the Spirit of the LORD" or "the Presence of God" dwells, when it descends or rest upon a Human and by further interpretation the Earth becomes "Paradise" or "the New Jerusalem" or "Jerusalem" as some religions expect.

This view could also be supported by the fact that Jesus Christ kept taking in the context of being sent on a mission by the Father. A mission I believe meant the "taking away of the sins of the world", or saving us from our sins. Our real sin is the fact that as humans we remain separated from the LORD by virtue of the decision taken by "Adam and Eve" the first humans.

It appears that Humanity from the on-set of creation had the capability to refuse doing the will of the LORD. And that is called our free-will, and it was this capability that led them to experiencing "the Forbidden fruit". Meaning this capability led us all into "the First sin of Humanity state", which we all exist in, which was what separated us from the LORD God or His Presence. Its other consequence is what can be considered "the Second sin of Humanity", becoming creatures "knowing good and evil". A phrase which simply means having our hearts and will become subject or open to the control of both the LORD and also the devil, or "good and evil" but by default configuration evil, for it was transformed to such a status by "the Forbidden tree" effects upon it. Now to bring us back to the LORD we have to desire reunion with Him.

It is worth understanding that all the talk about Jesus Christ taking away our sins appears misunderstood by us. Because if the LORD had not already forgiven us for our sins, He would not have sent Jesus Christ, or his only Son as Christian doctrine puts it, to create a reunion path for us in order to reconcile ourselves with Him. By giving us a chance for reconciliation is surely signal that the LORD had already forgiven us our sins.

Most of us will not even talk to some one who hurts us, neither will we respond to any of their phone calls until time passes and we forgive the person for their wrongdoing. That perspective may be similar to what happened with us and the LORD. Attempts by heavily sponsored religious doctrine to keep us focused on the notion that Jesus Christ came to take away our sins, is purely to conceal vital parts of the Truth concerning his mission.

In my view, our sins had already been forgiven by the LORD God. But like a lost sheep we needed a shepherd to find us and bring us back into the LORD's fold. And such was the role Jesus Christ played for us when he was dispatched to overcome the forces which separated us from the LORD's Glory namely "death and the grave".

Again the notion that Jesus Christ came to pay for our sins in a transactional context, is blasphemous doctrine in my view, because I cannot fathom any context in which the LORD God will have to pay anyone for anything, He is the LORD God. Who can say no when He says yes, who is it that can hold Humanity ransom and say unless you pay me a ransom with your son — Jesus Christ—in this case, these humans will not be released or their sins paid for?

There is no one that can contend against the LORD, but if anyone thinks otherwise I will really love to hear their views on that supported with facts, not the silly doctrinal argument that the price for sin must be paid to God, because such revokes His character as a Merciful God, if He must take His pound of flesh as Christian apologist suggests, such makes Him a vengeful God by logic.

> *Isaiah 43:11-13*
> *I, even I, am the LORD; and beside me there is no saviour. 12. I have declared, and have saved, and I have shewed, when there was no strange god among you: therefore ye are my witnesses, saith the LORD, that I am God. 13. Yea, before the day was I am he; and there is none that can deliver out of my hand: I will work, and who shall let it?*

> *Isaiah 44:6-8*
> *Thus saith the LORD the King of Israel, and his redeemer the LORD of hosts; I am the first, and I am the last; and beside me there is no God. 7. And who, as I, shall call, and shall declare it, and set it in order for me, since I appointed the ancient people? and the things that are coming, and shall come, let them shew unto them. 8. Fear ye not, neither be afraid: have not I told thee from that time, and have declared it? ye are even my witnesses. Is there a God beside me? yea, there is no God; I know not any.*

## Jesus Christ was half-human

Another reason for which I am firmly of the opinion that Jesus Christ was not "the expected Messiah" is that Jesus Christ was not a pure human breed, but rather "a half-human-half-divine" being. And by virtue of that composition, he does not fit perfectly into the sub-set called "a son of man", which means purely a human breed. That is an essential requirement for the one to be chosen as "the Anointed One", it is this one that the LORD strengthens in order for His Purposes to be fulfilled here not a hybrid human.

*Psalms 80:17-19*
*Let thy hand be upon the man of thy right hand, upon the son of man whom thou madest strong for thyself. 18. So will not we go back from thee: quicken us, and we will call upon thy name. 19. Turn us again, O LORD God of hosts, cause thy face to shine; and we shall be saved.*

If going by what we all know or are told, Joseph the husband of the virgin Mary was not the biological father of Jesus Christ, and rather it was the LORD's Spirit that came upon Mary, and if that is true, then it means Jesus Christ was not a pure Human, because his paternity was not by human action or copulation. And maybe that explains why he referred to himself sometimes as "a Son of Man" and sometimes also as "a Son of God", just a man whose father is American and whose mother Chinese can consider himself both an American or Chinese citizen in various circumstances.

It is also possible that in order to become a mortal or "a son of man", Jesus Christ may have had to give up his right to immortality as "a Son of God" and that may explain why both status applied to him and syncs with he being on a mission to help Humanity as directed by the LORD God. Perceiving him as a son of David is erroneous because the male attribute ( Y chromosome) came from Heaven.

## Jesus Christ did not bruise the serpent's head

*Genesis 3:14-15*
*And the LORD God said unto the serpent, Because thou hast done this, thou art cursed above all cattle, and above every beast of the field; upon thy belly shalt thou go, and dust shalt thou eat all the days of thy life: 15. And I will put enmity between thee and the woman, and between thy seed and her seed; it shall bruise thy head, and thou shalt bruise his heel.*

Those words or prophecy by the LORD to the serpent were about a "seed of the woman" which is also expected to be "a seed coming from Adam and Eve", who are both pure human prototypes. This seed that would bruise the serpent's head appears to have been misinterpreted by some, leading to a conclusion that Jesus Christ played this role or would play it in the future.

Seed in this context means an off-spring of the woman and one from her generation, and that was reason why Abel was slain, for he fitted perfectly into that subset, by being fathered by Adam & Eve, and also for the fact that his offering and ways were pleasing to God, such factors raised red flags to the devil that then tempted Cain to slay his brother. Tempt means to takeover or hijack his freewill in this context. It is something all humans who don't have the LORD's Spirit in them remain exposed to. Herein is wisdom.

Since Jesus Christ was not a pure human off-spring or of pure human generation according to the virgin birth accounts, but rather "half a seed of Woman and half a seed of God", that means he could not be the "seed of Adam and Eve" also "the seed of the Woman" or "one from the race Humanity" being referred to by the LORD, who was expected to bruise the serpent's head.

Besides that, the serpent is the same entity as the devil, and from what we know his head has not yet been bruised for he still troubles the world. That is a fact that throws up more questions concerning prophecies about "the expected Messiah" wiping off evil from our world, which remains unfulfilled. Such are compelling indication that Jesus Christ was not "the expected Messiah". Our Messiah must be a pure human or simply put "a pure seed of Adam and Eve", or similar configuration who will bruise the serpent's head.

In the earlier chapter I expounded on how the LORD means what he says and keeps to what he specified always. To clarify this view, I demonstrated it using "the Covenant" or "Birth-right" instance in reference to Abraham's Inheritance. I must add that I still hold steadfastly to that view because of such precedence set by the LORD. When He told Abraham that His Covenant "which is also the Birth-right Companion" will be with one from his and Sarah his wife's loins. When Abraham attempted to pass Ishmael off as the one to receive "the Covenant of the LORD", being his first born son from Hagar and by fact from Abraham's loins, the LORD said to him, no way, that was not what I meant when I promised you my Covenant. In my view the same applies with Jesus Christ becoming "the expected Messiah", if his virgin birth story is true, he has no chance being Humanity's Heir even if Humanity attempts to make him such.

*Genesis 17:17-22*
*Then Abraham fell upon his face, and laughed, and said in his heart, Shall a child be born unto him that is an hundred years old? and shall Sarah, that is ninety years old, bear? 18. And Abraham said unto God, O that Ishmael might live before thee! 19. And God said, Sarah thy wife shall bear thee a son indeed; and thou shalt call his name Isaac: and I will establish my covenant with him for an everlasting covenant, and with his seed after him. 20. And as for Ishmael, I have heard thee: Behold, I have blessed him, and will make him fruitful, and will multiply him exceedingly; twelve princes shall he beget, and I will make him a great nation. 21. But my covenant will I establish with Isaac, which Sarah shall bear unto thee at this set time in the next year. 22. And he left off talking with him, and God went up from Abraham.*

Though he referred to himself as "the Messiah", it should be noted that he still spoke of another one frequently. One called "a Son of man" whose descriptions and expectations sync perfectly with those of "the Anointed One" or "the Expected Messiah". If he was the person, Jesus Christ will surely have said I will return as "the expected Son of man", or tell those who quizzed him that I am that Son of man I speak of which is a mystery to you guys.

Again we need to take crucial notice about the LORD's reply to Abraham about he having as a heir, one born in his house to Eliezer his steward. The LORD expressly stated to him that when I mean your heir, I mean one born by you and nothing else.  With that expressed clearly by the LORD back then, if the LORD kept strictly to this rule in earlier context, why will He break it when same applies to "Jesus Christ" concerning "the expected Messiah" or "son of Man". Who was supposed to be "a pure seed of the Woman" and by further definition a pure-human is a question we need to ask ourselves?

> *Genesis 15:2-4*
> *And Abram said, Lord GOD, what wilt thou give me, seeing I go childless, and the steward of my house is this Eliezer of Damascus?  3.  And Abram said, Behold, to me thou hast given no seed: and, lo, one born in my house is mine heir. 4. And, behold, the word of the LORD came unto him, saying, This shall not be thine heir; but he that shall come forth out of thine own bowels shall be thine heir.*

The greater folly in trying to equate Jesus Christ, as "the expected Messiah" is in assuming because he overcame "death and the grave", that he has fulfilled the prophecy of bruising the serpent's head. Well, that may not be entirely correct, because what we should consider is that "death" is not "the serpent" neither is "hell or that called the grave" either. They are two different entities though they all work together or in alliances for the devil (or serpent).

The serpent is also the one called "the devil" also known as "the dragon" and he has not yet been defeated, his defeat is prophesied to occur later in the book of Revelation at a time after the resurrection of Jesus Christ. The dragon is the entity that is trying to kill "the Anointed one or man Child" or "the expected Human Messiah" when he was about to be born by a woman.

The dragon also called "the serpent" in that context is the one making war against the saints after failing to kill "the man Child or expected Messiah" at birth. And if we take note from details in the prophecy, we can see that this child has co-siblings called "remnant of the woman's seed" who are also persecuted by the serpent, but they are also able to overcome by what is called "the testimony of Jesus Christ".

That testimony is invoked by following the path laid out by Jesus Christ to receive "the Powers of the LORD" needed to overcome all evil, and I believe such can also be figuratively described as "the Blood of the Lamb", with which the dragon can be defeated or by which they overcame.
Such overcoming ability came by a shedding of "the Blood of the Lamb" who was Jesus Christ, when he laid down his body to overcome "death and the grave" on the cross as "a Lamb of God". And by doing that, he took away the seal separating humans from being able to use "the Powers of God" and such was needed to defeat death & hell like Jesus Christ did and ultimately the serpent. Everything expressed above can also be collectively perceived as "the

Testimony of Jesus Christ" for remnants of the woman's seed.

I will also draw attention to the fact that when "the seed of the woman" is referenced in such context above, it is not referenced as "the seed of the man and the woman", such is stated to strike out any supposition that as long as the seed comes from a human woman it bears sufficient qualifying attributes.

The woman depicts "the race of Humanity", any co-mingling of this subset with other entities does not produce a pure seed of the woman desired for their expected Messiah.

> *Luke 22:19-20*
> *And he took bread, and gave thanks, and brake it, and gave unto them, saying, This is my body which is given for you: this do in remembrance of me. 20. Likewise also the cup after supper, saying, This cup is the new testament in my blood, which is shed for you.*

Crucially we must see that if the co-siblings of "the man Child born" or "the expected Messiah" are overcoming the serpent with this testimony. This is because the testimony has been executed or put in place before "the expected Messiah" or "man Child" was born. Let us recall that the serpent was trying to kill this one born, at or prior to his birth and it is immediately after his birth that his co-siblings persecution commences.

> *Revelation 12:11*
> *And they overcame him by the blood of the Lamb, and by the word of their testimony; and they loved not their lives unto the death.*

The co-siblings are not people of blood relation, but rather a collective set of humans on the Earth. The dragon's aim to kill the man-child is in a bid to ensure that the one to overcome his reign or kingdom over the Earth is never born, because it is by his successful birth that the kingdom returns to the LORD God. This child has attributes and expectation that suggest clearly he is "the expected Messiah".

> *Revelation 12:1-17*
> *And there appeared a great wonder in heaven; a woman clothed with the sun, and the moon under her feet, and upon her head a crown of twelve stars: 2. And she being with child cried, travailing in birth, and pained to be delivered. 3. And there appeared another wonder in heaven; and behold a great red dragon, having seven heads and ten horns, and seven crowns upon his heads. 4. And his tail drew the third part of the stars of heaven, and did cast them to the earth: and the dragon stood before the woman which was ready to be delivered, for to devour her child as soon as it was born. 5. And she brought forth a man child, who was to rule all nations with a rod of iron: and her child was caught up unto God, and to his throne. 6. And the woman fled into the wilderness, where she hath a place prepared of God, that they should feed her there a thousand two hundred and threescore days. 7. And*

*there was war in heaven: Michael and his angels fought against the dragon; and the dragon fought and his angels, 8. And prevailed not; neither was their place found any more in heaven. 9. And the great dragon was cast out, that old serpent, called the Devil, and Satan, which deceiveth the whole world: he was cast out into the earth, and his angels were cast out with him. 10. And I heard a loud voice saying in heaven, Now is come salvation, and strength, and the kingdom of our God, and the power of his Christ: for the accuser of our brethren is cast down, which accused them before our God day and night. 11. And they overcame him by the blood of the Lamb, and by the word of their testimony; and they loved not their lives unto the death. 12. Therefore rejoice, ye heavens, and ye that dwell in them. Woe to the inhabiters of the earth and of the sea! for the devil is come down unto you, having great wrath, because he knoweth that he hath but a short time. 13. And when the dragon saw that he was cast unto the earth, he persecuted the woman which brought forth the man child. 14. And to the woman were given two wings of a great eagle, that she might fly into the wilderness, into her place, where she is nourished for a time, and times, and half a time, from the face of the serpent. 15. And the serpent cast out of his mouth water as a flood after the woman, that he might cause her to be carried away of the flood. 16. And the earth helped the woman, and the earth opened her mouth, and swallowed up the flood which the dragon cast out of his mouth. 17. And the dragon was wroth with the woman, and went to make war with the remnant of her seed, which keep the commandments of God, and have the testimony of Jesus Christ.*

*Revelation 20:2*
*And he laid hold on the dragon, that old serpent, which is the Devil, and Satan, and bound him a thousand years,*

"Death and hell" are different entities from the serpent. The casting of "death and hell" into everlasting fire is also pencilled to occur in the future, though "death and hell" have already been vanquished, they still exert their power over the human race, otherwise no human should be dying. But that is simply because humans fail at doing that which is desired of them to defeat these entities like Jesus Christ did. Though he taught his disciples, they too failed the course and died unlike their master. But the influence of "death and hell" will end after they are both cast into the lake of fire at the judgment day, when the LORD separates His people from all those who are already their captives in the realm controlled by "death and hell" also called Hades.

*Revelation 20:13-14*
*And the sea gave up the dead which were in it; and death and hell delivered up the dead which were in them: and they were judged every man according to their works. 14. And death and hell were cast into the lake of fire. This is the second death.*

On the other hand, we need to consider that if Jesus Christ was purely human meaning Joseph was his birth father rather than the Holy Spirit as promoted by Christian doctrine, then that makes him just like us "a pure seed of a human female and male", and by that status he perfectly fulfills the "seed of Adam" or "seed of the Woman" criteria for being "our expected Messiah". The one who would bruise the serpent's head. However that still leaves some criteria set out from other prophecies about "the expected Messiah", which are yet outstanding to qualify him as "the Anointed One" or "the Messiah" expected by various faiths.

What the Christian doctrines states and teaches, is that Jesus Christ was "a Begotten Son of God", in actual fact "the only Begotten Son of God" is suggested by their doctrinal text, which attempts to states to us that only he is and can be "a Son of God".

That sounds untrue, because there are several other occurrences of the phrase "the sons of God" within the bible. This term reveals or hints to us that there are other entities in our Universe not of human descent and not Jesus Christ by identity that are created by the LORD God. From such references we can discern some are good ones and there are also evil ones like satan, existing in our Universe, all such entities are called "the sons of God".  I like to infer that this phrase "sons of God", also means "angels" when referencing the good ones and "demons" when referencing the evil ones.

> *Job 1:6*
> *Now there was a day when the sons of God came to present themselves before*
> *the LORD, and Satan came also among them.*

In view of that we can understand how it could be that when Jesus Christ called himself "a son of God", he could have meant being one of those entities, albeit one of the good ones who ways are pleasing to the LORD unlike the devil and his followers whose ways displease the LORD.

Though Christian texts insist that Jesus Christ is "the only Begotten Son of God", a view I must confess I find hard to accept as true, considering the existence of these other sons of God. The question then becomes if these other ones were not begotten by God who begat them? Is there more than one God or entity begetting the sub-set of entities called sons of God? And why are they all called "sons of God"? If God was not the one that begat them?

There are two possible perspectives or scenario of Jesus Christ being "a son of God", and we really need to ask our selves or understand which category we want to place Jesus Christ in. Not because it affects him, but for the fact that it helps us in understanding the scriptures bringing about sound doctrines.

Was Jesus Christ the "only Begotten Son of God"? Or was he "one of the sons of God" referenced to exist in the scriptures?  Whichever category we choose to place him in, is a decision to be taken in a clear mind, considering all evidence.

One free of all religious perspectives or suggestions which appear already cast in stone, and remains steadfast in intent to reject anything contrary to their views or dogmatic doctrine.

It also appears that all Humans or "sons of men" too could become "sons of God". All we need to do in order to acquire this title, or to transform into that status is to receive God's "Light" and "Believe on His name". This is another way for referring to tapping into God's Power and Glory, by letting the LORD's Spirit rest upon or dwell within our hearts like it did with Jesus Christ. If really one of us fulfills that which transforms us in "a son of God", then can that supposition of Christianity that Jesus Christ is "the only Begotten son of God" still hold true after such an accomplishment by another human or "a son of man"?

> *John 1:9-13*
> *That was the true Light, which lighteth every man that cometh into the world. 10. He was in the world, and the world was made by him, and the world knew him not. 11. He came unto his own, and his own received him not. 12. But as many as received him, to them gave he power to become the sons of God, even to them that believe on his name: 13. Which were born, not of blood, nor of the will of the flesh, nor of the will of man, but of God.*

There is also the need to consider why the LORD God is noted to say to one, that he becomes His Son this day as echoed in the text below. This pronouncement means the one being referred to here transforms into "a Son of God".

This one who becomes a Son is also to be worshipped by angels too. That is strange and alarming, I thought only God should be worshipped according to prevalent doctrine. Why is He allowing another entity (or a Son of His) to take worship from his angels? Is that not what got the devil in trouble and got him cast out of heaven? Is it not strange that all accounts of angels — the good ones — interacting with Humanity indicate they refuse to be worshipped by Humans? Do they know something Humans are clueless about? These are question to be explored and understood in another perspective, which may explain why all the angels are commanded to worship this Son of Man.

Also we need to consider if it possible that God will not remember that His Son (in this case Jesus Christ) was already His Son as has been laid out by Christian religious dogma?

If such is impossible, by that I mean God forgetting He had Jesus Christ as a son, who then is the one being told by the LORD that you become my Son today by virtue of being begotten or becoming the First begotten?

> *Hebrews 1:5-6*
> *For unto which of the angels said he at any time, Thou art my Son, this day have I begotten thee? And again, I will be to him a Father, and he shall be to me a Son? 6. And again, when he bringeth in the firstbegotten into the world, he saith, And let all the angels of God worship him.*

Even with the scenario of Jesus Christ being a pure human like us at the outset of his life, considering that by the act of building a "Temple for the LORD" in his heart and "receiving the Light", which was from God, and that is "the Spirit of God".

He will have been instantly transformed into "a Son of God" or "a begotten Son of God" as religion chooses to labels him anyway. So really in several ways Jesus Christ did achieved or become "a Son of God".

Even if he wasn't one before birth, that is something no one can ever deny him or take from him.

The issue remains, whether that status "a Son of God" is exclusive to him alone as Christianity is trying to pass on? Because accepting that precludes others from striving for such a status, one which becomes acquired when "the Spirit of God" descends upon a human and that is what births another Messiah or Anointed One. This needs to be crucially considered and understood, to guide Humanity forward in our walk of faith or walk towards God.

> *John 1:32-34*
> *And John bare record, saying, I saw the Spirit descending from heaven like a dove, and it abode upon him. 33. And I knew him not: but he that sent me to baptize with water, the same said unto me, Upon whom thou shalt see the Spirit descending, and remaining on him, the same is he which baptizeth with the Holy Ghost. 34. And I saw, and bare record that this is the Son of God.*

Again, concerning the claim by Christians, that Jesus Christ was "the only Begotten Son of God", if that is true then I suppose it should surely imply that he is the "only Son of God" and by further interpretation "the First-born of God", and a Divine being.

Well there is another rather conflicting prophecy in Psalms 89. This speaks about "one chosen out from the people" who will be christened as "the LORD's First-born". This person is surely a pure human and was made to rule and take a position of "the LORD's First-born son", after being spotted in the sea of Humanity.

We seriously need to wonder why the LORD is waiting for humans to produce the birth of His First-born or Only Begotten Son, if it is something that has happened before humans were created. Because as Christian teachings suggest, the LORD already has "an Only Begotten Son" — Jesus Christ —, how then can the LORD via prophetic utterances say that this one chosen from among the people is to be "my First-born Son"? It shows some facts are missing or we are unclear of some things being stated here, for there can only be one First-born.

I will again rather defer to the LORD God being right in this case, and Christian doctrine being woefully wrong here. Because I know the LORD is not senile, if he had a "First-born Son" before this one was spotted, He will have named this chosen one "His Second-Son" or "His Second-Begotten Son".

I know by taking that position some of Christianity's apologists may attempt at shifting their goal post by suggesting that the prophecy is one actually referring to Jesus Christ.

But if that be true, it simply means that Jesus Christ was "One chosen among the people" and by fulfilling such a prophetic definition he instantly becomes a pure human like everyone of us. Not a divine entity sent from heaven or birthed by the Holy Ghost as initially claimed by Christian doctrines, hence they may have to recant such claims about him.

> *Psalms 89:19-27*
> *Then thou spakest in vision to thy holy one, and saidst, I have laid help upon one that is mighty; I have exalted one chosen out of the people. 20. I have found David my servant; with my holy oil have I anointed him: 21. With whom my hand shall be established: mine arm also shall strengthen him. 22. The enemy shall not exact upon him; nor the son of wickedness afflict him. 23. And I will beat down his foes before his face, and plague them that hate him. 24. But my faithfulness and my mercy shall be with him: and in my name shall his horn be exalted. 25. I will set his hand also in the sea, and his right hand in the rivers. 26. He shall cry unto me, Thou art my father, my God, and the rock of my salvation. 27. Also I will make him my firstborn, higher than the kings of the earth.*

The fact is that there exists several categories of sons of God. Such as "The Only Son of God"; "A Begotten son of God" or "The First Begotten Son of God"; and "a son of God", I plan to clarify or distinguish each one of those categories in further writings as I must say that I am still learning or seeking divine knowledge and understanding to make an accurate distinctions on each category of sonship.

## Jesus Christ is not "The Branch"

Christian views abound suggesting that all prophecies about "The Branch" refers to Jesus Christ. However, when he spoke in this context, he never referenced himself as either "A or the Branch". Rather he called himself "the Vine"; while he named the LORD God "the Husbandman"; and told all humans they are "the Branches" collectively.

Going by his words that humans are "the Branches" who need to abide in "the Vine", which to me suggests relying on "the testimony of Jesus Christ" or "the New testament he executed" on Earth for them, then most likely "the Branch" being referred to in these prophecies is a human and one of the humans. I come to such a conclusion since collectively all of Humanity were called "the Branches", it simply follows that one from among them will be "A or the Branch" referred to by such prophecies and depicted in context.

> *John 15:1-7*
> *I am the true vine, and my Father is the husbandman. 2. Every branch in me that beareth not fruit he taketh away: and every branch that beareth fruit,*

*he purgeth it, that it may bring forth more fruit. 3. Now ye are clean through the word which I have spoken unto you. 4. Abide in me, and I in you. As the branch cannot bear fruit of itself, except it abide in the vine; no more can ye, except ye abide in me. 5. I am the vine, ye are the branches: He that abideth in me, and I in him, the same bringeth forth much fruit: for without me ye can do nothing. 6. If a man abide not in me, he is cast forth as a branch, and is withered; and men gather them, and cast them into the fire, and they are burned. 7. If ye abide in me, and my words abide in you, ye shall ask what ye will, and it shall be done unto you.*

## Jesus Christ is not "the one from the vine or the vineyard"

We can also deduce from the verses of Psalm 80 below, that the Psalmist calls on the LORD to visit "this vine and the vineyard", which is a phrase to symbolise our world. This perception of "the vine" or "the vineyard" as our world can be validated in several of Jesus Christ's teachings about a vineyard too, and the perception of "the vine" representing our world is also validated by the prophecies of Prophet Jeremiah and Ezekiel.

*Jeremiah 2:21*
*Yet I had planted thee a noble vine, wholly a right seed: how then art thou turned into the degenerate plant of a strange vine unto me?*

*Ezekiel 17:8-10*
*It was planted in a good soil by great waters, that it might bring forth branches, and that it might bear fruit, that it might be a goodly vine. 9. Say thou, Thus saith the Lord GOD; Shall it prosper? shall he not pull up the roots thereof, and cut off the fruit thereof, that it wither? it shall wither in all the leaves of her spring, even without great power or many people to pluck it up by the roots thereof. 10. Yea, behold, being planted, shall it prosper? shall it not utterly wither, when the east wind toucheth it? it shall wither in the furrows where it grew.*

During this visit to "this vine or the vineyard" as clamoured by the Psalmist, the LORD who visits it is expected to put his hand upon a man. This man is expected to be "a pure human"; or "the seed of the Woman"; or "a son of man". And by that act of the LORD's hand being placed upon him, this human gets transformed into "the One of the LORD's Right-hand".
That phrase clearly suggests "One sitting on the Right-hand of the LORD's Power". This person will be made strong by the LORD for his purposes, at a time when He once again causes his face to shine upon our world and when Humanity is reconciled with Him in general.

It should be clear that "The Branch" in this context is the one made strong by the LORD. Not "the Vine" or the Vineyard for those who may be led into presuming this prophecy was referring to Jesus Christ, because he declared himself as "the Vine" while he walked upon the Earth. Discerning that the vineyard is also considered as the vine in some context will clarify any such ambiguities.

> *Psalms 80:14-19*
> *Return, we beseech thee, O God of hosts: look down from heaven, and behold, and visit this vine; 15. And the vineyard which thy right hand hath planted, and the branch that thou madest strong for thyself. 16. It is burned with fire, it is cut down: they perish at the rebuke of thy countenance. 17. Let thy hand be upon the man of thy right hand, upon the son of man whom thou madest strong for thyself. 18. So will not we go back from thee: quicken us, and we will call upon thy name. 19. Turn us again, O LORD God of hosts, cause thy face to shine; and we shall be saved.*

## The terrible one has branches too perspective

"The Branch" personality when considered in perspective of most scriptures is noted to be one from a subset of other entities, which I have attempted to illustrate is a pure human. But quite strangely the one named "the terrible one" is also noted to have its own branches. And this is an entity that is to be vanquished before those favoured by the LORD can have peace on the Earth, in various contexts of scriptures.

Crucially we need to know that if "the terrible one" has branches, and the LORD via Jesus Christ names humans as his branches which need to abide in him to bring forth fruits, it shows or clearly hints a duality in our Universe, and that reveals similar facts to what the parable of the Sower illustrates about humans.

> *Isaiah 25:5*
> *Thou shalt bring down the noise of strangers, as the heat in a dry place; even the heat with the shadow of a cloud: the branch of the terrible ones shall be brought low.*

> *Isaiah 29:19-20*
> *The meek also shall increase their joy in the LORD, and the poor among men shall rejoice in the Holy One of Israel. 20. For the terrible one is brought to nought, and the scorner is consumed, and all that watch for iniquity are cut off:*

## Becoming a Begotten Son of God?

There is this context of becoming "a Begotten Son of God". This can be gleaned by reading Psalms 2 which was sparsely expounded earlier. In that context, we hear the LORD God in conversation telling the person, who most Christians will suggest is Jesus Christ, that he has become "a Begotten Son" today, and this was after the person in question was set as King on the LORD's Holy Hill of Zion, which is also "the place where the LORD dwells or where His Throne" is located or domiciled.

If this person who became "a Begotten Son" accomplished this status by being set as King on the LORD's Holy Hill to rule or reign over Humanity, higher than all "the other Kings of the Earth"; and "as the LORD's Human representative"; all these qualities clearly suggests to me that becoming "a Begotten Son" is only accomplished, when a human accomplishes such a similar objective as this person has achieved.

A simpler interpretation is to say when a human becomes "One with God", or "abides in the Father" as Jesus Christ instructed us, which in a way is what happened before this status was bequeathed unto the benefactor. This is also to a certain extent what the person called "David my Servant" did to become "a First-born Son of the LORD". We must note that "The First-born Son"; and "Begotten Son"; positions depicts a rare closeness to the LORD at heart, in the very least perspective; and that it takes significant efforts to attain such a level.

> *Psalms 89:26-27*
> *He shall cry unto me, Thou art my father, my God, and the rock of my salvation. 27. Also I will make him my firstborn, higher than the kings of the earth.*

> *Psalms 2:4-9*
> *He that sitteth in the heavens shall laugh: the Lord shall have them in derision. 5. Then shall he speak unto them in his wrath, and vex them in his sore displeasure. 6. Yet have I set my king upon my holy hill of Zion. 7. I will declare the decree: the LORD hath said unto me, Thou art my Son; this day have I begotten thee. 8. Ask of me, and I shall give thee the heathen for thine inheritance, and the uttermost parts of the earth for thy possession. 9. Thou shalt break them with a rod of iron; thou shalt dash them in pieces like a potter's vessel.*

Apostle Paul also echoes that every one under the influence of "the Spirit of God" is "a Son of God". To be under the Spirit's influence you must be one who does not resist any will of "the Spirit of God", and you must have made room for Him to dwell (a temple) in your heart and to control you as it pleases. That is what being led by the Spirit connotes.

> *Romans 8:14-16*
> *For as many as are led by the Spirit of God, they are the sons of God. 15. For ye have not received the spirit of bondage again to fear; but ye have received the Spirit of adoption, whereby we cry, Abba, Father. 16. The Spirit itself beareth witness with our spirit, that we are the children of God:*

Also to be noted, is the scriptural context of humans being classified as "Children of the Most High" in Psalm 82. However, despite that classification all humans holding such a status were dying like mere mortals or fallen princes, simply because they walked on in darkness or remained separated from "the Spirit of the Most High"; or "the Light"; also known as "the Spirit of

God", which confirms to them their immortality also referred to as "Eternal Life" in certain doctrines or context.

This suggests they were bearing the status of fallen princes or mortal humans for failing to live up to the requirements of being called "Children of the Most High". Every one of us needs to pay attention to what is desired in order to acquire the status of becoming "Children of the Most High".

A status which in my view is the same as being called or becoming "sons of God". Such was that which Jesus Christ was sent to teach us about, a status hidden and only obvious to the discerning human, a status visible to those who walk in "the Light" rather than in darkness path laid out in the world.

> *Psalms 82:5-8*
> *They know not, neither will they understand; they walk on in darkness: all the foundations of the earth are out of course.  6.  I have said, Ye are gods; and all of you are children of the most High.  7. But ye shall die like men, and fall like one of the princes.*

It is worthy to note, that Jesus Christ stated that anyone who believed in him, will never die (Immortality), and he also affirmed that even those that are dead will live again. The living again of the dead ones is equivalent to resurrecting the dead upon the return of the LORD's Spirit to the Earth after judgment of all humans.

Believing is equivalent to accepting "the Spirit of the LORD" into our hearts so we become "One with God". If this process is completed our status changes and we become humans that can never die again, but for those who may get killed during the process of their metamorphosis by the enemy, such will be raised up at the last day.  In my view this privilege will only apply to those who truly establish a connection with "the Spirit of the LORD" during their lifetimes, like those at the upper room on the day of Pentecost.

The entity speaking those words to the people is "the Spirit of God" or God Himself, not Jesus Christ. We can see here that if humans becomes "children of the Most High" or "sons of God" by the process stated above, they stop dying which is what was hinted above under the context of humans knowing not or understanding as illustrated by text of Psalm 82 above.

> *John 11:25-26*
> *Jesus said unto her, I am the resurrection, and the life: he that believeth in me, though he were dead, yet shall he live:  26.  And whosoever liveth and believeth in me shall never die. Believest thou this?*

## The bloodline of David vs. Sons of God

The view that Jesus Christ was a direct descendant of King David's bloodline could only be true if he were purely human of fathered by a man. However, it is suggested by Christian doctrine, the chief promoter of this view that His birth was by an act of the Holy Spirit or "Virgin Birth". Meaning his paternity blood source was the blood from "the Spirit of God", not the blood of one of King David's descendants.

If that was so, it means Jesus Christ was not of King David's bloodline as Christianity teaches and that strengthens my earlier view about "seeds or sons of David" meaning bearers of "David-like Attribute".

There is this counter-supposition put forward by apologists, that Mary his mother was also a descendant of King David via Nathan. This supposedly makes Jesus Christ "a son of David" too, albeit by maternal descent.

Though such sounds contrary to what science tell us about the role the male plays in determining the blood-line or type of a child, leading me to wonder how his mother may have passed on the presumed Davidic heritage or blood-line.

That somehow brings us into a deadlock situation, where we have to reconsider if the "royal blood-line" presumption about Jesus Christ was simply another tactic by the promoters of Christianity to keep all humans in the dark, and away from the Truth. Which simply is that anyone (or pure human) who seeks the LORD as steadfastly as Jesus Christ did while he walked on the Earth, is also able to become "a son of God" like he was.

Going by scriptural precedence, it is obvious that the blood-line requirement is nullified, whenever the LORD gets displeased with His servants. Prophet Eli; King Saul; King Solomon;  are classic examples of such who either got their blood-line wiped off or suspended as beneficiaries of the LORD's Inheritance or Throne.

A priviledge which was designated to only their blood-line until such was nullified. The same fate applies to the son and grandson of King Josiah. If this be true, why some will still suggest that Jesus Christ was "a son of David" by blood-line or heritage is an issue worthy of serious consideration. For it shows cooking up of books specifically New Testament genealogy in this respect to put forward such facts.

In all prior cases whenever the LORD revokes his promises from a person or their household or blood-line, He announces who the new or temporary beneficiary of such revocation will be. But in the case of Coniah, the LORD simply cancelled the rights of such inheritance perpetually from David's biological lineage or blood-line.

If indeed it were that the rights of such inheritance were returned back to Nathan's lineage, it is not suggested or declared in anyway. That leads us to cautiously presume that it was not handed to Nathan's lineage and any suggestions that Mary passed it via that lineage may be a canard. If we also recall that Jesus Christ (or the Spirit of the LORD) declared that the Kingdom of God had been taken away from the Jews, such pronouncements draw a parallel with what is suggested here.

*Jeremiah 22:18-30*
*Therefore thus saith the LORD concerning Jehoiakim the son of Josiah king of Judah; They shall not lament for him, saying, Ah my brother! or, Ah sister! they shall not lament for him, saying, Ah lord! or, Ah his glory! 19. He*

All humans had access to "the Tree of Life", prior to the deceptions of "the serpent". And if we follow the teachings of Jesus Christ, we shall once again have right to that Tree, which is what gives us "Eternal life". And such also yields us a right to sit on "the Throne of God" or become a beneficiary to the LORD's Inheritance for Humanity. It also gives us a right to eat of what is called "the Hidden manna". It also gives us power to rule over the nations, nations in this context means those of other spiritual composition or from other tribes — bearing other spirits — in them that do no worship our God.

I know it may be hard for us to disentangle that geopolitical meaning of "nation" which we are accustomed to in our interpretation of that word, because such is what we are used to. Following these teachings also establishes a human's name in the book of Life and makes them a pillar in the Temple of God.

*a white stone, and in the stone a new name written, which no man knoweth saving he that receiveth it.*

*Revelation 2:26-27*
*And he that overcometh, and keepeth my works unto the end, to him will I give power over the nations: 27. And he shall rule them with a rod of iron; as the vessels of a potter shall they be broken to shivers: even as I received of my Father.*

*Revelation 3:5*
*He that overcometh, the same shall be clothed in white raiment; and I will not blot out his name out of the book of life, but I will confess his name before my Father, and before his angels.*

*Revelation 3:12*
*Him that overcometh will I make a pillar in the temple of my God, and he shall go no more out: and I will write upon him the name of my God, and the name of the city of my God, which is new Jerusalem, which cometh down out of heaven from my God: and I will write upon him my new name.*

*Revelation 3:21-22*
*To him that overcometh will I grant to sit with me in my throne, even as I also overcame, and am set down with my Father in his throne. 22. He that hath an ear, let him hear what the Spirit saith unto the churches.*

## Jesus Christ is the wisest

Posing the question, "Who is the wisest man that ever lived? To most Christians, is one that usually elicits the response King Solomon. How those with such response unanimously arrive at  such a view considering all the antics and misconducts of King Solomon remains unexplainable to me, and should be to any who has read 1 King 11.

Solomon was a man whose ways prompted the LORD to strip control of the ten tribes of Israel from under the influence of "the physical Throne of David". Which back then became the seat of the King of Judah after its influence was mightily diminished.

Solomon was also a man whose heart went after other lesser gods, bowing to and frolicking with other deities. I suppose if he was quizzed about the reasons for such a venture, his excuse would be, "I was just being open-minded or a person of equality". As is expected in our days of everyone where those who believe now feel muzzled, because they are expected to be open-minded or adopt a state sanctioned equality.

Solomon to me was "a son of King David" who laboured for nothing in his lifetime and squandered everything he inherited from a hard-working father. Just how anyone in their right mind can call such a person a wise man puzzles me? Right there you spot clearly how influences of faulty doctrines which are repeated over and over again become accepted without any critical analysis or thought. None of those who label Solomon as a wise man would want an off-spring like him, one who will do likewise with their legacy in ministry.

Solomon was a man who thought he could buy the LORD's attention, by offering more bulls and cows as sacrifices, just because the first time he did it, the LORD visited him in a dream.

In actual sense, that was not the way King David developed a relationship with the LORD, he didn't have privilege of sacrificing inherited cows. Rather King David caught God's attention because his heart was given to Praise and Worship inclined towards seeking the face of the LORD. King David was "the Chief Worshipper in the house of his God". He did not delegate this responsibility to others even though he could have done so with no questions being asked. It takes great interest and dedication to God for a man to write or compose as many Psalms and song as King David composed in his lifetime. These were things Solomon his son never did nor attempted to do.

He was too busy exploring women only to find out there was nothing in them as he later confessed through his writings. We must take note, that he averred that a good woman is one who fears God, and she is a treasure to the man who finds her. Solomon never kept any of his women as a precious treasure, which probably hints that his entire search was unsuccessful in his quest to find a good woman, one that worships the LORD with her whole heart.

If indeed it was the fear of the LORD that made a woman so precious, I often wonder why Solomon didn't fear God likewise. This is so he would have become a good man, because by doing that, he too would be a treasure to both the LORD, and any woman who finds him.

Although in his case, maybe I will have to say the over a thousand woman who found him, would have had to duel over who gets to keep that treasure called Solomon. That is something for everyone to ponder upon.

It is true and undisputable that the LORD told King Solomon he would be given wisdom to become the wisest one that ever lived. However, if we study the scriptures clearly, we would see that the LORD made several promises to people who He interacted with, and by virtue of their unsatisfactory conduct such promises got reversed or annulled later.

This action is best referred to as a breach of the LORD's promise. Because that is what He named it as can be gleaned from the verses below. I do not think Solomon ever achieved the peak of "the seed of wisdom", the LORD sowed in his life by such a promise, in my view he totally bungled it like several others who failed to live up to the expectations of "the Spirit of the LORD".

*Numbers 14:28-34*
*Say unto them, As truly as I live, saith the LORD, as ye have spoken in mine ears, so will I do to you: 29. Your carcases shall fall in this wilderness; and all that were numbered of you, according to your whole number, from twenty years old and upward, which have murmured against me, 30. Doubtless ye shall not come into the land, concerning which I sware to make you dwell*

*therein, save Caleb the son of Jephunneh, and Joshua the son of Nun. 31. But your little ones, which ye said should be a prey, them will I bring in, and they shall know the land which ye have despised. 32. But as for you, your carcases, they shall fall in this wilderness. 33. And your children shall wander in the wilderness forty years, and bear your whoredoms, until your carcases be wasted in the wilderness. 34. After the number of the days in which ye searched the land, even forty days, each day for a year, shall ye bear your iniquities, even forty years, and ye shall know my breach of promise.*

Though the LORD told Moses initially you will lead my people into the promised land, but right after Moses displeased the LORD, He told Moses, "you will not step foot on the Promised land for your misconducts". That again was a breach of His Words or Promise.

The LORD vowed to King David, "your seed will seat as King over Israel forever". However, when Solomon displeased the LORD, He annulled this promise and reduced the reign of the off-spring of David to just over Judah. Going by such precedence, it is safe to conclude that despite the promise of the LORD to Solomon, about giving him wisdom to be the wisest, that such did not happen due to his short-comings. It is obvious that he squandered it by his misconducts especially for bearing a heart after other women's gods. So we really can't hold the LORD responsible for the way things turned out. Rather, we have to learn from it and make sure our assumed promises from the LORD, are protected by an unflinching dedication to Him, and pleasing His will so they don't get revoked. Here I sound a note of caution to all those who supposedly swim in grace of the erroneous doctrine fed to them, let him with an ear hear it.

There was a message from the LORD to the prince of Tyrus, and within it was a question to the prince, which goes: "Do you think you are wise? Are you as wise as Daniel"? These comments were directly from the LORD's Spirit, though uttered by Prophet Ezekiel. It is wise to notice here that the LORD did not make any mention of King Solomon who most Christians considered as wise or the wisest.

Contrary to such expectations, the LORD named Daniel as the wisest man of the Earth. Despite that this event was one occurring after the lifetime of Solomon, who presumably should have set the record for the world's wisest human, as initially promised by the LORD. Does that not reveal everything we need to know concerning what wisdom is really about?

*Ezekiel 28:1-3*
*The word of the LORD came again unto me, saying, 2. Son of man, say unto the prince of Tyrus, Thus saith the Lord GOD; Because thine heart is lifted up, and thou hast said, I am a God, I sit in the seat of God, in the midst of the seas; yet thou art a man, and not God, though thou set thine heart as the heart of God: 3. Behold, thou art wiser than Daniel; there is no secret that they can hide from thee:*

If we really have a keen interest in understanding the LORD's comments here, we should wonder who Daniel was and how come he is pencilled as the wisest in an utterance coming from the LORD of Hosts?

Daniel was a man who would rather die than stop praying to the LORD. How many humans have such a deep desire to seek the face of God as Daniel did? Perhaps just a trace can be found in Humanity and our generation if there are any at all is my opinion.

Daniel was a man to whom the LORD revealed his works for the future of the Earth, and our generation. And we should realise that all these came from having "a fasted lifestyle". Not one corrupted by the Babylonian culture he lived in and was accepted into while on exile. It would have cost him nothing to become a Babylonian and forsake his roots for a sybaritic lifestyle existence, his position was opposite to the way Africans forsake their culture for those of the West in our times once they relocate.

How many humans walk such paths of dedication and sacrifice to faith in our days? The path walked by Daniel is the same path walked by King David. Though we may describe his as one of "praise and worship" because he did it with harps and other musical instruments. Both men were doing the same thing in different ways, and by such acts they sought and found the face of the LORD in purposeful dedication towards finding, worshiping or pleasing Him.

In my opinion, if the prophecy from the mouth of Prophet Ezekiel to prince of Tyrus came, after the days of Daniel, and by that I mean during or after the time Jesus Christ walked the Earth. It would have been, "Hey prince of Tyrus, do you think you are wise? Are you as wise as Jesus Christ"?

Why do I say that? It is because of the following verses in the bible, which suggests how well Jesus Christ was graded in his ways and life by the LORD, and to me that means he shifted the wisest human record to a higher level than that set by Daniel, it is time for us to take it higher.

*Matthew 17:5-7*
*While he yet spake, behold, a bright cloud overshadowed them: and behold a voice out of the cloud, which said, This is my beloved Son, in whom I am well pleased; hear ye him. 6. And when the disciples heard it, they fell on their face, and were sore afraid. 7. And Jesus came and touched them, and said, Arise, and be not afraid.*

Even without those words and just analysing what Jesus Christ did during his lifetime, it would be fair to suggest that he was wiser than Daniel. After all said, King Solomon displayed precocious abilities and insights. Such are depicted in his writing and are invaluable to anyone in search of "a true Knowledge of God".

The great conundrum remains why he did not follow through with these insights? He appeared to be one in search of greater things, why did he not practice all what he revealed in his writings remains a mystery. If he had done those things or practiced what he preached, he would have become the wisest man that lived prior to Jesus Christ being born in my view, but then maybe his record may still have been broken by Daniel's steadfastness in prayer, just maybe I opine.

Wrong doctrines and teachings suggest humans only need to believe in Jesus Christ promoted by Christianity. Such are simply attempts to throw Humanity off the scent of the Truth, or in other words, showing Humanity a treasure map bearing a wrong route to and a wrong location of "the Hidden treasure". The desires of the LORD God are that we become "disciples of Jesus Christ", aiming to surpass all achievements of his by doing greater works, by virtue of better relationships with "the Spirit of the LORD God".

In finality, I really must re-emphasise that I believe humans are born solely to strive at taking the manifestation of God in their generation to higher levels than those set before their birth. Just as every new software; or gadget; or computer processor; outstrips it predecessors performance. I know the lazy ones may find that opinion hard to accept, considering the alternative opinion of just say you believe in Jesus Christ and everything is fine that has been fed to them by sponsored Christianity. Well I'll simply say once again, such greatness is what we were all are made to accomplish, for those who have a hard time accepting this view, deal with it guys is my final word on that.

# THE THRONE OF GOD

"The Thorne of God" is where God sits, it is also where the LORD rules and executes His Judgments from, it is equally where "the Spirit of the LORD" dwells, and it is the place, city and location where God's Presence is encountered, exists or domiciled.

"The Throne of God" as a location is also named "the Temple of God" or considered as a "Heavenly domain". Because the place where "the Throne of God" is situated is traditionally called Heaven, such is also called "His Holy Temple" or "The Holy Temple" because it is where those who worship or pray to the LORD send their prayers and worship.

In addition to that, it is from there that responses to such prayers and any blessings coming forth from the LORD God emanates. It is in someway "the control centre of the Universe", because everything existing, can be controlled or influenced from it if the LORD so desires such manipulations.

The men of God who were able to control the Sun, manipulate the Sea, or make the Earth stand still, could do so because they had access to that control centre of the Universe. An access availed to them by uniting with "the Spirit of the LORD", or in other words, by it coming upon them, after which everything existing can now be accessed and controlled by them from this Throne or by means of their new status. That which they now bear as humans after uniting with "the Spirit of God" or becoming "One with God".

*Psalms 11:4*
*The LORD is in his holy temple, the LORD'S throne is in heaven: his eyes behold, his eyelids try, the children of men.*

The Throne of God as a city is called Jerusalem, Zion or the Holy city

The name for the location where the "Throne of God" is situated is "Jerusalem". Although we have now gotten used to the idea that Jerusalem is a city in the Jewish nation of Israel, the truth is that this city only acquired that name after it was conquered by King David. Prior to that, it was still a territory of the Jebusites bearing a different appellation, one given to it by another tribe who dwelt there.

It appears that the LORD may have inspired King David to re-name that territory Jerusalem, just like humans stick their flags on any land mass they conquer or win through any battle, to indicate it is sovereignty, as well as featuring it as an extension or part of their territory.

*Jeremiah 3:17*
*At that time they shall call Jerusalem the throne of the LORD; and all the nations shall be gathered unto it, to the name of the LORD, to Jerusalem: neither shall they walk any more after the imagination of their evil heart.*

*Revelation 21:2*
*And I John saw the holy city, new Jerusalem, coming down from God out of heaven, prepared as a bride adorned for her husband.*

*Revelation 21:10-12*
*And he carried me away in the spirit to a great and high mountain, and shewed me that great city, the holy Jerusalem, descending out of heaven from God, 11. Having the glory of God: and her light was like unto a stone most precious, even like a jasper stone, clear as crystal; 12. And had a wall great and high, and had twelve gates, and at the gates twelve angels, and names written thereon, which are the names of the twelve tribes of the children of Israel:*

*Isaiah 52:1-2*
*Awake, awake; put on thy strength, O Zion; put on thy beautiful garments, O Jerusalem, the holy city: for henceforth there shall no more come into thee the uncircumcised and the unclean. 2. Shake thyself from the dust; arise, and sit down, O Jerusalem: loose thyself from the bands of thy neck, O captive daughter of Zion.*

*Psalms 68:28-30*
*Thy God hath commanded thy strength: strengthen, O God, that which thou hast wrought for us. 29. Because of thy temple at Jerusalem shall kings bring presents unto thee. 30. Rebuke the company of spearmen, the multitude of the bulls, with the calves of the people, till every one submit himself with pieces of silver: scatter thou the people that delight in war.*

As a city, the "Throne of God" is also referred to as "Zion". This is another name ascribed to the "dwelling place of the LORD's Spirit". At other times it is a reference to where the LORD's Throne is at, and since the LORD God sits on the Throne all the times, it means He reigns from wherever it is located, which is also called Jerusalem or in some cases depicted below as Zion.

*Zechariah 8:2-3*
*Thus saith the LORD of hosts; I was jealous for Zion with great jealousy, and I was jealous for her with great fury. 3. Thus saith the LORD; I am returned unto Zion, and will dwell in the midst of Jerusalem: and Jerusalem shall be called a city of truth; and the mountain of the LORD of hosts the holy mountain.*

*Isaiah 24:23*
*Then the moon shall be confounded, and the sun ashamed, when the LORD of hosts shall reign in mount Zion, and in Jerusalem, and before his ancients gloriously.*

*Isaiah 52:1-2*
*Awake, awake; put on thy strength, O Zion; put on thy beautiful garments, O Jerusalem, the holy city: for henceforth there shall no more come into thee the uncircumcised and the unclean. 2. Shake thyself from the dust; arise, and sit down, O Jerusalem: loose thyself from the bands of thy neck, O captive daughter of Zion.*

## The Throne of God as a geographic location is considered

## "a Holy Mountain or Hill"

The Holy City (which is also called Holy Hill or Holy Mountain), is an abstract way of describing any place or location inhabited or occupied by "the Spirit of the LORD". This view can be discerned when we extract from the bible various context about, the specific name given to a place or geographic location from where the LORD's help is emanating.

Logically we can say such a place is obviously where His Throne is located, thereby making it also the place where His Spirit dwells, and sometimes also termed as his "Holy dwelling place".

All "Holy" suffixes are appended to these appellations and descriptions. This indicates no evil, dark or unholy entities can access such places or zones. A strict vetting policy is enforced before humans or other entities are given access to the LORD who dwells within such a domain.

We were sent away or had our right to access to such a zone located in Eden because we became compromised creations. The vetting of access is executed by the LORD's gate-keepers and security services, those we fondly call His angels.

They protect His Presence, because an encounter with the LORD God bequeaths to those who experience it a sweet-smelling, essence which never diffuses or wanes. That essence is labelled generically as "Eternal Life" by some doctrines or "Immortality" in other context.

*Psalms 3:4*
*I cried unto the LORD with my voice, and he heard me out of his holy hill. Selah.*

*Psalms 68:15-16*
*The hill of God is as the hill of Bashan; an high hill as the hill of Bashan. 16.*
*Why leap ye, ye high hills? this is the hill which God desireth to dwell in; yea,*
*the LORD will dwell in it for ever.*

*Daniel 9:16*
*O Lord, according to all thy righteousness, I beseech thee, let thine anger and*
*thy fury be turned away from thy city Jerusalem, thy holy mountain: because*
*for our sins, and for the iniquities of our fathers, Jerusalem and thy people are*
*become a reproach to all that are about us.*

*Zechariah 8:2-3*
*Thus saith the LORD of hosts; I was jealous for Zion with great jealousy, and*
*I was jealous for her with great fury. 3. Thus saith the LORD; I am*
*returned unto Zion, and will dwell in the midst of Jerusalem: and Jerusalem*
*shall be called a city of truth; and the mountain of the LORD of hosts the*
*holy mountain.*

*Psalms 15:1*
*A Psalm of David. LORD, who shall abide in thy tabernacle? who shall dwell*
*in thy holy hill?*

*Isaiah 56:4-7*
*For thus saith the LORD unto the eunuchs that keep my sabbaths, and*
*choose the things that please me, and take hold of my covenant; 5. Even unto*
*them will I give in mine house and within my walls a place and a name better*
*than of sons and of daughters: I will give them an everlasting name, that*
*shall not be cut off. 6. Also the sons of the stranger, that join themselves to*
*the LORD, to serve him, and to love the name of the LORD, to be his*
*servants, every one that keepeth the sabbath from polluting it, and taketh hold*
*of my covenant; 7. Even them will I bring to my holy mountain, and make*
*them joyful in my house of prayer: their burnt offerings and their sacrifices*
*shall be accepted upon mine altar; for mine house shall be called an house of*
*prayer for all people.*

*Psalms 24:1-4*
*A Psalm of David. The earth is the LORD'S, and the fulness thereof; the*
*world, and they that dwell therein. 2. For he hath founded it upon the seas,*
*and established it upon the floods. 3. Who shall ascend into the hill of the*
*LORD? or who shall stand in his holy place? 4. He that hath clean hands,*
*and a pure heart; who hath not lifted up his soul unto vanity, nor sworn*
*deceitfully.*

An invitation to all of Humanity "Come into the Throne of God"!!!

Coming unto the "Throne of God", means coming into "the Presence of the
LORD God". That automatically means those who come there become

denizens of "the City of God" or of "Heaven ". This is the place where the LORD dwells and reigns from. There exists an open and outstanding invitation for all of Humanity to come up to this Throne. It is our inheritance. However, in order to honour this invitation, we all need to cast-off the old garment of sins upon our hearts and then put on a new garment fit for being in "the Presence of the LORD", such must be done in order to be granted access by the LORD's gatekeepers back to where "the Tree of Life" is located.

> *Genesis 3:23-24*
> *Therefore the LORD God sent him forth from the garden of Eden, to till the ground from whence he was taken.  24.  So he drove out the man; and he placed at the east of the garden of Eden Cherubims, and a flaming sword which turned every way, to keep the way of the tree of life.*

This invitation is like one to us for a marriage ceremony, we have to prepare ourselves, our schedules and our hearts for it, because when consummated, it yields a union of "the Spirit of the LORD" with our human hearts.

It is our responsibility to prepare our hearts for this union, before the last call for such is sounded. Those humans, who are ready for it, will be those who enjoy what is figuratively described as "the feast with the LORD". That is simply because they have their wedding garment on when the ceremony begins, and also for the fact that they were prepared for this invitation, which is one perpetually open at present. Sadly I have to stress that those humans whose hearts are not ready for this wedding, when time runs out and the feast begins, will be cast out, into a place called "the real hell or outer darkness". This view is signified by the parable below spoken by Jesus Christ as he gave a perspective about Heaven.

> *Matthew 22:1-14*
> *And Jesus answered and spake unto them again by parables, and said,  2. The kingdom of heaven is like unto a certain king, which made a marriage for his son,  3.  And sent forth his servants to call them that were bidden to the wedding: and they would not come.  4.  Again, he sent forth other servants, saying, Tell them which are bidden, Behold, I have prepared my dinner: my oxen and my fatlings are killed, and all things are ready: come unto the marriage.  5.  But they made light of it, and went their ways, one to his farm, another to his merchandise:  6.  And the remnant took his servants, and entreated them spitefully, and slew them.  7.  But when the king heard thereof, he was wroth: and he sent forth his armies, and destroyed those murderers, and burned up their city.  8.  Then saith he to his servants, The wedding is ready, but they which were bidden were not worthy.  9.  Go ye therefore into the highways, and as many as ye shall find, bid to the marriage. 10.  So those servants went out into the highways, and gathered together all as many as they found, both bad and good: and the wedding was furnished with guests.  11.  And when the king came in to see the guests, he saw there a man which had not on a wedding garment: 12.  And he saith unto him,*

*Friend, how camest thou in hither not having a wedding garment? And he was speechless. 13. Then said the king to the servants, Bind him hand and foot, and take him away, and cast him into outer darkness; there shall be weeping and gnashing of teeth. 14. For many are called, but few are chosen.*

In order not to be deceived or misled about our right to "the Throne of God", we must realise that within this phrase is encapsulated other meanings calling for wise discernment. But before that, let us look at those labelled as "the bad" in the parable, who are those without a wedding garment and one of such was he that got cast into outer darkness. Concerning the "Throne" in a classic instance Jesus Christ affirms to his disciples, that each of them will have a throne to sit upon in "the New Kingdom on Earth".

In another instance, he stresses to the mother of James and John, that it wasn't within his power to declare who will seat on his right or left hand, but rather it was a choice to be made by the LORD. We can spot two different perspectives of "the Throne", from both contexts of his comments, a discovery not to be ignored or glossed over. And somehow we must also realise that, if Jesus Christ was the one to sit on the LORD's right hand, he would have known prior to making such a statement. He would simply have told the mother of James and John that the right hand of the Father is already taken by me, but i have no control on what happens on the left side of the LORD. I add that to all earlier submissions about "the expected Messiah" — who is the one on the LORD's right hand.

*Matthew 19:27-28*
*Then answered Peter and said unto him, Behold, we have forsaken all, and followed thee; what shall we have therefore? 28. And Jesus said unto them, Verily I say unto you, That ye which have followed me, in the regeneration when the Son of man shall sit in the throne of his glory, ye also shall sit upon twelve thrones, judging the twelve tribes of Israel.*

*Matthew 20:20-23*
*Then came to him the mother of Zebedee's children with her sons, worshipping him, and desiring a certain thing of him. 21. And he said unto her, What wilt thou? She saith unto him, Grant that these my two sons may sit, the one on thy right hand, and the other on the left, in thy kingdom. 22. But Jesus answered and said, Ye know not what ye ask. Are ye able to drink of the cup that I shall drink of, and to be baptized with the baptism that I am baptized with? They say unto him, We are able. 23. And he saith unto them, Ye shall drink indeed of my cup, and be baptized with the baptism that I am baptized with: but to sit on my right hand, and on my left, is not mine to give, but it shall be given to them for whom it is prepared of my Father.*

## The Human Heart is the vessel for accessing the "Throne of God"

The heart of a human is the vessel through which humans come up or ascend into "the Throne of God". Or that with which access to the place where "the

Spirit of the LORD" dwells is secured, a place which is also called "Heaven" and known as where "the realm of Eternal life" exists for Humanity to reclaim. For the human heart to become enabled to accomplish the objective of accessing "the Throne of God", it has to go through certain processes, best perceived as purification procedures, and that is simply because in its present state our hearts are "unholy or unfit" to be granted access to the LORD's Throne, that is why we were sent away from "Eden or Paradise".

A set of terms or sub-phases in the bible, and others adopted by various faiths abound which describe the required purification processes or procedure. Examples of such terms are "circumcision of the heart"; "taking away the foreskin of the heart"; "taking away the veil on the heart"; "making the eye single"; "rending of the heart and not the garment"; "penance"; "quest for enlightenment";  "searching for the light;" and "a battle or Jihad for Jerusalem".

Upon full completion of such a process, the human's heart becomes fit to be availed access to "the Throne of God". In such a circumstance the human heart transforms and becomes considered as pure or holy. We should note that without being pure, the heart of a human will never be allowed to access "the Presence of the LORD" by the gate-keepers who guard His Presence.

*Matthew 5:8  Blessed are the pure in heart: for they shall see God.*

Being pure in heart is assumed to be a religious requirement nowadays, but prior to the establishment of most religions, it has been known as an essential requirement to achieve the impossible, which is uniting with God.

This view is validated by various legends or stories not religiously inspired, and such shows up as the core narratives of various Hollywood movies such as "The Golden child"; "Raiders of the lost Ark"; "the Forbidden Kingdom"; etc. Where the main character possesses an attribute so rare, it avails them abilities to overcome all obstacles or hindrances that others fail at.

In order to understand the need to be pure in heart, we must realise or come to accept that all humans have at present "a body of sin". This is simply one made up of matter, or that called or described as "dust" within scriptural perspective which we are made from.

Dust is a material that demands more resources to keep it perfect or stable, than our hearts presently have available. For such reasons our human body withers, blows away and decays with passage of time in life, causing us to become weak and frail, giving us experiences such as loss of strength; memory; sickness; pain and ultimately death.

All these happens because our "body of sin" also called "our flesh"; or "dust"; is not receiving the appropriate amount of resources, better described as "Living Waters", needed to keep it in perfect shape or condition which the LORD designed for it at our creation and placement here on Earth.

The "Eternal body" that will be given to those fit for it, at the end times after "Judgment Day" an event also termed "the Regeneration" by Jesus Christ", is really our same human body in a way. The only difference is that their hearts will have become enabled to provide above the sufficient amount of life force; energy; nutrients; or "Living Waters"; which it needs to nurture the so-called "body of sin" they all bear presently. Their hearts will from that moment on keep their body in a perfectly stable condition where it does not experience the present limitations or fragilities iterated earlier, and such happens by a transformation to the heart.

> *Matthew 19:28-30*
> *And Jesus said unto them, Verily I say unto you, That ye which have followed me, in the regeneration when the Son of man shall sit in the throne of his glory, ye also shall sit upon twelve thrones, judging the twelve tribes of Israel. 29. And every one that hath forsaken houses, or brethren, or sisters, or father, or mother, or wife, or children, or lands, for my name's sake, shall receive an hundredfold, and shall inherit everlasting life. 30. But many that are first shall be last; and the last shall be first.*

To help us understand that further, I'll use this analogy. We are all familiar with how a street light-bulb produces poor illumination, simply because of low-voltage electric current supplied from the electric utility company to it. The same bulb will deliver a brilliant illumination, spanning several metres, if the voltage supplied, perfectly meets the street light-bulb's requirements. Such is what happens to our body presently and likewise the expected changes at the regeneration. This change must be preceded by the transformation of the heart which is figuratively the same as having a wedding garment ready for the feast or wedding.

The human heart is the control centre of our body, and it is from this centre that the power or resource which fuels our body comes. Just as the central processing unit is the core of a computer system, from which all its components such as printers, scanners, display screens, microphones or speakers etc., can be controlled to perform their respective functions. If the computer does not possess enough processing power to run all those functions simultaneously, it is further designed to run one while the others processes wait and queue up, until engaged resources are free to execute them.

In the case of humans, our heart is the core of our body. It was disconnected from its main power source, "that which we also call God" because of what is now known as "the First-sin of Humanity" or "the Original Sin", at an event also generically labelled as "the Fall of man". When that happened, a lot of changes occurred, which can best be described as the sort of changes to water flow rate  and other ecological life forms changes downstream, whenever a river is dammed for power generation purposes.

Usually when such damming occurs, the river does not stop flowing downstream. What happens is that water now flows at fractions of the rate at which it used to flow downstream, because of the restrictions from the dam wall which was constructed to generate electric power.

The reduced quantity of water passing through the dam creates a reduction in water supply downstream, affecting all vegetation and life forms that depend on it. Some areas don't get enough water as they got previously anymore, several plants or trees die-off, humans and other wild animals living downstream have to adjust and cope with the water austerity situation that befalls the entire region.

Likewise it is with humans, our bodies equally suffer a similar effect as those downstream a dammed river, in respect of its separation from the unlimited "Power or Presence of God". What is available to us is far less than that which our body was initially designed to operate under, this resource best perceived as "Living Waters" but also described as "Eternal Life" in certain faith's context, is that sent out to various parts of our body from our heart in trickles of "Life forces" presently, it is what makes us conscious and a living being.

The paucity of this resource also explains why we get tired from doing little work, and why we need to stop and rest in order to regain our strength. In situations when all the trickles of these "Life forces" flowing from our heart through the dam wall into our body falls below the essential requirement needed to maintain our body, humans begin to suffer what is called aging. Our skins begin to wrinkle; our body parts creak and crumble due to absence of sufficient life forces to nourish it. A process which as it persists, leads ultimately to death, the stage at which our body can no longer cope or survive with the minimal life force supplied to it by our heart in this realm or dimension.

Prophet Elijah running faster than the king's chariot of horses, was simply because his heart had been undammed, thereby transforming it into one sufficiently able to supply enough power or strength to his limbs. Such was needed to make them move faster than those of the horses linked up to king Ahab's chariots, rarely can humans outrun horses.

This was a feat which no ordinary human could accomplish, unless their hearts became transformed like Elijah's, this transformation needs to occur in all humans. A likewise transformation to that was responsible for the sheer strength we attribute to Samson, one which he harnessed to fight and with which he conquered many Philistines as just one man. Although in his case it was God triggered rather than a man sought phenomenon, better perceived as "the Spirit of the LORD" coming up Samson as opposed to Samson craving "the Spirit of God".

Getting our hearts undammed and allowing an unlimited flow of "Life forces from God" into our being, is a task we all need to accomplish in our lifetimes. Figuratively, we should see it as a mission of blowing up the dam-wall which prevents all the powers from God "or Living Waters", from being available to our bodies "in this realm". The inability of our hearts to deliver this to us is a phenomenon which limits our capabilities as humans on Earth.

If we succeed at that task of transforming our hearts, we will begin to experience what is figuratively described as "seeing the Glories of God" or "manifesting the Powers of God". All of which also can be imagined as experiencing the full unhindered effect of the river-currents flowing downstream, because the dam wall limiting the flow rate has been obliterated.

In such a situation, because we can never run out of "the Power coming to us from God" ever again, that is after this dam wall is breached, this could also be expressed as being directly in "the Presence of God" the source of such. From then onwards we begin to exist in a state considered as "living forever" or "Eternal Life". And just like God does not die, we also exist in such state and can never die, because we have with us sufficient resources from "the One who does not die". This resource is that symbolised as the "the Tree of Life" and such is needed to overcome the force known as "that of death" in our realm.

It was because Jesus Christ's heart existed in such a state that he was able to vanquish "death" or the force which kills all living things when he encountered it.

It is crucial that as humans we have to realise that the disconnection of our hearts from its source of unlimited power "that which we call God", or sometimes describes as "Living Waters", or figuratively as "the Tree of Life", was a plot planned and executed by the entity called the serpent, "also known as the devil".

He did this simply because he wanted to keep the LORD's influence, which is "the unlimited Power or Presence of God" away from or out of reach of humans in this realm, or place we call Earth. And that is simply because in absence of such, he is and remains the controller of this world.

In order to rule over the human race and make them worship him, this had to happen because without God or His Presence being with us, the devil was an entity, stronger and more experienced than us down here, and he remains in control because of our feebleness by virtue of estrangement from the LORD who is way smarter and stronger than him. It is his mission to maintain that status quo hence the way things are in our world.

All over the Earth several countries bully other weaker nations because they have a larger army, or possess more advanced warfare weaponry than those weaker nations. These countries act just like the devil does, they also do all they can under the context of "geo-politics" to ensure that the weaker nations do not grow stronger, or develop their own weapons which will enable them to challenge the existing political hegemonies of the stronger nations military might and its dominance or hyper-puissance.

In the history of mankind, several humans have been known to attempt the task of blowing up the dam walls and seal upon their hearts. Such is that withholding God's Power from them, and this wall is in reality a prison wall that separates "Humanity from God" or any influences of His Power being with us. That is why it is referenced as "a veil" in religious parlance.

Sometimes, whenever a human partially succeeds at pulling back the veil, or breaking down the dam wall, such a person gains partial access to the unlimited resources of God and access to "the Throne of God". By such access, the person appears to now possess unusual abilities, such a person begins to manifest what we describe or consider as miracles or miraculous abilities. These are those unusual differences exhibited by those called "servants; prophets; or anointeds of God;" chronicled in the scriptures.

Although we must realise that in some instances the pushing-back of the veil is done by angels or "the Spirit of God", rather than the humans within whose hearts the veil is pushed back or rendered.

In the case of humans who pushed back the veil by their own efforts, what these men have done by their lives is simply to show us a glimpse of what Humanity can be like, if we all do that which they have done, such is needful and we all should copy or imitate them.

However, our new potential if we do what is needful is a threat to the enemy controlling this realm. This threat is the reason why the devil "or enemy" remains also busy at work doing everything to dispel truths that will prompt us into understanding anything about transforming our heart's status. That is why he laces every religion that could guide us to this truth with perversions of such truths or expurgates the essence of the actual message that may spark such an intention, or any illumination about it which can bring the desired "Freedom....from the shackles thrust upon the human Heart", to those who may hear, understand and purpose to accomplish it.

This evil aim of holding back "the Truth" is now fully developed into one where doctrines are concocted to vilify those who manifest "the powers of God" on Earth, thereby labelling the miraculous or power of miracles as something which shouldn't be desired.

The devil being a hater of all humans bullies, oppresses, and frustrates everyone of us, simply because we don't have enough strength to stand up to or fight him in our heart's current state.

For that reason, it remains his duty to ensure we don't change or transform the current states of our hearts. Because such changes transforms us into beings stronger than him, powered by God and able to contend his or his demons authority.

In my view after such a change occurs we are best described as "sons of God". However anyone of us who succeeds in fully blowing up that shackle, which was wound around our heart through the process of "the Original Sin", also becomes one with full access to "the Throne of God".

And surely, with full access to the Throne, a person has available to him or her, all the resources or power needed to confront and vanquish the devil, or any of his legions of demons under any circumstances. That is another context of illustrating the man-child being born whose birth was plotted against by the serpent.

> *Luke 4:32-34*
> *And they were astonished at his doctrine: for his word was with power. 33. And in the synagogue there was a man, which had a spirit of an unclean devil, and cried out with a loud voice, 34. Saying, Let us alone; what have we to do with thee, thou Jesus of Nazareth? art thou come to destroy us? I know thee who thou art; the Holy One of God.*

The final battle between good and evil on Earth, which is expected to happen when Humanity, or "One among them" finally acquires the wherewithal to confront the devil and his demons. Or collectively all those that have been troubling Humanity and it will surely happen someday since it has been decreed by the LORD God and is purposed as "a Messianic Enigma".

The first human who accomplishes this objective of gaining full access to "the LORD's Power or Presence" becomes "the Anointed One", that person is the human who in a duet with the LORD will vanquish all those considered as "the enemies of the LORD", who are dwelling in the midst of Humanity. And he will cast such who are also called "strangers" off the Earth, into a place known biblically as "hell". Or better imagined as the Universe's refuse dump or incinerator, for none of them (the strangers) can stand against him, because God is with him and his mission is to repossess the Earth from the evil forces occupying it, by waging a battle in "a duet with God" against such evil forces.

> *Psalms 18:42-45*
> *Then did I beat them small as the dust before the wind: I did cast them out as the dirt in the streets. 43. Thou hast delivered me from the strivings of the people; and thou hast made me the head of the heathen: a people whom I have not known shall serve me. 44. As soon as they hear of me, they shall obey me: the strangers shall submit themselves unto me. 45. The strangers shall fade away, and be afraid out of their close places.*

From that moment onwards, all the inhabitants of the Earth will dwell in peace. Because the one or those ones who troubles them also called strangers or heathen, are no more for they all have been vanquished.

There is a similarity in that expectation of "a peaceful accomplishment" expected by this "First human who gains access to God's Presence", to do what the others before haven't, one that accentuates all the references to King David, or "a seed of David" in last day prophecies. If we recall that King David while in a duet with "the Spirit of the LORD" vanquished Goliath the giant, and other territorial enemies of the nation Israel, and after these battles, Israel dwelt in peace on their land. Such is the similarity to "the Anointed One" and expectations of being the one to vanquish the devil and his cronies, by accessing "the Presence of the LORD" or "the Throne of God" via a duet with the LORD God's Spirit, which avails him the power needed for such a mission.

> *Amos 9:10-11*
> *All the sinners of my people shall die by the sword, which say, The evil shall not overtake nor prevent us. 11. In that day will I raise up the tabernacle of David that is fallen, and close up the breaches thereof; and I will raise up his ruins, and I will build it as in the days of old:*

> *Isaiah 16:5*
> *And in mercy shall the throne be established: and he shall sit upon it in truth in the tabernacle of David, judging, and seeking judgment, and hasting righteousness.*

Most especially, "the Anointed One" becomes the custodian of "the Presence of the LORD" on the Earth. After defeating the enemies of the LORD, by virtue of being the one with access to the LORD, as such he becomes a "Priest to the LORD", in religious parlance. The inhabitants of the earth are expected to dwell in peace thereafter because he is "the one who Judges the Earth to enforce Righteousness" as "a son of God" or one being at "One with God".

Judge in this context means to rule over as the LORD's Servant, it also means to separate good from evil, and ensure peace reigns, that is also why the Earth will from that moment bear a new name "the New Jerusalem" or "a Kingdom of Heaven" which are names given to anyplace where "the Presence of the LORD" exists, dwells or is domiciled.

This crucial objective to break down the dam wall around the human heart is literally or is figuratively illustrated in all cultures and various religions all over the world. It is a message brought to all races and cultures, although it should be known that the devil has steadily been at work to efface any representations or descriptions of such an objective wherever it exists or is relayed to humans. Just like an incumbent willing to do anything possible to retain a hold of political power will busy himself with such acts to undermine the opposition for his political gain.

The well-circulated picture depicting Jesus Christ pointing towards his heart, which appears tied up by a thorn-bush but radiating light by overcoming the hedge put around it, is essentially a pictorial image and representation of this objective. Various cultures have hinted praying, meditation, chanting, singing or worshiping "the Eternal One" as methods to accomplish this mission of breaking that hedge.

Whenever humans engage in any of these processes, what happens is they begin a process of striking the wall built around their hearts with a hammer.

The size of the hammer is determined by the passion in their heart to encounter God. With every strike, a piece of the stones making up this dam wall chips off and falls down. The more they do it, the more cracks that appear on that dam wall set around the human hearts to withhold or limit God's Presence. With persistence they will get to a point where the dam wall around their hearts, will collapse and crack into bits and cascade, just as an almond seed hit with a rock cracks into pieces, to reveal the nut hidden inside it.

That which is revealed inside the human heart after the dam wall is broken down is called "a Golden seed". It was placed in the heart of all humans at the beginning of creation. It is a device which provides us access into "the Throne of God", or allows a human's heart to connect with or draw upon "the Powers of the LORD". Or in another descriptive phrase, it fills a human up with "the Spirit of the LORD" because once the barrier hindering its entrance is destroyed, the LORD's spirit flows unhindered or through a human's heart.

To get "that Golden seed" revealed in them, every human who desires such must be prepared to wrestle the entrenched views of religion, because such are laced with doctrines to keep them away from ever accomplishing this objective. Every human who desires access to God, must be prepared to better any of the current religions of the world and their preaching, because they all are somewhat set up as smoke-screens to keep humans away from discovering anything about "the Golden seed" placed within them by the LORD.

It is every human's responsibility to unwrap that gift given to us from God. This really isn't a gift, because it has been with Humanity all along and was part of us since creation. But if we consider that after all that has happened to humans tagged "the Fall of man", and that it will take a reverse of what happened back then to bring us back to our initial state of creation. By that I mean "taking away the fore-skin of the heart" in order for us to reclaim what is actually ours and has been with us even though we knew it not and were unaware of its presence or uses.

In that perspective, it is safe to call it a gift. Simply because everyone gets excited about discovering what is hidden within a box or package handed to them as a gift. We need such excitement to prevail in our hearts and rule over all our emotions, because such will help us work towards revealing that which allows us to once again have access to "the Throne of God" or "His Presence" and become "sons & daughters of God", or in other words see "the Glories of the LORD" in our generation.

Most of all existing religions in their pristine state are not bad, but in their corrupted states they have become simply perverse and blasphemous. This is because they are now rewritten and preset with agenda of not provoking humans to seek for "that treasure hidden within their hearts" which is simply same as seeking for God because that is what that treasure brings Humanity.

Their doctrines simply deceive and persuade humans not to do anything but live a life sanctioned or dictated as ideal by the promoters of such a religion or faith, claiming that it is only by doing so, that the followers will make a place they call "Heaven or Paradise". And that view is absolutely untrue, anyone who doesn't find that treasure within their heart, will never make it to Heaven or dwell eternally with the LORD God, for "the real Heaven" is inside the human heart and that is also where "the Temple of God" exists and access to it manifests "the Kingdom of God or the Kingdom of Heaven" on Earth.

> *Luke 17:20-21*
> *And when he was demanded of the Pharisees, when the kingdom of God should come, he answered them and said, The kingdom of God cometh not with observation: 21. Neither shall they say, Lo here! or, lo there! for, behold, the kingdom of God is within you.*

The location of "the Kingdom of Heaven" is hidden and can only be found by humans who are ready to dedicate a lot to discovering it, because there are a lot of entities who do not want humans to find their way to it.

> *Matthew 13:44*
> *Again, the kingdom of heaven is like unto treasure hid in a field; the which when a man hath found, he hideth, and for joy thereof goeth and selleth all that he hath, and buyeth that field.*

Every human who desires to discover "the hidden treasure in the field of their heart" must aim for "a perfect relationship with GOD". Such which is desired by the LORD God, it contrast with the type of relationships dictated by the edicts of the various religions or faiths which abound worldwide, with claims to know what God wants but with no proof of a relationship with Him as demonstrated by Jesus Christ or those who came before him.

> *Matthew 13:45-46*
> *Again, the kingdom of heaven is like unto a merchant man, seeking goodly pearls: 46. Who, when he had found one pearl of great price, went and sold all that he had, and bought it.*

> *Psalms 17:14-15*
> *From men which are thy hand, O LORD, from men of the world, which have their portion in this life, and whose belly thou fillest with thy hid treasure: they are full of children, and leave the rest of their substance to their babes. 15. As for me, I will behold thy face in righteousness: I shall be satisfied, when I awake, with thy likeness.*

"A true Knowledge of God" will be found by discovering "the hidden treasure" in our hearts, and this can be achieved by dedicating utmost priority towards this purpose and giving or committing the best of our time, efforts and resources in order to "buy this field".

Or owning the real estate of our hearts, because of the treasure to be discovered there, rather than allowing the cares of life or flesh existence such as money, fame power, social acceptance and other worldly lust to consume our hearts and distract us from owing our hearts, which is a field where the hidden treasure is buried.

Those humans who discover this knowledge or treasure are called "the wise"; "the righteous"; "pure in heart"; and "those without sin". Such individuals are those who can truly give others directions about how to locate "that hidden treasure", also described as entering "the Kingdom of Heaven" when it is found; or "the Throne of God" when it is discovered. Not any quacks or charlatans with claims of knowing all about pleasing their religious God, by simply quoting dogmas with nothing to show for it or prove such claims as worthy of its words. For it is only after a human has discovered "the Golden Seed" in their hearts that access to "the Source", that which we call God, can truly be granted to him or her, and such access is validated by manifesting miracles, signs or wonders similar to those who found God in past generations.

Those directions about worshiping the Father which Jesus Christ gave to the woman at the well, were actually directions about how to access "the Kingdom of Heaven". Such was coming from someone who had encountered the LORD with his own human heart.

These were contrary to those instructions to find God dictated by the lady's culture or religious doctrine preached in her nation. Finding God is surely not about how to pray or worship a Father to which we have no access in a physical temple or location, where His Presence cannot be found or does not exist anymore.

Even though most religions doggedly insist on such teachings, the simple truth is that the heart of a human is "the Temple of God" and those who want to worship or find Him must seek Him with and within such.

> *John 4:21-24*
> *Jesus saith unto her, Woman, believe me, the hour cometh, when ye shall neither in this mountain, nor yet at Jerusalem, worship the Father. 22. Ye worship ye know not what: we know what we worship: for salvation is of the Jews. 23. But the hour cometh, and now is, when the true worshippers shall worship the Father in spirit and in truth: for the Father seeketh such to worship him. 24. God is a Spirit: and they that worship him must worship him in spirit and in truth.*

Those directions given by Jesus Christ were about connecting with "the Father", "the One" who we call "the LORD God", the source of "Eternal Life". They were to guide us towards reaching Him where He truly dwells using the most appropriate tool for such, which is one buried deep within our human hearts. For whenever such a tool is activated, an event occurs figuratively depicted as "taking away of the veil"; or "rendering of the veil of the temple"; and this is because "a veil" prevents us from becoming what we really are "sons of God". A "vail" prevented us from acquiring our true nature as Humans until Jesus Christ took it away on the cross.

> *Luke 23:45*
> *And the sun was darkened, and the veil of the temple was rent in the midst.*

> *2 Corinthians 3:14-16*
> *But their minds were blinded: for until this day remaineth the same vail untaken away in the reading of the old testament; which vail is done away in Christ. 15. But even unto this day, when Moses is read, the vail is upon their heart. 16. Nevertheless when it shall turn to the Lord, the vail shall be taken away.*

Considering the advice by Jesus Christ to the woman from the LORD's address perspective, it wasn't that the LORD changed His location or address as the statement appears to specify superficially. Rather it was that the woman "and all other humans" were being advised and guided by one who had succeeded in securing accessing to "the LORD" and "His Powers", where "He Dwells, also known as "His Temple or Throne", using his heart as a human.

Such access he secured by removing of "the veil" or also referenced as "vail" clouding his heart, and all those before him who connected with the LORD God did likewise, and he also promised to hand down the knowledge about such accomplishments onwards to his disciples — those ready to follow his teachings. Concerning "veil and vail" which were rendered by the Christ, one prevents humans from accessing "the Throne of God" while the other prevents human from dying anymore, if they do the needful to merit its benefits.

> *Matthew 16:18-19*
> *And I say also unto thee, That thou art Peter, and upon this rock I will build my church; and the gates of hell shall not prevail against it.  19.  And I will give unto thee the keys of the kingdom of heaven: and whatsoever thou shalt bind on earth shall be bound in heaven: and whatsoever thou shalt loose on earth shall be loosed in heaven.*

A similar advice to that given to the woman at the well is also that being referred to when Jesus Christ promised to hand "the keys to the Kingdom of Heaven" to his disciple Peter. Those keys depicted a right to an authority or power dwelling in a place known as "Heaven", which could be invoked on the Earth to reign.

The keys were means and knowledge about how to access that domain called "Heaven", in order to secure an authority or power greater than every other one existing in the Universe. To reign on the Earth, any human who accesses this domain experiences a transfer of such power or key to him or her, also considered as coming into "the Presence of God"; or "Decoding the Enigma of God"; or "Unlocking the Messianic Enigma"; or "Fulfilling the Quest for Enlightenment"; or "Walking fully the path to Illumination"; and so on.

Such is an experience all humans need to pursue with their hearts until it occurs, because when it happens we are transformed into bearers of "the Supernatural Attributes of God" as humans.  This transformation is the next stage of human evolution, once it occurs to a human, such a human could then be said to have become "a Son of God". It is simply a point at which "the Spirit of God", also known as "His Name" in some scriptural contexts comes to dwell in "the Temple" or body of a human just as it did with Jesus Christ.

> *John 1:12*
> *But as many as received him, to them gave he power to become the sons of God, even to them that believe on his name:*

Transhumanism is the process of "the Spirit of God" coming upon Man

A friend of mine lamented about having just fired one of his good staff, because of her unbecoming conduct and nonchalance towards her job responsibilities. After listening to him I told him, that I understood his problem more than he could ever express it in words.  Then I proceeded to state to him that even the LORD God has had to fire several of His servants, sent into the world because they begin to grow wings and behave irrationally, the moment they became empowered or "anointed as the LORD's Representative" or bearer of His Authority and Power. This is simply because of their right of freewill and lack of knowing and doing what the LORD would desire of them in certain situations in which they find themselves.

I further explained to my friend that such was why the LORD was still seeking for "the Perfect One" called "the Messiah" from "the Sea of Humanity". Because this person, just like Jesus Christ will have submitted his or her free will to the LORD, such that whenever the individual desired to do anything that displeases the LORD, He will override such intentions because the individual's freewill belongs to and can be manipulated by the LORD God.

I explained to my friend that what he really was searching for was a staff, who will run his business for him as he would himself if he were there. So that in the event that such a staff wanted to do something which he won't approve of if he was there, he would also like to retain the power or ability to stop or prevent that staff from proceeding on such a course of action even during his absence. Likewise is what the LORD seeks from Humanity, one to be "His First-born Son" to handle his affairs and do the LORD's Will on and throughout the Earth.

In reality what my friend was looking for was a clone of himself to run and manage his business the way he would manage it, so that he could get on with other things. Likewise is what the LORD seeks from Humanity. He wants humans "who will fully bear His Image" and represent Him. And that means such a human has been transformed into "an uncorrupted Image of God", one bearing or manifesting "the true Attributes of God" as "a Seed of Human", just like Jesus Christ did.

What is peddled under the doctrine of Christianity as forgiveness of sins is actually an open gate of opportunity for humans to re-transform themselves back into their original status as bearers of "the Image of God". And by such free themselves from what is called "Sin" or "the blazing fires of material existence" also known as "matter or Maya".

It is worthy to note that my friend was drawn into the option of firing his staff because he was fully convinced that such an employee was not fit for his business or capable to fulfil his desired purposes anymore, and this decision was based on how the staff had performed in the course of being my friend's staff.

Likewise is what the LORD is going to do to humans who are not fit for his new Kingdom coming upon the Earth at His return. Which occurs when he finds "the Anointed One"; or "the Son of Man"; or "His Firstborn Son"; they all will be cast into a place considered as "other darkness or the real hell" as stated in various narratives, some will be spared such a judgment for even though they have not accomplished what the Firstborn has, they will already be set on their journey towards such a similar accomplishment.

So if we consider it in a different context, what is desired from humans is a leap in evolution in scientific perspectives, which also could be considered as a transformation of Humanity into a better breed of mankind, one bearing "God-like traits and attributes" or "the Image of God".

Though there are diverse interpretations to the term "Trans-humanism", despite that all definitions have something in common which is progressing to a next-level destination for Humanity.

And strangely it appears such stepping up the ladder for humans either by self-actualization or technological innovations appears blasphemous or perverse to the regular human who seems to perceive it as a pipe-dream or tall order of imagination.

In all renderings, Trans-humanism suggests "a New Beginning"; or "New Era for Humanity"; because the people have acquired the ability to overcome certain limitations or difficulties plaguing their race presently.

The generation of humans capable of making such a stride, are surely wiser and better than their fore bearers. In scriptural context, they are tagged as "sons of David" or in post-Jesus Christ era such were tagged as "baby Christ" or "disciples of Christ". Both phrases suggest a league of people better in performance than their progenitors or pace-setters in this case King David and Jesus Christ. Or at worst these phrases suggests humans bearing similar attributes as them, with the potential to achieve more than they did. The moment we get to realise that God does not celebrate failures and that He does not select faulty humans and place them as objects of excellence, we will come to understand a pressing need to progress in our walk with His Spirit from wherever our pre-decessors passed the baton over to us. It is a responsibility.

We can see clearly in scriptures that He criticises those He raises up, when they falter or misbehave. Such action is for the next generation to observe and learn from their predecessor's short comings, and by doing so becoming better breeds of humans. That is a strategy towards transformation in Humanity, and that is Trans-humanism in a perspective induced by the LORD.

The clamour for Humanity's repentance yelled out by various faiths is a call for Trans-humanism too, though it usually shrugged of with a dash of insignificance in our generation. It is a call for humans to begin to walk in lock-step with God's Spirit, so He can transit us into the next level of existence.

That which we should call "the expected Kingdom of Heaven" where all things are made perfect. Some humans resist such views by boldly suggesting that imperfection of Humanity and an imperfect state of existence on Earth or Creation is the norm. This is just to validate their disinterest in God, Religion or Faith and the need to repent from their evil ways.

The fact remains that God has in plan a brighter future for our world than our imaginations may ever fathom. But because we are used to seeing and experiencing things in what He will label as a perverse order of things on Earth. Which to us appears somewhat normal, for such reasons, it may be difficult for us to realize and understand His desires to transform our world. But such transformation can only begin when Humanity produces "His expected Messiah", the tool needed to accomplishing His Will in our world. He is "the One" who will reveal "the Glory of God" to us again, and this happens only when that which we call Transhumanism occurs in our world, that achieved by adopting "His Spirit" in order to redeem our body so we can become "sons of God" too.

Even though most faiths may not re-state the facts as they need to, in order to enlighten Humanity of what is suggested, all religions that highlight the need for a relationship with "the Divine" are very precious cultural attributes that require fine-tuning in other for Humanity to have "a New Order" restored to us on Earth. One which promises peace, tranquillity and everlasting joy in a New Heaven and New Earth context when God dwells with humans.

*their swords into plowshares, and their spears into pruninghooks: nation shall not lift up a sword against nation, neither shall they learn war any more.*

Does our world need "a New Order" which can transform our lives and generation? Do we need "the Spirit of God" to come and dwell in our world? Surely the answer is yes! I would love to see lions and bullocks dwell in peace, eating grass together on the same field as prophesied by Prophet Isaiah in my days. I would love to see a world where no more wars are fought, one where Humanity dwells in peace with each other, and I am quite sure I am not the only one with such longings. Considering expectations of wild animals dwelling in peace and eating straw or grass together. That always suggests to me a state on the Earth where predators do not prey up on other animals, and such is a forsaking of the food chain order we are quite accustomed to.

We all get saddened when we watch on television as a Lion or Crocodile kills a bull for food or nourishment, I presume we feel like this because we don't want the Lion to die of starvation, neither do we want the bull to get killed to nourish the Lion, which is an insolvable paradox. In my view such exists because we know or can sense that "the One" who created them, can feed them without they having to kill each other for food or nourishment.

That feeling of displeasure we get is a protest from that of the LORD's Spirit being displeased by perceiving such happenings in our world. We must remember He fed the Israelites in the wilderness with manna and such gave them all the nutrients which their body needed. He can likewise transform grass into a source of all nutrients for all creatures in my view thereby deleting off any predatory traits in wild animals, and that to me is what is suggested by those expectations of lions and ox feeding together.

*Isaiah 11:6-10*
*The wolf also shall dwell with the lamb, and the leopard shall lie down with the kid; and the calf and the young lion and the fatling together; and a little child shall lead them. 7. And the cow and the bear shall feed; their young ones shall lie down together: and the lion shall eat straw like the ox. 8. And the sucking child shall play on the hole of the asp, and the weaned child shall put his hand on the cockatrice' den. 9. They shall not hurt nor destroy in all my holy mountain: for the earth shall be full of the knowledge of the LORD, as the waters cover the sea. 10. And in that day there shall be a root of Jesse, which shall stand for an ensign of the people; to it shall the Gentiles seek: and his rest shall be glorious.*

The call for transformation to Humanity and search for "the Messiah" is one bearing similarities to an Olympic contest, where the winner leads the rest towards fulfilling the LORD's Purpose for our world. The first to answer this call gets the prize and simultaneously opens up access for the LORD God's Spirit into our world. Considering the prize at stake, I must confess that I already made head start as a front runner in this contest, catch me if you can.

The day of the "New Human or A Second Adam", begins after "the LORD's Spirit" descends back to Earth. At such a period, humans will become smarter and stronger than "the First Adam". They will be able to resist all temptations of the devil and fleshly lust; they will bear freewill to please the LORD God in all their ways, just as Jesus Christ did while playing the prototype role for "A New Man". Pleasing the LORD is basically doing only things that He purposed His Creations for as guided by His Spirit.

A sizable fraction of humans will agree that we have spent enough time as a race, being subservient to the evil one and the execution of its evil order on Earth. It becomes equally strange that in spite of that, many among such people are not prepared for the LORD's return or willing to accept His Influence or Presence returning into our world.

This is because when the LORD returns, and by that I mainly refer to His Influence on the Earth, by proxy of "the expected Messiah" or "man Child who is born" and acts as a custodian for "the Spirit of God", what we expect is simply the manifestation of "a New World Order".

Humanity has to be weary of voices that suggest all is well with our race, such voices swiftly proclaim that anything not human or from our world is evil and must be thoroughly resisted.

In my view "the Spirit of the LORD" is alien to our world presently and will only return here when "the expected Messiah" is assisted to bring it back here, as depicted in Daniel's vision where "a son of Man" is brought to the Most High for such purposes.

> *Daniel 7:13-14*
> *I saw in the night visions, and, behold, one like the Son of man came with the clouds of heaven, and came to the Ancient of days, and they brought him near before him. 14. And there was given him dominion, and glory, and a kingdom, that all people, nations, and languages, should serve him: his dominion is an everlasting dominion, which shall not pass away, and his kingdom that which shall not be destroyed.*

The LORD's Spirit cannot do anything on Earth without being united to a human. The human who engages it in all such duets are those who play "the Anointed One" or "Christ" roles. The verses below depict "the Spirit of God" as "Christ" in its context and expresses what it did in duet with a human in the past and what it will do with another human in the future.

> *Romans 10:6-7*
> *But the righteousness which is of faith speaketh on this wise, Say not in thine heart, Who shall ascend into heaven? (that is, to bring Christ down from above:) 7. Or, Who shall descend into the deep? (that is, to bring up Christ again from the dead.)*

Such humans are also depicted as "the Lamb" in other prophecies that symbolises their roles. Anytime "the Spirit of God" rests upon a pure or mixed breed human, such humans becomes "a Lamb of Christ" or "Lamb for the Spirit of God" to accomplish that for which He desires such a Lamb. In the cases of the verses above that will be bringing "the Spirit of God" down from above, to be done by the "son of man to be born" or he who the angels bring up to God's Throne to be anointed as ruler of an everlasting Kingdom on Earth. Just as it was brought up from the dead (or grave) by "the Lamb" called Jesus Christ. There are two distinct references of "the Lamb" in the book of Revelations; the first is for "a Lamb that was slain" which is also "the one who loosens the seven seals". This character is Jesus Christ and he is also called "the first begotten of the dead" and "the prince of the kings of the Earth". Such titles merited by his accomplishments for the LORD GOD.

*Revelation 5:7-10*
*And he came and took the book out of the right hand of him that sat upon the throne. 8. And when he had taken the book, the four beasts and four and twenty elders fell down before the Lamb, having every one of them harps, and golden vials full of odours, which are the prayers of saints. 9. And they sung a new song, saying, Thou art worthy to take the book, and to open the seals thereof: for thou wast slain, and hast redeemed us to God by thy blood out of every kindred, and tongue, and people, and nation; 10. And hast made us unto our God kings and priests: and we shall reign on the earth.*

*Revelation 1:5*
*And from Jesus Christ, who is the faithful witness, and the first begotten of the dead, and the prince of the kings of the earth. Unto him that loved us, and washed us from our sins in his own blood.*

The second Lamb is the one who seats on "the Throne with God". This is achieved by overcoming all hindrances to such accomplishments after which this Lamb gets to share all the benefits of "the Throne of God" with the LORD. This Lamb is also known as "the LORD of LORD and KING of KINGS" and "a Son of God" by virtue of such accomplishments.

*Revelation 21:6-7*
*And he said unto me, It is done. I am Alpha and Omega, the beginning and the end. I will give unto him that is athirst of the fountain of the water of life freely. 7. He that overcometh shall inherit all things; and I will be his God, and he shall be my son.*

*Revelation 17:14*
*These shall make war with the Lamb, and the Lamb shall overcome them: for he is Lord of lords, and King of kings: and they that are with him are called, and chosen, and faithful.*

The titles in the verses above are not those that Jesus Christ lays claims to in any context, he is even noted to have invited other humans to come and sit with Him on "the Throne of God". This shows the Throne is open for others.

*Revelation 3:20-22*
*Behold, I stand at the door, and knock: if any man hear my voice, and open the door, I will come in to him, and will sup with him, and he with me.  21. To him that overcometh will I grant to sit with me in my throne, even as I also overcame, and am set down with my Father in his throne.  22.  He that hath an ear, let him hear what the Spirit saith unto the churches.*

The human who hears and heeds to his voice of invitation is the one who plays the role of "the Lamb" to be called "the KING OF KINGS", also to be called "the New Jerusalem". These titles are associated to being both a "Temple" and "Throne for the LORD". The temple is built for God within the Lambs heart, and that is also where "the Name of God" or "His Spirit" is written or placed.

*Revelation 3:11-12*
*Behold, I come quickly: hold that fast which thou hast, that no man take thy crown.  12.  Him that overcometh will I make a pillar in the temple of my God, and he shall go no more out: and I will write upon him the name of my God, and the name of the city of my God, which is new Jerusalem, which cometh down out of heaven from my God: and I will write upon him my new name.*

After this temple is built, "the Spirit of God" descends to dwell with "the Lamb", that is after he was taken up to God's Throne for the purpose of becoming a vessel to bring down the LORD's Spirit by the angels. Once the LORD's Spirit is placed in his heart (the Lamb) he becomes "the New Jerusalem". That acquired name associates him as the vessel and temple bringing "the Spirit of God" back into the Earth to dwell with humans. We have to remember here that without a vessel "the Spirit of God" cannot dwell with humans, and the vessel in this case is the heart of the Lamb, who brought it down from above by ascending up by angelic assistance. The Lamb's heart becomes "a temple of God" or "a tabernacle of God".

*Revelation 21:2-3*
*And I John saw the holy city, new Jerusalem, coming down from God out of heaven, prepared as a bride adorned for her husband.  3.  And I heard a great voice out of heaven saying, Behold, the tabernacle of God is with men, and he will dwell with them, and they shall be his people, and God himself shall be with them, and be their God.*

Ascending to heaven depicts being taken up to "the Throne of God" and after it occurs "the Lamb" accomplishing this will then guide other humans to the LORD God or "the fountain of Living waters" and also put an end to all human misery, acting similar roles to that which Jesus Christ played.

*Revelation 7:17*
*For the Lamb which is in the midst of the throne shall feed them, and shall lead them unto living fountains of waters: and God shall wipe away all tears from their eyes.*

That happens as expected by various faiths and religions of their Messiah, who by virtue of bringing "the Spirit of God" down to the Earth and becoming a "Son of God" or by encountering "a knowledge of God" can accomplish it all such includes destroying all those who have destroyed the Earth. They are the ones scheming in everyway to ensure such an event never occurs.

*Revelation 11:15-18*
*And the seventh angel sounded; and there were great voices in heaven, saying, The kingdoms of this world are become the kingdoms of our Lord, and of his Christ; and he shall reign for ever and ever. 16. And the four and twenty elders, which sat before God on their seats, fell upon their faces, and worshipped God, 17. Saying, We give thee thanks, O Lord God Almighty, which art, and wast, and art to come; because thou hast taken to thee thy great power, and hast reigned. 18. And the nations were angry, and thy wrath is come, and the time of the dead, that they should be judged, and that thou shouldest give reward unto thy servants the prophets, and to the saints, and them that fear thy name, small and great; and shouldest destroy them which destroy the earth.*

Being in the midst of "the Throne of God" occurs to a human after "the Spirit of God" descends to Earth or "the Christ is brought down from above". This is where those with claims that Humanity is perfect have anchored all their arguments, in their bid to forestall that which is currently alien from coming into the Earth and dwelling with us.

*Revelation 22:1-5*
*And he shewed me a pure river of water of life, clear as crystal, proceeding out of the throne of God and of the Lamb. 2. In the midst of the street of it, and on either side of the river, was there the tree of life, which bare twelve manner of fruits, and yielded her fruit every month: and the leaves of the tree were for the healing of the nations. 3. And there shall be no more curse: but the throne of God and of the Lamb shall be in it; and his servants shall serve him: 4. And they shall see his face; and his name shall be in their foreheads. 5. And there shall be no night there; and they need no candle, neither light of the sun; for the Lord God giveth them light: and they shall reign for ever and ever.*

Quite strangely, there are multitudes of people already submerged in deeply dug trenches of oppositional stances and rhetorics, to the impact of "the New

Jerusalem" with the Earth by the Lamb's accomplishments, and by him bringing "the Throne of God" back here, which in my personal view is what births "a New World Order".

That new order is already despised, hated, loathed and considered bad for Humanity, if we are to consider the sponsored and frenzied clamour against it by promoters everywhere. Most shocking is that multitudes of humans appear already neurologically programmed to resist it, or any mention of such a change occurring on Earth with the last drop of blood in their veins.

Almost everyone has a picture for the battle of Armageddon in their minds, because for decades Hollywood has pitted Humanity against anything not human in narratives that typify aliens or anything not terrestrial as evil while we are the good or perfect ones.

The question which begs asking is why has "a New World Order" or such change been prejudged as bad for Humanity? Why do we have multitudes of humans bearing negative expectations for what no human has experienced?

We need to wonder about the sources of such suggestions, their motives or intents? Could it be those entities co-dwelling with us on Earth presently? Those best labelled as strangers and our oppressors, or the evil and wicked one? Those who are with fore knowledge that someday their time here will run out, and their ability to trouble and exploit Humanity will become fully diminished.

With awareness about such possibilities of change to the order of things on Earth, one which transforms it into a domain they cannot dwell in or operate within, what do we think they will do with such a foresight? Sit back and await their displacement to manifest or do everything possible to ensure it never happens, even if such includes proclaiming false propaganda messages against its occurrence. I leave that to your pondering.

If indeed such entities exist, they must be those who are responsible for orchestrating and sponsoring all railings and accusations against "a New World Order" or any close encounter with "the Spirit of God" by Humanity.

For such is what comes after their time runs out here, and that may explain why they oppose changes which brings peace and progress to mankind or takes the human race into its next level of existence.

If what happened to "Adam and Eve" at the beginning of Creation is described as "the Fall of Man", then any reverse to such a status is fitting for the description "the Rise of Man".

This reversal is what happens when "the Spirit of the LORD" returns to dwell with Humanity, and when His reign begins here on Earth, it will bring peace, unity and a banishment of evil away from Humanity's midst, that is my clear definition of "a New World Order".

Sadly, such appears to be what certain sacred texts proclaim as arrival of evil on Earth. I say that because several faiths have embedded within their doctrines, writings or suggestions to the effect that when one comes, arises or appears, who is able to syncretise faiths and cultural differences, who is able to enforce peace among humans, who is able to transform the Earth into one where "a New World Order" exists contrary to that which prevails presently and by such acts unites Humanity, that such a human is one empowered by the devil to accomplish such objectives on Earth.

There are suggestions in certain doctrines that say this human is the devil incarnate and label him as "the bete noire of Humanity", better known as the anti-Christ.

Sound biblical scholars know the Greek word "Avτi" translated into English as "anti" could also means "in the place of". If we have that word combined with another Greek word "Khristos" which means "Christ or the Anointed One", what should we get from its meaning?

There are countless references to "a Heir of God" or "a seed of one of His faithful servants", who inherits all things belonging to the LORD God in this world.  By following scriptural narratives, we can observe a transfer of this heir's inheritance from Abraham unto Jacob, Joseph and then to David's lineage as its beneficiary.

> *Romans 4:13*
> *For the promise, that he should be the heir of the world, was not to Abraham,*
> *or to his seed, through the law, but through the righteousness of faith.*

> *Hebrews 1:2-3*
> *Hath in these last days spoken unto us by his Son, whom he hath appointed*
> *heir of all things, by whom also he made the worlds;  3. Who being the*
> *brightness of his glory, and the express image of his person, and upholding all*
> *things by the word of his power, when he had by himself purged our sins, sat*
> *down on the right hand of the Majesty on high;*

If transfers of this inheritance have occurred in the past, who can say for certain that it isn't bound to occur down the line again. It is only with the benefit of hindsight that we could even spot such transfers in scriptural narratives.

That transfer of "a heir's inheritance" is an exclusive preserve of the owner, and such are sanctioned without human consultation. The LORD God remains the owner, and from what I know He always does what pleases Him.

In addition to that it can be clearly discerned that He appears to be in search for "this Heir" among Humanity, not from a specific clan, race or tribe of Humanity. Another clear pattern to notice is that whenever one tribe or nation messes up or displeases Him, He simply moves on to the next available one, He does not wait on the crooked to become reformed.

How sure can we be that He hasn't transferred this inheritance unto the Gentiles nation when the Jews rejected Him? If we recall, He said in what to me is clearly a prophetic utterance from Jesus Christ that, "the Kingdom of God had been taken from them and given to another nation that will bring forth it fruits". The voice of a prophet is the voice of God and God cannot lie.

*Matthew 21:43*
*Therefore say I unto you, The kingdom of God shall be taken from you, and given to a nation bringing forth the fruits thereof*

I opine that the Kingdom referenced in that context means and suggests the same as "the Inheritance" for "the Heir of God" and the same one promised to "a son of David". It is that which "the LORD's Heir" or "the Anointed One" and "the expected Messiah" from Humanity's midst, who gets to "sit on the LORD's right hand" will secure. This individual or heir is also the one who in my view brings about the anticipated "Rise of Man", that which other evil entities in this world have been working to prevent or forestall. They prefer humans to exist perpetually in their fallen state.

When it comes to the benefits or changes expected in our world, as a result of "the Rise of Man", we must ask critical questions. Why will the devil desire peace for humans? Has such a motive ever come forth from him to Humanity? Let us ponder upon this issue really deeply, why will the devil desire to rid our world of all evil in it? Does the existence of such a world, meaning one without evil in it benefit the serpent or its seeds?

Why will the devil opt to unite faiths and cultures, when by dividing them, it has sustained hatred and kept humans perennially at war with each other? Some pundits opine guided by their doctrines that the devil may have opted to execute all these things because he wants the whole world to worship him?

We all know what most religions and faith in God promise to Humanity, and we clearly can discern what the absence of such consequences upon our race. If we are not worshipping the devil presently, who are we worshipping? Shouldn't we wonder who is presently controlling this world?

Will the LORD God be nursing a desire to control a world that He already controls? Will He labour tirelessly to give it to "a Heir", if it was already under His Kingdom's control? Can we really suggest that this broken world is one run by the LORD God? Does all that which we experience in our world suggest an order or manners we would expect the LORD God to run a world? Do we really think a caring God will allow evil to disturb the peace he purposed for His creations? Don't we always long to ask God, why He allows evil to happen to good people or those we consider as the innocent?

The presence of such curiosities on our minds suggests clearly that God didn't set evil loose or sanction its operation in our midst is my submission.

Most disturbing to me is the position taking by those who consider themselves faithful to God or religious adherents, because such seem to have resigned expectations that their God will allow an evil entity to take over their world in future, and torment them to death. Simply because they have read about it in a book which they are told contains only truths inspired by God's Spirit. Such unquestioned doctrines prevalently promoted amidst mainstream faiths, is another classic example of the, "my people suffer for they lack knowledge" cries, which was voiced by prophet Hosea, while under the influence of "the Spirit of the LORD".

It beats my imagination why those who supposedly are believers in a Great, Mighty and Loving God, or people considered as those with faith in God, fail to realise that they should have transitioned themselves, from those who speak against evil, injustice and wickedness in this world, into those who enforce good, righteousness and love among Humanity, because that is what the LORD God desires of them.

How such people can remain steadfastly unprepared to take hold on "the testimony of Jesus Christ", and walk in his path to advance both their faith and generation, by manifesting the works of Christ just as he did with the testimony of those who came before him, remains a mystery to me.

I remain convinced that by so doing any generation can fiercely contend against every works of evil within their society or their world, till all of such flees and disappears from amidst Humanity.

It remains saddening how humans or people, who look up to the LORD, suffer for lacking knowledge about power already given to them by Him. One with which they should do that which He expects of them. How such people fail at grasping the plain truth that, unto Humanity has been bequeathed an authority that no other power can withstand remains a mystery.

*Mark 16:15-20*
*And he said unto them, Go ye into all the world, and preach the gospel to every creature. 16. He that believeth and is baptized shall be saved; but he that believeth not shall be damned. 17. And these signs shall follow them that believe; In my name shall they cast out devils; they shall speak with new tongues; 18. They shall take up serpents; and if they drink any deadly thing, it shall not hurt them; they shall lay hands on the sick, and they shall recover. 19. So then after the Lord had spoken unto them, he was received up into heaven, and sat on the right hand of God. 20. And they went forth, and preached every where, the Lord working with them, and confirming the word with signs following. Amen.*

*Matthew 28:18-20*
*And Jesus came and spake unto them, saying, All power is given unto me in heaven and in earth. 19. Go ye therefore, and teach all nations, baptizing them in the name of the Father, and of the Son, and of the Holy Ghost: 20. Teaching them to observe all things whatsoever I have commanded you: and, lo, I am with you alway, even unto the end of the world. Amen.*

Alarming is the thought that, when "One among Humanity" awakens from their collective slumber, perceives and discovers what they all failed to grasp, or understand, and by such knowledge begins to manifest its privileges and authority. Then they all go, surely this is the evil one we read about mentioned in our holy books and suggested to us by various doctrines.

Quite strange though, is the fact that from all expectations of the evil one, extracted from their sacred books and professed doctrines, he is going to be doing what they have been crying out to their God for. I should rephrase and say, crying to the false gods who they worship, created in image of their faulty doctrines, the gods who they believe does good for them and also permits evil to exist in their world.

When the real God who does only good and gets rid of all evil in the world arrives, they appear auto-guided by various corrupted sentences in their sacred text and erroneous doctrines to presuming this is the evil one.

I must declare here that having studied the bible for years I am fully convinced it is God inspired text. Despite that in course of studying various versions I discerned that this text has suffered a lot from human tampering, interpretations, suggestions and effacements.

The classic one is suggesting that an angel of God told Mary and Joseph to name their son Jesus. That is a pure lie, the word Jesus has Latin or Roman origins. The angel instructed the boy be called "Yehoshua" a Jewish name.

The question becomes, how many more of such embellishments abound in all these sacred texts? Nevertheless, I have clearly gleaned that everything which is crucial information within the Bible seems to have eluded those bearing hostile jamming or effacement intents because these details are spread out in what I will call "a line upon line precept upon precept manner" visible only to the discerning or those who study the text deeply.

All subjects and contexts of prophecy are scripted to transmute, such that one must be at full blast of ones wits to keep up with this encryption rhythm, one deployed to protect the message and its integrity.

Without having studied any other sacred text as deeply as I have the bible, I can guess the same pattern applies and I can understand why such details may have been encrypted or marked for only the eyes of the wise ones who truly search for it or those who know what to look for. Without such safeguards all traces of the truth will have been effaced by those in whose interest it is to keep such revelations from human cognition

Despite all such, just why at the moment when humans awakens and begin to use their brains, to realise the truth and thereby bring about the decoding of "the Messianic Enigma" and "the Rise of Man" such humans will get labelled as children of the devil worries me.

Why should the one who manifests what faithfuls longed and prayed for daily for centuries, and accomplishes feats which other humans failed at get rewarded by a crown of villainy? Is that not the height of stupidity?

Why should any human who lays hold upon "the testimony of Jesus Christ" and manifest such to its fullest, now become the one who some doctrines label as the devil? Manifesting such will only bring into our midst miraculous healings, abilities to feed multitudes of those suffering in famine raged lands by blessing a small meal like Jesus Christ did, raising the dead etc.

Hard questions must be asked like, are any of these doctrines set up to advance Humanity or clamp our race down. We live in a world where all evil deeds are executed by humans. Never for once has the devil done evil here, such is accomplished by human who have given or rented out their hearts or souls to him.

The counter opposite to that is emergence of humans who will equally give their hearts and soul to the LORD God in order to act on His behalf. By such submissions, humans can become vessels to execute His purposes on the Earth too.

Such purposes are what "the expected Messiah" should and will be executing, but these are now scripted into holy books or suggested by some doctrines as deeds of the devil meant for controlling the world. I smell a rat.

Peter was promised an authority to reign on Earth, such that no other authority could contend against it by Jesus Christ. Peter was a pure human. Does that make him a worthy suspect as the expected son of evil too?

Considering that the roles Peter was expected to play bore similarities to the accomplishments of "the expected Messiah". If really such abilities or authority were to be kept away from Humanity, until Jesus Christ returns as Christian doctrines promotes, why then was it handed over to Peter to reign here with?

In my view Peter failed at harnessing the utmost potentials of the authority given to him. I firmly believe that if he had done as expected of him with this authority, "the New World Order" which I speak about would have begun back in Peter's days, bringing about the end of evil and its reign in our world.

> *Matthew 16:16-19*
> *And Simon Peter answered and said, Thou art the Christ, the Son of the living God. 17. And Jesus answered and said unto him, Blessed art thou, Simon Barjona: for flesh and blood hath not revealed it unto thee, but my Father which is in heaven. 18. And I say also unto thee, That thou art Peter, and upon this rock I will build my church; and the gates of hell shall not prevail against it. 19. And I will give unto thee the keys of the kingdom of heaven: and whatsoever thou shalt bind on earth shall be bound in heaven: and whatsoever thou shalt loose on earth shall be loosed in heaven.*

It can be said without dispute, that Peter was given an authority to act on Earth on behalf of "the Kingdom of Heaven" which Jesus Christ represented in our world by his anointing. Does such an authority not make Peter a human who "acts in the place of Christ"? Lest we forget, that phrase resolves back to meaning he is an "anti-Christ". What exactly does this word mean or signify?

"The power or keys of the Kingdom of Heaven" giving to him and the others disciples were meant for such accomplishments. Not for creating various factions of the gospel as "Peter et al" ended up doing by infighting amongst themselves, thereby taking their eyes of the ball by promoting their own version or opinions about "the gospel of Christ" as the official one.

Again we must discern here that if Jesus Christ was the one to contend or wipe off evil from the Earth as Christian doctrine suggested, he would not be handing over or promising to give the power to execute such unto Peter or any of the other disciples after his resurrection or promising such to anyone who overcomes in the book of Revelations.

The potentials of what the power or anointing which "Peter et al" all bore as pure humans, and what it could accomplish was the sole reason why they (meaning all early Christians or followers of Christ teachings) were sought out and killed off. This was simply because they were threats to the evil kingdom reigning on the Earth, one which still reigns till today. Such happened because they failed to do the needful with what they were given by Jesus Christ, and by the needful I mean taking the anointing power or authority they bore to greater heights of manifesting the "Kingdom of God" and ridding the Earth of evil.

An Islamic text chronicles a refusal of the devil to bow to Adam when he was created and named the inheritor of the Earth. At "the Rise of Man" the devil and his kingdom will unfailingly bow to "a New Human" or "the Second Adam" who is custodian to "the Spirit of God" for humans.

This bowing will be one enforced by "their expected Messiah" another human empowered by the LORD God, who will accomplish such with power and anointing coming from the LORD via His Spirit to humans.

This power is best perceived as "the testimony of Jesus Christ". Such accomplishments were things that the early Christians failed at harnessing for their lacking knowledge about the power given to them. It simply goes that if humans bear power to prevail but remains unaware of this power or its potentials that is weakness.

*Hebrews 2:5-8*
*For unto the angels hath he not put in subjection the world to come, whereof we speak. 6. But one in a certain place testified, saying, What is man, that thou art mindful of him? or the son of man, that thou visitest him? 7. Thou madest him a little lower than the angels; thou crownedst him with glory and honour, and didst set him over the works of thy hands: 8. Thou hast put all things in subjection under his feet. For in that he put all in subjection under him, he left nothing that is not put under him. But now we see not yet all things put under him*

Everything has been prepared for us, if only humans will seek to approach "the Throne of God", and aim to engage "the Spirit of God" with their hearts, bearing "a zeal for God" as that of athletes vying for medals at an Olympics contest. Then as a result of such intents Humanity shall collectively experience a greater manifestation of "the Glory of God" in our generation than any previously experienced on Earth.

Such has been prophesied to occur in last days and such intents in humans will birth "the Rise of Man". It also brings forth "the Anointed One of God" from among Humanity and effects the transfer of the LORD's Inheritance to "His Heir". Who is one from their midst, who is the one to act "in the place of" their "Christ or Messiah" and he it is who is brought to seat at the LORD's right hand or is strengthened by the LORD for His purposes.

"The Glory of God" begins to manifest on Earth when nothing is impossible to humans anymore. This Glory is that manifested when humans can heal their sick, feed multitudes of those dying in starvation, cast out demons, raise the dead etc. Such was manifested by humans who interacted with this entity known as "the Spirit of the LORD God" in our past history.

By such interactions when these humans prayed to this entity, He hears them and grants their request. Such is the clear definition of praying. In our days, it sounds more like asking God for things and thinking of an excuse why we wont get what we prayed to Him for. That explains why we pray for sick but get no healing, it is why those who claim they love and serve God remain servants to those who publicly loathe and denounce Him. These are mismatches that should show us there is something wrong, why will God make His people or faithfuls servants to those who hate Him. In my view such situations persist because those who should reach out to God are fed with wrong doctrines teaching them things that please the evil one and keeps the evil kingdom in control here. The time is ripe for us to begin to strive for true manifestations of God in our midst by prayers.

Surely there are those who benefit from the present way things are set in our world, those who exploit "the Fall of Man" and the absence of "the Glory of God" or "His Spirit" in our world. They will resist my opinion and shout down any clamour for change in the way we approach the LORD.

Such they do with an aim to maintain the status-quo already preset by their faulty religious dogma or doctrinal hegemony over Humanity, purposed to hold back "a New Age on Earth" or "a New World Order".

That defines two factions at play in this plot, one seeking to transform the world into a better one, and another one seeking to maintain the status-quo it benefits from presently and to perpetually enslave mankind.

It remains everyone's choice to select which side they join, work in league with and support having read all I have written. If it all does not make sound sense at first reading please read again.

I submit saying, there is nothing wrong in presuming that one's views was right especially without any evidence to prove such views wrong. However, once evidence which overwhelmingly contends against such views and proves them inaccurate are presented, then it becomes gravely wrong for one to still insist that such previously held views are right.

Nevertheless it is time for us to awaken from any attempts of any faith to place a copyright on God's Name or His doctrines. God was known by various names in the bible, never did He say you must only call on me by such and such a name, these are doctrines of men used to prop up religious suggestions. Irrespective of that it must be known that not all religions or doctrines are set out to serve the true God, so caution is demanded before any man may say to the other man my God is your God, but something remains incontestable. We all are made in "the Image of God".

Professing belief in a different God or views different to the generally accepted ones about God, should not be swiftly considered as blasphemy until the details put forward and proof (if any) concerning such are examined.

Prophet Elijah was only able to prove that his God was actually the living God by calling on all those who considered themselves prophets of God in his days to prove, that their God wasn't an impotent construct of their religious ways, by this I mean one that couldn't make rainfall in the land after Elijah had declared that there will be no rainfall until he says so a pronouncement spurred by his disgust of religious practices. Such a declaration was made to highlight that his God was the real God and it was proven true by the LORD.

It must be understood that when any human rises up to condemn prevailing perverse religious practices in any generation. Such humans are simply acting for the same God (or entity) that raised up such humans in the past. This He periodically does to state clearly to respective generations that their ways are not pleasing to Him. Similar roles were played by Jesus Christ; Elijah; Jeremiah and several other prophets in biblical days. A true Prophet of God will always perceive with disdain and strong resentment the perverse religious ways of his generation or times.

Placing of doctrines of any religion above what the LORD God desires will only make those who do so become like the Jews of the days of Jesus Christ, who placed their oral traditions and laws above the mandated desires towards their belief in God. This writing bears no iconoclastic aims but rather conformist intents for Humanity with respect to the LORD God's will and desires from humans.

The time is right and is now for our generation to take control of this world, to reign as "sons of God", to bring His Kingdom and ensure only His will is done. It is our world! ; It is our inheritance!! ; It is the will of the LORD God!!!.

For all who will heed my voice, this I'll say, "Let us go back to God".

Ìransẹ Èlédúmarè is the sobriquet for an individual bearing these convictions.
It takes just "one human" ready to do "the will of God";
For "the Kingdom of God" to return upon the Earth,
It takes "one human" ready to forsake the ways of a generation gone astray
from God;
For "the Spirit of the LORD" to return and dwell in Humanity's midst,
It takes "one human" realising that God isn't responsible for Humanity's
sorrow or pains;
To birth desires that will ultimately end all such misery on Earth,
It takes "one human" that realises God's presence amongst Humanity has
waned;
To birth a clamour for His return by all who truly care about such,
It takes "one human" ready to bear the sacrifice and endure its opprobrium,
For "the Knowledge of God" to be re-discovered by Humanity.

He is a personality who will say to those who care to listen, that the path back
to the LORD is a long, lonely, and deserted lane, where only few humans have
treaded, but yet few desire to venture, one where even the closest people to
you will consider you insane for deciding to venture towards.

He is a personality with an anachronistic pre-dilection for worshipping the
LORD, in such a manner that would pleases His Heart. Many have opined and
commented to him that such is just another strain of being religious.
Ìransẹ's view steadfastly remains: "You are never wrong doing what is right!"



Ìransẹ Èlédúmarè wishes to says this to all those with an ear,
If one can see what another perceives not, it is because they are not equal.
Can two walk or dwell together except they see the same future?
A part of me boils with anger for all evil that has been done to Humanity.
Another part of me has knowledge that free-will to do evil to other humans is
actually free-will to serve the evil one.
Another part of me knows that humans bear within them, the will power not to
serve the evil one, however they fail to harness it for lack of knowledge.
And then, there is one part of me that has to act mindful of all these said, yet
bearing a passion for the will of God to be done on Earth.

Contact me via:-

Email: iam@iranse-eledumare.com
Twitter: @IranseEledumare